WAR AND SOCIETY IN COLONIAL ZAMBIA, 1939–1953

War and Militarism in African History

SERIES EDITORS: ALICIA C. DECKER AND GIACOMO MACOLA

Sarah J. Zimmerman
*Militarizing Marriage: West African Soldiers'
Conjugal Traditions in Modern French Empire*

Alfred Tembo
War and Society in Colonial Zambia, 1939–1953

War and Society in Colonial Zambia, 1939–1953

Alfred Tembo

OHIO UNIVERSITY PRESS ～ ATHENS, OHIO

Ohio University Press, Athens, Ohio 45701
ohioswallow.com
© 2021 by Ohio University Press
All rights reserved

To obtain permission to quote, reprint, or otherwise reproduce or distribute material from
Ohio University Press publications, please contact our rights and permissions department at
(740) 593-1154 or (740) 593-4536 (fax).

Printed in the United States of America
Ohio University Press books are printed on acid-free paper ⊗ ™

31 30 29 28 27 26 25 24 23 22 21   5 4 3 2 1

Library of Congress Cataloging-in-Publication Data

Names: Tembo, Alfred, 1978– author.
Title: War and society in colonial Zambia, 1939–1953 / Alfred Tembo.
Other titles: War and militarism in African history.
Description: Athens, Ohio : Ohio University Press, [2021] | Series: War and militarism in African
history | Includes bibliographical references and index.
Identifiers: LCCN 2021016492 (print) | LCCN 2021016493 (ebook) | ISBN 9780821424629
(hardcover) | ISBN 9780821447482 (pdf)
Subjects: LCSH: World War, 1939–1945—Zambia. | War and society—Zambia. | Zambia—
History—1924–1953.
Classification: LCC D766.99.Z36 T46 2021 (print) | LCC D766.99.Z36 (ebook) | DDC
940.54096894—dc23
LC record available at https://lccn.loc.gov/2021016492
LC ebook record available at https://lccn.loc.gov/2021016493

This book is published
through the generous support of the
Ohio University Press
Young Scholars Fund

Contents

List of Illustrations	ix
Acknowledgments	xi
Place Names	xiii
Abbreviations	xv
Introduction	1
1 Military Labor Recruitment and Mobilization	23
2 Southeast Asia, a Desperate Britain, and the Revival of African Rural Industries	56
3 War and the Economics of the Home Front	79
4 Strangers in Our Midst *The Dilemma of Hosting Polish War Refugees*	97
5 The Copper Mining Industry and the Allied War Effort	115
6 Demobilization and the Great Disappointment of War Service	142
Conclusion	169

Contents

Notes   177

Bibliography   225

Index   243

Illustrations

FIGURES

1.1 Recruitment poster I	37
1.2 Recruitment poster II	37

TABLES

3.1 Northern Rhodesia supply position of cotton piece goods, 1944	84
3.2 Cost of living index for Africans, 1939–44	95
5.1 Estimated world copper production by country ('000 long tons)	117
5.2 Maize sales in the line-of-rail provinces, 1941–44 (bags)	134
6.1 Gratuities paid to African servicemen of the Northern Rhodesia Regiment, 1939–45	152
6.2 Gratuities paid to European servicemen of the Northern Rhodesia Regiment, 1939–45	154

Acknowledgments

Scores of people and institutions helped or humored me while I worked to produce *War and Society in Colonial Zambia, 1939–1953*. First, I am grateful to my employer, the University of Zambia, for granting me a one-year paid leave in 2017, during which period I mooted ideas about this book.

I would like to register my appreciation to those at Ohio University Press. First, the series editors of War and Militarism in African History, Giacomo Macola and Alicia Catherine Decker, for accepting my work for publication, and for their constructive criticism as I put my ideas together. I would also like to record my debts to the two anonymous reviewers of my manuscript for their incisive evaluation of the work. Lastly, I would like to thank the entire publications team led by Acquisitions Editor Ricky S. Huard for facilitating the production process, and Nancy Basmajian of E. T. Lowe Publishing for the attention-to-detail copyediting of the manuscript.

I am hugely indebted to my former supervisor and academic father Ian Phimister for being a pillar of inspiration and support. My appreciation also goes to Andrew Cohen, Kate Law, Ivor Mhike, and Kalonde Siulapwa, who, in various ways, lent a hand to me over the course of writing this book.

Chapter 4 of this book was presented in different form as a paper at seminars and workshops in Zomba, Bloemfontein, and Berlin. Numerous Africanist participants at these events are to be thanked for their insightful comments and questions. I am particularly grateful to the *Journal of Southern African Studies*, the International Studies Group at the University of the Free State, and Forum Transregionale Studien and Max Weber Stiftung for the generous travel grants accorded to me to make these presentations. I owe a special debt of gratitude to Marja Hinfelaar for reading an earlier version of the same chapter.

Acknowledgments

A section of chapter 5 originally appeared as "Coerced African Labour for Food Production in Northern Rhodesia (Zambia) during the Second World War, 1942–1945," *South African Historical Journal* 68, no. 1 (2016): 50–69. I am grateful to Taylor and Francis for authorizing me to reproduce excerpts from this article. The University of Wisconsin Press allowed me to use extracts from my article "Rubber Production in Northern Rhodesia during the Second World War, 1942–1946," *African Economic History* 41 (2013): 227–59. I would also like to thank the management at the Livingstone Museum for granting me permission to use photographs reproduced in figures 1.1 and 1.2. The staff at the National Archives of Zambia was helpful, as always, when I consulted various documents held there. For this, I say thank you.

My mother, Mary, and siblings, Gerry and Sibu, were always at hand to provide emotional support. Lastly, my wife, Namakau, and son, Lusungu, put up with this manuscript for four years. I owe both of them a lot more than can be adequately expressed on an acknowledgments page. I hope that I have a very, very long time to repay this debt.

Place Names

OLD NAME	NEW NAME
Abyssinia	Ethiopia
Balovale	Zambezi
Barotse Province	Western Province
Ceylon	Sri Lanka
Dutch East Indies	Indonesia
Fort Jameson	Chipata
Fort Rosebery	Mansa
Kaonde-Lunda Province	North-Western Province
Malaya	Malaysia
Mankoya	Kaoma
Northern Province	Northern, Luapula, and Muchinga Provinces
Northern Rhodesia	Zambia
Salisbury	Harare
Southern Rhodesia	Zimbabwe
Western Province	Copperbelt Province

Abbreviations

ALAB	African Labour Advisory Board
BBC	British Broadcasting Corporation
BSACo	British South Africa Company
CAF	Central African Federation
c-i-f	carried-in-freight
CO	Colonial Office
COLA	Cost of living allowance
d.	pence
DC	District Commissioner
EPT	Export Profit Tax
f-o-b	free-on-board
KAR	King's African Rifles
LME	London Metal Exchange
MIA	Mining Industry Archives
MoI	Ministry of Information
MWU	Mine Workers' Union
NAZ	National Archives of Zambia
NCO	Noncommissioned Officer
NRAC	Northern Rhodesia African Congress
NRG	Northern Rhodesia government

Abbreviations

NRR	Northern Rhodesia Regiment
OB	Ossewabrandwag
PEMS	Paris Evangelical Missionary Society
POSB	Post Office Savings Bank
RAA	Rhodesian Anglo American
RST	Rhodesian Selection Trust
s.	shilling
SEC	Secretariat Series
UK	United Kingdom
UNRRA	United Nations Relief and Rehabilitation Administration

WAR AND SOCIETY IN COLONIAL ZAMBIA, 1939–1953

Introduction

WARS, LIKE EPOCHS OF PEACE, ARE CHAPTERS IN THE LIFE PROcess of societies the world over. Modern warfare alters all social conditions of life not only in the countries where the fighting rages but also in those on the periphery that may be linked in some way to the belligerents. These wars have social and political topographies that are fluid and unstable, constantly changing in response to external and internal forces affected by state-level decisions and other actors involved.[1] In seventeenth-century wars ravaging Europe, for example, the civilian populations of countries such as Sweden and Danish Norway bore the brunt of war, whether economically or as refugees or indeed as fatalities. Thus, state development and warfare in ancient Europe were intimately linked, making it difficult to disregard the importance of war to peoples' lives and societies as new nation states arose.

In the centuries that followed, wars waged by state actors still affected ordinary people's ways of life. In order to fully understand a war, we must know the societies that wage it, as it affects each social institution—not only the state, the army, and business, but the churches, the schools, and ordinary families as well. However, it must be noted that the way in which wars have been fought in society has evolved over time, with respective accompanying consequences. The nature of war thus changes with the changing structure of society, and not all wars affect the social order in the same way and to the same extent.[2] Modern society has been transformed by technology, and so, too, has the state of warfare. War has become total war. Up to the end of the nineteenth century, no more than 3 to 5 percent of the population was economically dispensable for war.[3] During the First World War, however, the number of mobilized soldiers in relation to the total population fluctuated from one belligerent nation to another between 10 and 20 percent, with the exception of the United States, at about 4 percent, because it participated in the war for a shorter period than the other countries.[4] This high rate of recruitment of military personnel is ascribed to the fact that these nations were hugely industrialized, thereby freeing manpower for war service.

This book offers a critical lens through which to analyze the military and warfare, and how a global violent conflict—a world war—affects societies on the periphery of the fighting at the epicenter. It gleans sociological insights about the nature of warfare and how it reflects and shapes social dynamics and institutions in colonial Zambia. In writing this book, I adopt a "war and society" approach to show that warfare always has serious ramifications—in this case, social, economic, and political. Bill Nasson's *Abraham Esau's War* offers an examination of the life of rural African and "Coloured" populations of the Cape during the South African War (1899–1902) to illuminate the demands that war places on labor, patriotism, identity, martyrdom, and resistance. Abraham Esau's story is thus about how war shapes a community and how a community shapes a war.[5] Wars incur massive expense to make weapons, to send servicemen to the front, and to supply them with food and ammunition. In addition, wars stimulate economic growth as wartime mobilization leads to increased technological innovation. Wars, including the Second World War, produce an increase in the number of jobs available to groups such as women and youth in the United States, whose participation in the economy had been historically limited.[6]

On the home front, war hurts the well-being of citizens by disrupting the socioeconomic and political life of a given country. Marriages and family relationships, for instance, may get strained due to stress, anxiety, guilt, grief, and other such mental disorders. Women usually lead their households without their men, and some of them end up raising children on their own following the death of their husbands at the front. Food shortages created by a war directly influence the future state of children's health. For instance, those who suffer a period of famine as children are at higher risk of a weakened immune system later in their life.[7] In addition, servicemen may return home with illnesses and physical handicaps that may not have been addressed by military authorities. Emotions that emerge from war experiences disrupt families and change social life. An armed conflict may cause the movement of a large refugee population to neighboring countries, which may not be

Introduction

ready to accept them. Similarly, participation in peacekeeping or peace enforcement operations can cause physical and psychological wounds for soldiers and their families.[8] On a more positive note, a state of war can lead to the defeat of problematic regimes, the correction of injustices, advances in technology and medicines, industrial growth, and an increase in employment levels. At the governmental level, a large wartime mobilization can lead to an increase in governmental centralization as the state develops and maintains institutions specialized in the exercise of coercion.[9] In *War and Society in Colonial Zambia, 1939–1953*, I examine how the social, economic, and political processes set in motion by the Second World War led to the development of a new Zambian economy and state, even as African servicemen did not invest their political agency in the rise of nationalism in the country.

When asked at the occasion marking the fiftieth anniversary of the start of the Second World War how he had found himself fighting on behalf of Britain—an imperial country he had never been to before—veteran Chama Mutemi Kadansa remarked:

> We had only a vague explanation of why and how the war started. They told us that fighting broke out between Britain and Germany, allied with Italy and Japan over their colonies. . . . The fighting that broke out spread to all colonies of the British, as well as our country, then called Northern Rhodesia. At once, all the chiefs were alerted about the raging war by the District Commissioner who requested them to contribute in form of personnel.[10]

In terms of lives lost and material destruction, the Second World War (1939–45) has been the most devastating conflict in human history. More than 21 million combatants and about 38 million civilians died.[11] Having started as a European conflict on 1 September 1939, when Nazi Germany attacked Poland, it soon turned into a global war. Two days after Germany launched its invasion of Poland, Britain declared war on Germany.[12] In this war against Germany, Britain enlisted the support of its closest ally, France. Due to Britain's declaration of war, up to one-fifth of the world's population found itself at war, owing to the mobilization of the far-flung empire Britain controlled.[13] Britain called on vast colonial resources to defend its global empire and trade. In addition to direct military participation, the British Empire provided financial and material resources for the Allied war effort.

3

The empire's main contribution in the early months of war, however, was the deployment of its human assets. Initial assistance came from the dominions. Canada made the first contribution of soldiers on 10 December 1939, while Australasian troops reached the Middle East on 12 February 1940, and joined those from India.[14]

The British colonies in Africa were of strategic significance to the empire. The continent played a prominent part in the war as a battleground for its overland, sea, and air lines of communication. This was because of the demands of global resource mobilization by various colonial powers that sought either to extend or to protect their territorial possessions on the continent.[15] In addition, some 500,000 men and women from British African countries served in the Allied forces in campaigns in the Middle East, North Africa, and East Africa.[16]

The North African campaign consisted of a series of battles and actions involving the Axis and the Allied forces in Libya, Egypt, and Tunisia from 1940 up to 1943. The fascist leader of Italy, Benito Mussolini, had long harbored ambitions of domination over French and British colonies in the Mediterranean region and the Middle East. The opportunity came when France fell at the hands of Germany on 10 June 1940. Mussolini declared war and stepped into Britain's North African empire, thus ensuring that the Mediterranean became a major theater of conflict.[17] The fall of France shattered the balance of power in the Mediterranean, where the British had based their strategic calculations for the containment of Italy on the strength of the French army in North Africa and its Mediterranean fleet.[18] Mussolini's aim was to extend Italian control from Libya and Abyssinia to Tunisia, Algeria and Morocco, and Egypt. He felt that Italian greatness required domination of the Mediterranean and, therefore, British defeat.[19] At the same time, the main aim of the British in the region in the 1930s was to defend Egypt to ensure control of the strategic Suez Canal, thereby maintaining British influence throughout much of the Middle East and South Asia.[20]

Italy's declaration of war in the Mediterranean also prompted the commencement of fighting in East Africa.[21] From June 1940 to November 1941, forces from the British Empire and other Allies fought fascist troops from the colonies of Eritrea, Italian Somaliland, and Abyssinia in what became known as the East African campaign. This was after Mussolini's units from the Italian garrison in Ethiopia had occupied frontier towns in the Anglo-Egyptian

Introduction

condominium of the Sudan on 4 July 1940. On 15 July they penetrated the British colony of Kenya, and between 5 and 19 August occupied the whole of British Somaliland, on the Gulf of Aden.[22]

Servicemen from British Africa were also utilized in the Middle East campaign to offset the labor shortages faced by the Allied nations in 1941. This campaign led directly to the recruitment of 40,000 men from the High Commission Territories of Bechuanaland, Basutoland, and Swaziland to serve there.[23] As the war progressed, the colonies in Africa became increasingly vital in supplying the Middle Eastern theater not only with labor but with food.[24]

Naturally, Northern Rhodesia (modern Zambia), as a British colony, joined the war on the side of its colonial master on 3 September 1939.[25] This followed the British War Cabinet's request that the Colonial Office and the War Office produce a report on the manpower resources of the entire colonial empire.[26] It was in this context that servicemen such as Chama Mutemi Kadansa were enrolled by colonial authorities in the Northern Rhodesia Regiment (NRR) to help imperial Britain defeat the Axis. The military restricted recruitment to African men for engagement in the Second World War. Gender and the military recruitment process were thus profoundly linked. Colonial military values associated macho virility with violence and martial gallantry—values which stay-at-home women could not be expected to personify. By excluding women from joining the Northern Rhodesia Regiment, the military and colonial authorities were reinforcing a heteronormative definition of masculinity, one that embraced ruggedness, virility, and strength.

As the outbreak of war loomed, officials in Europe anticipated that, except for Ethiopia, Africa would only be tangentially affected by the war; however, the fall of France in 1940 and the loss of Britain's Far Eastern colonies after 1942 transformed Africa's engagement in the conflict and brought changes to all levels of society.[27] Kadansa noted that "it was quite likely that German [sic] would have possibly captured Northern Rhodesia had it not been for the [A]frican contribution to the war."[28] In this regard, the colony raised eight battalions comprising about 15,000 African servicemen and between 700 to 800 Europeans.[29] Serving in Kenya, Somaliland, Madagascar, Ceylon, Burma, Palestine, and India, three of these battalions were infantry while the rest performed garrison duties. "From Lusaka we were taken by lorries to Nairobi in Kenya. We had to travel day and night because we were urgently required there to help our exhausted colleagues," recalled ex-serviceman Kadansa on how he found himself in the NRR 1st Battalion serving in East Africa.[30] After a stint of training in East Africa, the servicemen left for the various theaters of the war. For these men, as Rabson Chombola, another veteran, noted, "it was the first time to see the Indian Ocean and to board a ship."[31] The war experience was "fearful" and "the thought of being far away from home [always] came to my mind."[32]

In addition to providing servicemen, Northern Rhodesia was vital in the defense of British and Allied interests, as the colony was a major supplier of copper, the most crucial metal in the manufacture of munitions for the Allies. Mobilization for war brought about marked changes in African colonies. Almost everywhere intense pressure on the colonies to produce more goods to meet war needs led to increased imperial direction over colonial economies.[33] Additionally, the British African colonies' overseas trade was regulated even more than before by the metropolitan government. Bulk purchase schemes in East and West Africa turned colonial governments into monopoly purchasers of local cash crops, sometimes paying only half the price fetched on the open world market.[34] Prices paid to producers of essential commodities were held down, and the ensuing profits temporarily appropriated by the British Treasury in the overriding cause of imperial survival.[35] The colonies also had to accept new conditions imposed by exchange controls, rising inflation, restrictions on trade with non-sterling countries, rationing, and labor conscription.

The war demanded a cooperative effort not only between Britain and its Allies, but also between Britain and its imperial subjects, be they members of the fighting forces or civilians engaged in war work, or factory workers in the metropole or African industries. The war's major impact was economic, and most other changes emanated from this. The war transformed the world economy from one of excess commodity supply to one of raw material shortage, and it changed the role of government in mediating the market and organizing production.[36]

Historian Rosaleen Smyth once argued that "Africans in Northern Rhodesia experienced the Second World War vicariously through news and propaganda."[37] My contention is that this view obfuscates more than it reveals, as there was scarcely an aspect of social life in Northern Rhodesia that was not affected by the war. As one veteran put it, "It was a painful

Introduction

experience. . . . We had to sacrifice our lives to a war effort which was not of our own making."[38] Although no military action took place in the colony, the temptation to view the war as external to the local people should be resisted, primarily because the effect of the war on Northern Rhodesia was not confined to the approximately fifteen thousand servicemen recruited in the territory.[39] As in Ashley Jackson's Bechuanaland, the "concept of the 'home front,' so familiar in the historiography of wartime Britain and used as an umbrella for all of the war's domestic manifestations," applies to Northern Rhodesia as well, for even there "the war affected the social and economic lives of people in a direct way."[40]

In comparison with the British home front, of course, the effects on Northern Rhodesia were on a relatively small scale.[41] Nonetheless, between 1939 and 1953, the colony endured commodity shortages, inflation, the black market, and the profiteering of traders that directly impinged on ordinary people's livelihoods. As in Britain, moreover, the tasks facing African colonial governments because of the disruption of war and its production demands led to an increase in the size of the state's apparatus and an unprecedented involvement in people's daily lives.[42] The colonial state became more closely associated with the running of the economy through the adoption of austerity measures, such as rationing and price controls. Furthermore, import substitution industrialization, agricultural labor conscription, military labor enlistment, and the increased mining of base metals all meant that the war had a direct impact on the Northern Rhodesian home front. This impact, I contend, was greater and more far-reaching than has hitherto been acknowledged.

This book is the first comprehensive historical study to examine the ramifications of the war on colonial Zambia. My book is not primarily about the experiences of Zambian servicemen abroad, but rather about the home front. The task is all the more urgent since central Africa remains peripheral to the growing body of literature devoted to the relationship between the continent and the Second World War.[43] And yet—as Jackson has argued—it is only by means of in-depth case studies that a full appreciation of the lived experiences of Africans during the Second World War can be gained.[44] In Zambian historiography, in general, the theme of "war and society" remains relatively undeveloped. This book investigates one dimension of such history: the Second World War. By critically examining the nature of this war, I contend, we can better begin to understand its influence on the colony's economy and society, particularly with regard to how traditional leaders, mining magnates, traders, and local producers responded to new imperial policies, and how the war affected production and labor relations.

The dearth of studies on the impact of the Second World War on Zambia's colonial history makes this book an original contribution to the country's historiography. This account begins in 1939, the year in which the war started, and ends in 1953, with the establishment of the Central African Federation (CAF). The decision to extend my investigation beyond 1945 has to do with the fact that the effects of the conflict continued to be felt for many years after its official ending. In particular, 1953 was also the year when the bulk purchasing of copper which Britain had initiated at the onset of the war came to an end and free trading in copper on the London Metal Exchange (LME) resumed.

AFRICA AND THE WAR

As the wartime shortage of consumer goods took its toll on the African colonies, many territories followed directives from London to introduce an array of austerity measures similar to those implemented in the United Kingdom. The inception of a centralized economic policy in British Africa was exemplified by the adoption of such measures as the rationing of commodities and price control in almost every colony. These issues have attracted the attention of scholars with an interest in the economic history of colonial Africa.[45] Michael Cowen and Nicholas Westcott, for instance, examined the extent to which the conflict reduced colonial autonomy and contributed to the centralization of imperial economic policy around the British national economy. On the other hand, John Lonsdale's study asserted that the combination of economic collapse and military conflict transformed Kenya from a segmentary to a centralized, but ungovernable, state.[46] Brian Mokopakgosi and Hoyini Bhila compared oral and archival material to determine the war's long-term effect on those left behind by the Bechuanaland servicemen who had enlisted.[47] Their conclusion is that the policies adopted in wartime "greatly underdeveloped peasant agriculture and exacerbated the existing social and economic imbalances in Tswana society."[48] I argue that to make sense of the war's varied economic impact on Northern Rhodesia, a deeper understanding of such issues as inflation, profiteering, shortages, hoarding, and the black market is required.

Introduction

Another area of scholarly concern has been the recruitment and mobilization of military labor for the war effort. Several scholars have analyzed the manner in which African men were encouraged to enlist for war service and the different responses that the enlistment drive elicited.[49] In the High Commission territories of Swaziland, Bechuanaland (Botswana), and Lesotho, successive stages of recruitment for the war service were closely connected to events taking place at different times of the fighting. In South Africa, on the other hand, issues of race took center stage in determining the role that Black men were to play at the front, since the government worried about a possible backlash at the end of the war should local men be equipped with guns. In contributing to this discussion, this book demonstrates that while traditional authorities in Northern Rhodesia were utilized to recruit men, not all of them supported the imperial war effort. Furthermore, local people also had their own personal motives for enlisting in the colonial army. In this sense, my approach foregrounds African agency in this process.

The early successes of Germany in the war and Japan's conquest of Southeast Asia cut off Allied supplies from many sources of tropical raw materials in 1942. This made Britain increasingly dependent on its African colonies for primary products and food supplies. In this way, the war boosted crop production in some African countries to meet the high demand emanating from the metropole. This demand and its consequences have been examined by several scholars.[50] Their works have a direct bearing on the case of Northern Rhodesia, where the production of such commodities as rubber and beeswax was revived following the fall of Allied-controlled colonies in Southeast Asia.

If metropolitan demand called for the extraction of minerals on an unprecedented scale from African colonies,[51] it also brought changes to the way African agricultural produce was marketed, especially after the loss of Britain's Southeast Asian colonies in 1942. This resulted in the creation of agricultural marketing boards in Nigeria, Ghana, Sierra Leone, and the Gambia run directly by the colonial governments.[52] The boards took over marketing activities from trading companies and were granted monopolies over the sale of cocoa, groundnuts, palm oil, palm kernel, and several other minor crops. This change in policy led colonial states to participate directly in running the economy, buying commodities from African peasant farmers at low prices on behalf of the British government. This helps contextualize the role played by imperial institutions, such as the Ministry of Supply, in the production and marketing of wartime Northern Rhodesia's natural resources, which this book investigates.

Another popular theme among Africanists is the extent to which the events of 1939–45 contributed to the decolonization process on the continent. To some, the war represented a watershed, setting in motion the rapid withdrawal of European powers from the continent. These scholars argue that African opposition to the indicators of imperial socioeconomic development programs, as well as general political tension, led to demands for greater independence in the period after the war. It was these problems which worked toward hastening decolonization.[53] Similar arguments have been advanced by David Throup and David Anderson in their studies of the rise of the Mau Mau movement and its role in the struggle for independence in Kenya.[54] Conversely, other scholars have argued that the war merely accelerated a process that had already started during the Great Depression of the early 1930s and the adverse colonial conditions it generated.[55] In this book I demonstrate that the end of the war brought colonial Zambia even closer to Britain than was the case during the war. Rather than letting go of the colony after the war, Britain drew it closer so as to benefit from Zambia's copper, which fetched high prices on the dollar market.

One of the most hotly debated aspects of the relationship between the Second World War and Africa has been the political impact of military service on African colonial soldiers. It has usually been assumed that the men who were recruited and participated in the war came back with new ideas, wider experiences, and broader horizons that made them fight for the independence of their countries. Early works on this theme claimed that soldiers returned home politicized by their wartime experiences and eager to put into practice the new ideas they had acquired through contacts with nationalists in Asia.[56] Ex-servicemen's participation in the Gold Coast riots of 1948 seemed to offer the ultimate proof of the role of demobilized soldiers in postwar nationalist politics. Such views are shared by Michael Crowder. In his interrogation of the effects of the war on West Africa, Crowder concluded that "some returning soldiers were to play a vital role in the formation of the political parties that gained independence in the fifteen years that followed the war. Many were no longer content with the colonial situation as they left it."[57]

Subsequent studies of the impact of servicemen on the societies to which they returned took a different tack. Some scholars even dismissed the ostensible rise of nationalist feelings among ex-combatants as a mere myth.[58] They argued that ex-servicemen in colonial Ghana did not constitute a coherent activist group within the nationalist movement and that the view that African servicemen were directly influenced by personal contact with Indian nationalists "stretche[d] the imagination."[59] A more nuanced approach to this theme was adopted by Adrienne Israel, who, unlike Richard Rathbone and Simon Baynham, suggested that the contribution of ex-soldiers to the politics of independence depended on local conditions, ethnicity, educational levels, military occupations, and class origins.[60] In a 1978 article, Rita Headrick suggested that more important than political awakening *sensu stricto* was the social transformation experienced by African soldiers.[61]

Many recent studies contend that the return of ex-servicemen to their home areas after the war had little impact on the rise of African nationalism.[62] Yet, some of these same studies have also shown that the return of demobilized soldiers was characterized by dissatisfaction where and when men did not obtain what had been "promised" to them during the recruitment process.[63] In general, however, the consensus is that ex-servicemen made a less significant contribution to nationalist politics than was once thought. In this book, I argue that the case of colonial Zambia is consistent with the above findings: insofar as African servicemen are concerned, the war was more remarkable for its social—as opposed to directly political—effects.

In the years that followed the Second World War, rapid changes in the political framework of the French empire forced the issue of veterans' loyalties to the forefront of politics. Rather than adopting the anticolonial cause and demanding independence, many veterans defended their own material interests.[64] Some, especially former career servicemen, even desired a continuing French presence in West Africa, even if such a presence was vaguely articulated. The complexity of the veterans' social positions and their mixed political allegiances stemmed partly from their experiences abroad and their ability to play a role in their communities while they were away.[65] To the contrary, Nancy Lawler has made a strong argument for veterans' participation in the anticolonial political movement in French West Africa led by Felix Houphouët-Boigny in the Ivory Coast.[66] At the center of this thesis is the preeminent influence of the *chef de province* (provincial chief) of Korhogo, who threw his weight behind Houphouët-Boigny's nationalist movement early on and persuaded local veterans to do the same. Gregory Mann's context and argument differs from this. To him, a crucial cleavage emerged among Malian veterans and is representative of divisions between veterans across that territory and the rest of L'Afrique Occidentale Française (French West Africa). The climax to these divisions occurred in November and December 1944, in the form of mutinies by ex-servicemen at Thiaroye, outside Dakar, in which thirty-five of them died. To Mann, these were not "planned and premeditated" mutinies, as Myron Echenberg has argued.[67] They were motivated not by politics, but by money, honor, and an array of acute grievances faced by veterans. Veterans made no larger demands, but in the immediate aftermath of the rebellion, Senegalese politicians, particularly Lamine Guèye, adopted their cause.[68] In the long run, veterans mobilized collectively to address a more complex set of demands to the colonial state rather than to the military. An especially clear example is provided by Guèye, who appealed to veterans' grievances and won their loyalty in his struggle against the French administration and certain *chefs de canton* (district chiefs). However, it must be noted that although politically they were a force to reckon with, veterans were not necessarily nationalists.[69]

In the case of Zambia, the social and political processes set in motion by the war, the growth of the copper mining industry, the new state-controlled economy, and even the distinctive approach to Polish refugees all actually set the country on a path to independence—even though African servicemen did not become the central agents for this movement. In this book, therefore, I nuance the idea that the mobilization and demobilization of African servicemen contributed to nationalist, pro-independence sentiment and organization. This brings into sharp relief the contradictoriness of political processes on the eve of decolonization on the continent: on the one hand, servicemen took part in the Second World War as imperial subjects; on the other, the momentous socioeconomic changes occasioned by the same conflict set Zambia on the path to autonomy and ultimately independence.

The Second World War period witnessed the emergence of new pressure groups as a result of the economic stringencies faced by the continent. Among the most critical of these were African-run trade unions. The rise of these trade unions came about as African workers received less and less remuneration for their labor owing to war conditions. The result was a strike wave in the most commercially active centers on the continent: ports in Mombasa, Dakar and Dar-es-Salaam; railways in the Gold Coast; and, indeed, the

Introduction

copper mines of Northern Rhodesia.[70] Inadvertently, African trade unions contributed to the rise of nationalist feelings in respective countries. By the 1950s, trade unions were adding their voice to the challenge to paternalistic authority in Africa. They joined the ranks of emerging political leaders in seizing the openings of the postwar moment by making a variety of claims: for access to material resources, for their voices to be heard, and for the exercise of power.[71]

African colonies mobilized civilian labor for war production on a large scale. Increased wartime demands, however, led to labor and food shortages, which induced Britain to authorize the use of conscripted labor with a view to securing adequate supplies of either food or minerals, or both. The resurgence of conscripted labor in British colonial Africa during the Second World War was an imperial initiative rooted in war and crisis. It was introduced in early 1942 following Axis victories in Southeast Asia, which curtailed the supply of raw materials to the Allies. Ian Spencer notes that Kenya was the first British African colony to use forced labor for agricultural purposes.[72] In Southern Rhodesia, forced labor was drawn upon to construct the airfields used by the Empire Air Training Scheme (EATS) and to produce more food in response to increased wartime demand.[73] Tanganyika, meanwhile, initiated labor conscription for European plantations with a view to increasing the production of sisal and rubber.[74] The most notorious form of labor conscription in wartime Africa took place on the tin mines of the Jos Plateau in northern Nigeria, where 100,000 Africans were recruited, resulting in the deaths of hundreds of them due to poor sanitary conditions.[75] What can be deduced from these instances is that, in times of war, Britain was desperate to attain victory at whatever cost. Labor conscription thus became an important strategy of survival—one to which, as will be seen, the Northern Rhodesian administration also proved ready to resort.

The most comprehensive analysis of a specific British colony during the Second World War has focused on Bechuanaland.[76] In this study, Ashley Jackson explores the social, economic, political, agricultural, and military histories of colonial Botswana. He examines the country's military contribution to the war effort and what impact that participation had on its own home front. The book also considers wartime colonial Botswana's interaction with, and impact on, events and personalities in distant imperial centers, such as Whitehall. Jackson's work amounts to a unique and "total" history of an African country—one which draws much of its strength from the author's reliance on oral sources alongside archival material.[77] Using a similar approach, this book builds upon the foundation laid by Jackson by examining, for the first time, the major facets of the war's impact on Northern Rhodesia.

The flurry of focused, subject-specific studies discussed above has lately paved the way for the compilation of more comprehensive overviews of the relationship between Africa and the Second World War. David Killingray's *Fighting for Britain* is to date the most comprehensive single-authored study of the relationship between British colonial Africa and the Second World War.[78] Paying special attention to the experiences of the African rank and file, Killingray aims to "tell in their own words the story of African soldiers who fought for Britain and Africa."[79] Taking a different approach, Ashley Jackson's *The British Empire and the Second World War* is the first publication to set Britain's war effort in its imperial context. Jackson's study is especially commendable for demonstrating that even small colonies contributed to the imperial war effort. Jackson's insight shapes the present work, which is primarily about reverberations—about how war events in the major theaters of the war affected a distant colonial backwater.

Issues of race, gender, and labor during the Second World War feature prominently in recent scholarship on the impact of the war on Africa. These *problématiques* lie at the heart of *Africa and World War II*, a collection of essays.[80] Taken together, the essays included in this important work grapple with critical issues of periodization, with contradictions in colonial policy, and with the impact of war on ordinary African livelihoods. Contributors to the volume identify signal events that had the most sustained impact on Africa's communities, such as the fall of France and Japan's conquest of Southeast Asia.[81] They illustrate the continent's critical role in sustaining the Allied war effort, particularly after early 1942, when British colonies in the Far East were overrun by the Japanese.

For Northern Rhodesia, I demonstrate that events taking place in Europe had a direct bearing on the recruitment of servicemen for the Allied war effort. Following France's defeat in 1940, Britain was under pressure to fight a war without the assistance of its closest ally. It thus began to rely more and more on its African colonies for the human resources needed at the front. From that point onward, an intensified drive recruited more African servicemen to join the Northern Rhodesia Regiment than before. Additionally, beginning in early

Introduction

1942, the colony came under intense pressure from imperial authorities to revive the production of such commodities as rubber, beeswax, rope, leather, and iron. This was a direct result of the Japanese takeover of Allied-owned colonies in Southeast Asia, which were traditional sources of these commodities. As Judith Byfield observes, in many ways, especially after 1942, African resources sustained the Allied effort. This support, however, entailed high social costs.[82]

Another critical point of discussion in *Africa and World War II* is how the mobilization of communities to provide labor, food, and other resources for the war exacerbated some of the contradictions of colonialism, thus making the war an equally significant watershed in African history.[83] The productivist drive of colonial governments encountered increasing obstacles, as some communities experienced food shortages in the wake of the relocation of agricultural labor or the redeployment of food to troops instead of to ordinary citizens. In Northern Rhodesia, I argue in the present study, the most critical point of contradiction had to do with the price structure of the commodities needed in the metropole. While authorities in London wanted materials such as rubber and beeswax to be supplied from Northern Rhodesia, they were reluctant to pay fair prices for the same commodities. It was the colonial authorities on the ground in Northern Rhodesia who had to contend with protestations from local peasant producers over the low prices offered by the British Ministry of Supply.

The last theme addressed by *Africa and World War II* is the varied impact of the war on ordinary Africans and their communities. Despite the hardships, many African men and women took to heart the stated aims of the Allied forces and volunteered to support the war in numerous ways to demonstrate their commitment to the shared ideals of the cause.[84] Africans made financial contributions by supporting war charities and paying taxes. The war affected the African home front in such ways as commodity shortages, profiteering, and forced labor, which I discuss in chapter 4. While the Northern Rhodesian home front was very far away from the battlefronts of wartime Europe, the war's effects did not spare the territory. Its citizens experienced commodity shortages and hoarding, hyperinflation, and the black market for much of the war period.

The Second World War was in many ways a refugee crisis. A faint echo of the massive population displacements taking place in Europe was provided by the resettlement of Polish refugees in Africa. Inspired by a pioneering study by Samwiri Lwanga-Lunyiigo,[85] David Kiyaga-Mulindwa explored the trajectory of Polish wartime refugees in Uganda, arguing that the colonial government's hostility to non-British settlement led to the isolation of the Poles; this isolation, in turn, accounts for their lack of impact on the hosting territory.[86] Recently, there has also been an examination of the discriminatory nature of the Rhodesian immigration policy toward Poles during and after the Second World War.[87] While noting the relevance of economic and political considerations, the authors of this last study foreground the central role of ethnic prejudice against Central Europeans in accounting for the way British Rhodesians treated Second World War evacuees. Such an attitude, however, was not peculiar to Polish citizens, as it was well entrenched in the region against all non-British Whites.[88] A recent and comprehensive discussion of the experience of Polish refugees in Africa, however, is to be found in Jochen Lingelbach's doctoral thesis.[89] Overcoming colonial borders, and focusing on east-central Africa as a whole, this fresh study tackles the interactions between Polish refugees and different actors of the hosting populations—their conflicts, mutual perceptions, and influences—from a wider perspective than country-specific studies permit.

NORTHERN RHODESIA AND THE WAR

A general and small corpus of literature does exist profiling the experiences of Northern Rhodesians during the war, but it is largely focused on copper mining and the fractious labor relationship that existed between European settler farmers and the local African population.[90] Not even L. F. G. Anthony's chapter in *The Story of the Northern Rhodesia Regiment* is concerned with the specificity of the impact of the war on the servicemen whose expeditions were the focus of the study.[91] The present book is the first comprehensive academic study of the ramifications of the war on colonial Zambia. It builds upon the foundation laid in 1954 by the colony's "official" war historian.[92] William V. Brelsford's edited collection consists of a definitive survey of the movements and tasks of Northern Rhodesian servicemen during the war. The present book attempts to broaden and deepen Brelsford's focus by examining other aspects of the war's impact on the colony's agricultural, political, economic, and social sectors.

There are only a few article-length studies of the role of the Second World War in the life of colonial Zambia. Rosaleen Smyth's 1984 article

Introduction

brought Northern Rhodesia historiographically into line with other former colonial territories during the war period.[93] Smyth analyzed the effect of war propaganda in hastening the rise of an African political voice. This book has profitably built upon Smyth's foundations through an examination of the government's desperate propaganda activities in the colony in its quest to recruit military personnel for the war effort. In this study, however, I demonstrate that, aside from the use of propaganda, there was also African agency in the recruitment drive for servicemen. Moreover, I argue that while there was a general rise in African political thought in the country during the war—as Smyth observed—this movement was led by ordinary citizens, and not by ex-servicemen.

Other studies, by Kusum Datta and Kenneth Vickery, have focused on White-Black labor relations and copper mining during the war.[94] They argue that the Second World War presented an opportunity for undercapitalized European farmers to enlist state support in securing African labor that could not be obtained on the free market. As a result of war imperatives, a wartime agricultural crisis, and a diminished supply of labor, settler farmers pressured the colonial government and London to introduce labor conscription on their farms in 1942. This was similar to measures adopted in Kenya, Nigeria, and Southern Rhodesia during the same period. This study shows how this policy was replicated in Northern Rhodesia.

Both Andrew Roberts and Lewis Gann have examined the prosperity of the Northern Rhodesian copper industry both during and after the war period, and the impact that the growth of the mining sector came to have on the political economy of the territory and the region at large.[95] Lawrence Butler has provided a recent study of business-government relations under colonial rule and the decolonization period in Northern Rhodesia.[96] According to him, the copper mining industry in the country was affected by three central issues since its founding in the late 1920s: overproduction, the introduction of government monopoly purchase schemes during the Second World War, and the threat of nationalization. As the copper mining industry was completely reliant on external demand for its product, events beyond the industry's control underscored the cyclical nature of the Copperbelt's fortunes. By the end of the war, Britain needed Northern Rhodesia more than ever before because of the importance of dollar earnings from copper. Thus, the present study charts the ways in which Northern Rhodesia was transformed from a neglected to a highly strategic possession in the late colonial period due to the Empire's shifting financial and monetary priorities.

In his examination of tariff and railway freight rates, Ackson Kanduza posits that Northern Rhodesian capital continued to face stiff resistance from the state in its quest to industrialize the country both during and after the war.[97] Due to this state laxity in protecting local industries, Northern Rhodesia was slow to accumulate capital in comparison to its southern neighbors. Northern Rhodesia was found unprepared to take advantage of that wartime scarcity which favored local manufacturing in Southern Rhodesia and South Africa. This book demonstrates that there were also factors other than tariff policy that hindered the attainment of import substitution industrialization in wartime Northern Rhodesia.

Samuel Chipungu's analysis of the relationship between peasant farmers, the state, and technological development notes that the Second World War acted as a catalyst for agricultural change in the Southern Province of Northern Rhodesia.[98] The war forced the colonial government to review the condition of African peasant agriculture to meet increased food requirements on the Copperbelt, whose labor force had expanded. Although Chipungu's study is not free from statistical errors, it has been used as the basis for my examination of the impact of the war on the agricultural sector in chapter 5.

Aside from scattered references in general histories, European refugees in wartime Northern Rhodesia have not received dedicated attention in historical studies.[99] This book addresses this little-known aspect of Zambian history.

A NOTE ON METHODOLOGY AND STRUCTURE

This monograph draws on a variety of primary sources. The archives at the Livingstone Museum, in Livingstone, provided previously untouched materials on the history of the Northern Rhodesia Regiment that have only recently been made available to the public. These include war diaries, recruitment posters, magazines, and photographs pertaining to the war period. I also used the Mining Industry Archives (formerly the Zambia Consolidated Copper Mines Archives), in Ndola, which contain data pertaining to mining operations and associated aspects. I relied as well on the extensive press coverage of the country's mining companies in international finance and mining publications during the period under study.

Introduction

However, I sourced the bulk of the archival materials from the Secretariat and Provincial Series of the National Archives of Zambia (NAZ), in Lusaka. The merit of using this archive is that it provides seamless linkages between the grand political levels informing the "on the ground" participation in the conflict in colonial Zambia; London is connected to Lusaka, and Lusaka to the territory's outlying districts and villages. The records in question consist of tour reports, annual reports of various government departments, newsletters, and correspondence between colonial and imperial government officials. Various newspapers and Legislative Council debates also provided much relevant information. Although the government-run *Mutende* newspaper was mainly used for propaganda purposes intended for the local reader, it also proved a useful source of evidence on Africans' perspectives on the war. The postwar economic and social ambitions and expectations of Northern Rhodesian ex-servicemen are richly set out in the letters they wrote, some of which were intercepted by military and civilian officials. Absent from this monograph are sources from British archives such as the National Archives at Kew owing to logistical challenges I encountered in trying to access these.

While I did not personally conduct oral interviews with any ex-servicemen, this book still makes room for the voices of the men who fought in the war. For this, I relied on twelve transcripts of interviews with Zambian ex-servicemen that were conducted by the British Broadcasting Corporation (BBC) in 1989 to mark the fiftieth anniversary of the outbreak of the war. These transcripts are lodged at the Imperial War Museum in London. These oral sources contain rich information concerning the experiences of African servicemen in the various theaters of the war: East Africa, the Middle East, and Asia. The African veterans' experiences provided a useful supplement, and sometimes a corrective, to what could be gleaned from official documents and secondary sources. Importantly, these interviews made it possible to hear the voices of Africans actively involved in the recruitment and demobilization processes—aspects generally missing in official records.

While using oral sources, I was also mindful of the drawbacks of relying too much on this type of data. A good deal has been written on the pitfalls of collecting and using oral evidence. A major problem, of course, is the reliability of the memories of aging informants about the events of a war in which they fought many years earlier.[100] Reliance on personal narratives also raises questions of representativeness, and the extent to which generalizations may validly be drawn from a limited number of interviews. The task of the historian dealing with oral evidence, however, is to take particular phenomena and elucidate their more general meanings. As Claude Lévi-Strauss observed, all the historian and ethnographer can do, and all we can expect of them, is to enlarge a specific experience to the dimensions of a more general one.[101] Gayatri Spivak further argued that it is impossible to "capture" the full reality of subaltern consciousness and memory across barriers of class and colonialism.[102] So, too, this book cannot imaginatively capture the full reality of Northern Rhodesia's servicemen who participated in the Second World War. More modestly, it has drawn upon a disparate group of servicemen's experiences to speak about their history. At best, oral evidence has been illuminating, detailed in recall, and powerfully descriptive. The voices of African veterans offer a rich and valid contribution to the history of the Second World War—important and decisive years in modern Africa's recent past.[103]

This book consists of six thematic chapters. In chapter 1, I address the recruitment of servicemen for the NRR. After showing how the British monarch took the lead in calling upon colonial subjects in Northern Rhodesia to support the imperial power as soon as the war broke out in Europe, I demonstrate that the government drew on both chiefly institutions and propaganda to recruit personnel for the army. I also argue that there were both pull and push factors behind the participation of Africans in the war and that, throughout the process, Africans were not deprived of agency. Lastly, I explain that the country's participation in the war was not without resistance from certain sections of the populace, primarily from African and European members of the Jehovah's Witnesses and the Afrikaner settler community.

In chapter 2, I explore the Northern Rhodesian reverberations of the defeat of the Allied-controlled colonies in Southeast Asia, which were major sources of raw materials needed for the war effort. To fill the void in the supply chain created by Japanese victories in early 1942, London instructed Lusaka to revive the age-old rubber and beeswax industries as alternative sources of raw materials for Allied use. The country also rejuvenated the production of iron tools, rope, and string to meet the demand for home consumption as these commodities could no longer be easily imported from overseas due to war conditions. The imperial government hoped this measure could lift the burden placed on it by providing scarce consumables for its colonies. I demonstrate that the prices paid to local producers of these

Introduction

commodities were lower than British propaganda had predicted at the start of the war and that this discrepancy led to a degree of tension between colonial officials on the ground and their superiors in London.

Next, I focus on the wartime economic challenges faced by the Northern Rhodesian home front. I investigate how the shortage of consumer goods, inflation, the black market, profiteering, and hoarding impacted the lives of ordinary people. Due to these challenges, the government abandoned its laissez-faire policy by taking a more active role in the running of the colony's economic affairs than it had in the past. Colonial administrators tried to solve some of these economic woes through rationing schemes, price control, and import substitution industrialization, and by curbing a rise in the levels of inflation. The chapter also shows that this trend continued in the postwar period, due to persistent commodity shortages resulting from convertibility challenges in the sterling area.

In chapter 4, I deal with issues pertaining to how Northern Rhodesia hosted Polish refugees on behalf of Britain. I examine the rationale, course of the migration, and eventual settlement of the Poles in various parts of the colony. In reconstructing the wartime history of Polish settlement in Northern Rhodesia, I repeatedly note the interconnectedness of events in the broader empire and in local society. A recurring point of discussion is that of racial hierarchy based on colonial pseudoscientific theories that influenced the relationship between the "aliens" and local British settlers. I argue that British colonial racial attitudes to a large extent determined how the Poles were treated in Northern Rhodesia. Local colonial authorities encountered numerous problems in the process of safeguarding the lives of these hapless souls. Although many of these problems were brought to the attention of Whitehall, no easy solution was forthcoming.

In the fifth chapter, I investigate the impact of the war on the colony's economic mainstay—copper mining. The scheme for bulk purchasing of copper developed by the British Ministry of Supply ensured that the commodity was bought at a uniform price throughout the war period and supplied only to Britain and its allies. Following the devaluation of sterling in 1949, the British government put pressure on the colony's copper mining industry to produce more copper for sale to dollar-earning countries. This state of affairs accounts for Britain's continued hold on the colony in the postwar period. Free-market conditions in the copper trade were restored only in

April 1953, following the reopening of the LME, which had been closed at the start of the hostilities.

Chapter 6 outlines the demobilization exercise undertaken at the end of the war. Many African servicemen felt cheated by a racialized process according to which European ex-servicemen received more favorable rewards than they did. I argue that the dissatisfaction of African ex-servicemen over perceived broken promises, however, was a universal phenomenon that also affected colonial personnel in other parts of Africa, Asia, and the Caribbean. In fact, complaints about conditions of service in colonial armies occurred even before the end of the war, as protests and mutinies over differential treatment based on race occurred in many theaters before 1945. Contrary to older academic opinions, I argue that African ex-servicemen did not collectively participate in nationalist politics but remained predominantly concerned with personal and domestic matters.

In conclusion, I draw out common and contrasting themes to demonstrate the wider economic, social, and political significance of the Second World War for colonial Zambia during the last phase of British imperialism. Although important aspects of the conventional view on Africa and the war have already been revised, more study is required to showcase national experiences and, by so doing, attain a more complete picture of the war. By making a case for the relevance of in-depth, country-specific case studies, this book adds to the historiography of the Second World War in Africa as a whole. I suggest that we still have much to learn about and from the war, which has mainly been studied from the global or continental perspective rather than by focusing on country-specific societal effects.

1

Military Labor Recruitment and Mobilization

O N SUNDAY, 3 SEPTEMBER 1939, KING GEORGE VI SPOKE TO THE empire from London via radio. Part of his speech, as reported in *Mutende* on 12 September, read:

> In this grave hour, perhaps the most fateful in our history, I send to
> every household of my peoples[,] both at home and overseas, this
> message, spoken with the same depth of feeling for each one of you
> as if I were able to cross your threshold and speak to you myself.
> For the second time in the lives of most of us, we are at war. . . . We
> have been forced into a conflict, for we are called with our allies
> to meet the challenge of a principle which, if it were to prevail[,]
> would be fatal to any civilised order in the world. . . . For the sake
> of all that we ourselves hold dear and of the world's order and
> peace, it is unthinkable that we should refuse to meet the challenge.
> It is to this high hope [purpose] that I now call upon my people
> at home and [my peoples] across the seas who will make our cause
> their own.[1]

It was in this context that Northern Rhodesia came to play a significant part in the mobilization and execution of the war effort on behalf of Britain. While Northern Rhodesia's major contribution to the British war effort was the provision of base metals, human resource mobilization counted second in priority. In this chapter I examine how the colony went about recruiting and mobilizing personnel for the Northern Rhodesia Regiment (NRR), in line with the appeal issued by the British Crown. I argue that while the government used chiefly institutions and propaganda to entice Africans into joining the army, the local people also had their own reasons for enlistment. I also depart from older academic arguments to show that war service was not wholly destructive to African socioeconomic life, because those who remained behind devised coping strategies in the absence of their male relatives. Finally, being concerned with local reactions to the outbreak of the conflict and the ensuing call to arms, the chapter touches upon how subversive elements in the form of the Watch Tower Sect and the settler Afrikaner community resisted and campaigned against the Northern Rhodesian war effort.

GOVERNMENT PROPAGANDA ON THE OUTBREAK OF THE WAR

Africans in Northern Rhodesia reacted to the news of the war as soon as the British king's speech was aired in the territory. This speech was not only broadcast in Northern Rhodesia—as in the rest of the British Empire—but also translated into various local languages and published in *Mutende*, the government newspaper for Africans. Before the outbreak of the war, government propaganda in the colony had presented King George as the symbol of empire, a kind of "super paramount chief" to whom all Africans owed loyalty and the linchpin of a "monarchical ideology" linking rulers and ruled.[2] It was to this "super chief" that the people of Northern Rhodesia were to pledge their loyalty during the Second World War. Secretary of State for the Colonies Malcolm MacDonald also added his voice in seeking the help of colonial subjects to win the war against the Axis powers. He stated: "The long and happy association of so many peoples of different races and creeds under the British Crown is itself the best proof that the ideal of peaceful and fruitful cooperation between diverse peoples, who are willing to understand and respect each other, is attainable."[3]

When Britain declared war on Germany on 3 September 1939, the government of Northern Rhodesia was interested in reassuring itself that its African charges would back the colonial master in the conflict.[4] Its attitude toward African participation in the war was disarmingly straightforward. Northern Rhodesia would participate in the war as a loyal member of the British Empire because the mother country had given protection to the

Military Labor Recruitment and Mobilization

territory since the start of colonization in the 1890s. It was thanks to British rule, government officials reasoned, that people enjoyed freedom in the territory. Governor John Maybin's message to Northern Rhodesia's Africans was couched in an appealing tone. Thus, in a special edition of *Mutende* published on 3 September 1939, he stated that "the Government will require recruits for the Regiment and drivers for its transport and I am confident that Africans will prove their desire to serve their King by promptly offering their service."[5] This plea was directed at chiefs, the official custodians of the country's traditional power structure in the context of indirect rule, and was issued through government bureaucrats and the press. The governor informed all chiefs in the country that war had been declared in Europe and requested a guarantee of their loyalty to the British Crown.[6] The policy of using traditional leaders, rather than government officials, in appealing for support from the African masses was candidly stated by the editor of *Mutende* in a letter to a provincial commissioner on 14 September. "From experience," he wrote, "I find that a letter from a chief or comments by a reader (or by the Editor under a Native name!) cut a great deal more 'ice' than a dozen 'leaders' or messages from Europeans."[7] Such requests were routine procedure all over the empire during the war.[8] In this way, the war contributed to the revival of the powers of chiefs by assigning them significant responsibility for the recruitment of personnel for the army, a role they had already fulfilled during the First World War.

Each of the four principal chiefs responded with positive statements pledging loyalty to the "mother country" and to help "their king." Chiefs and their senior officials drafted these messages. For example, Paramount Chief Mpezeni of the Ngoni people was one of the first to pledge his loyalty to the imperial government's war effort. Mpezeni, whose ancestors had fought the British at the end of the previous century, referred to his people's physical fighting qualities and assured the colonial government that the Ngoni stood loyally by the British king. Mpezeni informed the governor that he was "sorry to hear that war has broken out in Europe. . . . We have derived such blessings and benefits from British rule that we Angoni all stand loyally by our Governor and our King in this hour of need."[9] There were many such pledges of loyalty from other chiefs throughout the country.[10] As in much of colonial Africa, however, these avid chiefly expressions of allegiance to Britain were made without the knowledge of their subjects.[11]

Not all chiefs, of course, proved similarly amenable to the wishes of the British Crown and the colonial administration. A notable example was provided by the Tonga chief, Mwanachingwala, of Mazabuka district. When asked to help with the recruitment of servicemen, his reply, described by the district commissioner as "typical of his undistinguishable career," was: "Bwana, we are all . . . women; and we are afraid [of going to war]."[12] By voicing his reservations in these terms, Mwanachingwala indicated that gender and the military recruitment process were deeply interwoven. It is fascinating that the chief was essentially emasculating the men in his community by calling them "women." This was a clever tactic, but one that also suggested that women were weak, cowardly, and not valued. Here, Mwanachingwala was echoing the values in the military which equated masculine virility with violence and martial valor[13]—values stay-at-home women could not be expected to embody. By attempting to resist the recruitment of his male subjects on the basis that they were "women," the Tonga leader was actually playing up gender role stereotypes for subversive ends. He was undermining the men for strategic purposes! This is not surprising, since, as Alicia Decker ably demonstrates for Uganda, ideologies of masculinity and those of femininity are culturally and historically constructed, their meanings continually contested and always in the process of being renegotiated in the context of existing power relations.[14] The chief's powerful claim, however, did not work as expected, because some of his subjects registered for military service precisely to prove their masculinity.

To mobilize public opinion in support of the war, the colonial government began to pay more attention to African views than it had done before the outbreak of hostilities. It tried to influence public opinion by means of a thorough propaganda campaign involving newspapers, leaflets, talks by district commissioners, radio broadcasts, and cinema shows—all designed to explain the war, account for the economic strains brought about by the hostilities, and encourage men to join the army. Government policy was aimed at keeping educated and urbanized Africans as fully and accurately informed about the war as possible; conversely, it sought to avoid giving excessive detail to rural Africans, who were commonly regarded as too unsophisticated and isolated fully to understand the war's technicalities.[15] Published by the Information Office, and written in simple English and four other widely spoken local languages (Bemba, Nyfa, Tonga, and Lozi), the aforementioned

Mutende was a key tool in the hands of policy makers. At the outbreak of the war, the newspaper's circulation was about 5,600; by 1944, this figure was estimated to be 18,000. Its message, moreover, reached a much greater audience, as it was believed that each copy was seen by an average of ten people.[16] Fortnightly issues replaced monthly ones from September 1939 until the end of the war. Also, as a war measure, a free issue of *Mutende* was supplied to every chief in each district until the end of December 1939. In cases where a chief already subscribed to the newspaper, the extra copy was made available to other members of his council, thus disseminating Allied war propaganda news as far and wide as possible.[17] In January 1940, Native Authority Funds took over the responsibility of buying copies at three pence each. Also circulating among Northern Rhodesia's African intelligentsia were the two liberal European-owned commercial newspapers published for Africans in Southern Rhodesia, the *Bantu Mirror* and the *African Weekly*; both were published in English and selected African languages.[18]

Broadcasting targeted at African audiences was inaugurated in October 1939 from Nkana, on the Copperbelt, with the assistance of members of the Radio Society. The radio broadcasts, in the four major local languages, consisted of war news bulletins (broadcast on Mondays and Fridays) and a war news discussion program every week.[19] The broadcasts proved so successful with listeners throughout the southern African region that another broadcasting station was opened in Lusaka in September of the following year. Traditional leaders, of course, featured among the prominent people enticed to speak to African audiences. Chief Mwase Kasungu of Nyasaland, for instance, was flown into Northern Rhodesia at government expense in August 1940 specifically for propaganda purposes, following his trip to Britain early that year. He was especially chosen because he was regarded as an extremely intelligent chief who exerted significant influence over his people. Most importantly, he was perceived to have a great deal of sympathy for the Allied cause.[20] During his three broadcasts in Cinyanja, he urged his African listeners to remain loyal to the Allied war effort.

The main source of descriptive war news was the newly established British Ministry of Information (MoI). The ministry provided news articles about the war and related photographs to the local Information Office for distribution to media houses in Northern Rhodesia. By 1 December 1939, 435 articles and 500 photographs had been received from London and made available to *Mutende*.[21] Copies were also supplied to schools and mission stations. The European settler community was serviced by the *Northern Rhodesia Advertiser, Livingstone Mail, Northern Rhodesia Newsletter*, and *Southern Rhodesia Newsletter*. The *Indian Information Newsletter* was circulated in 100 copies to the Asian community once fortnightly in addition to the two newsletters from both Rhodesias.[22] The Afrikaner community was provided with the fortnightly *Afrikaans Newsletter*, whose circulation in early 1940 was 300 copies.[23] This newsletter consisted of South African and local news items, as well as information counteracting German propaganda.

Toward the end of the 1930s, Britain had become concerned about its image as a colonial power. To bring the empire together, it was decided that Britain needed a new organizing concept to portray its relationship with its colonies. During the war, "partnership" became the new slogan; the earlier concept of "trusteeship" was abandoned because it was thought to be too paternalistic.[24] The cornerstone of this propaganda was the conventional cliché of Anglo-Saxon democracy and its right to fight for and defend "freedom." Part of this hypocritical campaign appealed to Africans to support the British war effort. Failure to do so would be exploited by German colonialists, who, it was alleged, would buy colonial produce at unfavorable prices to African producers.

The Colonial Office in London realized that mobilization for total war required a coordinated propaganda campaign to combat dissension and aid recruitment for the army. The main organizer of this propaganda campaign was the MoI. In Northern Rhodesia, this responsibility fell to Kenneth Bradley, the country's first information officer, and, from 1943, to his successor, Harry Franklin. The Colonial Office nonetheless continued to formulate its own propaganda campaign aimed at the colonies. The Colonial Film Unit based in London made propaganda films which they supplied to African colonies. By 1944, 101 titles had been shown in the territory.[25] The local Information Office sent its only cinema van around the country to show propaganda films to as many people as possible. By the end of the war, an estimated 80,000 people had seen films shown by the mobile van in various parts of the country.[26] Yet some of these 16mm films, especially those lacking human action, were criticized for not appealing to intelligent African audiences.[27]

The publicity campaigns devised by the Colonial Office and MoI were designed to convince colonial subjects of three interrelated elements concerning the war: that Britain was fighting evil (Nazism); that the moral and material development of the British Empire after the war depended upon victory; and that this victory could be assured through the united efforts of "right-thinking persons."[28] Campaign material written in a typical war propaganda vein simplified the conflict by framing it as one between oppressed and liberated peoples. The message was strengthened through the use of folk tropes and imagery with the aim of constructing Germany and Adolf Hitler as the embodiment of an evil that needed to be defeated at all costs. For instance, a story published in the *Bantu Mirror* stated that "the leaders of [the] British and French people have been working hard for the past year to try and persuade the leader of the German people to stop his bad custom of stealing other countries like a thief who beats people on the road with a stick and then takes their goods."[29]

Colonial authorities tried to convince the local people that their lot would be significantly worse under German rule by exposing the ruthlessness of Hitler and his Nazi Party in dramatic language and pictures.[30] It was constantly brought to the attention of Africans that if the Axis occupied Northern Rhodesia, the position of local people would be scarcely better than that of Polish slaves.[31] Government officials thus emphasized that it was up to everyone to defend Northern Rhodesia and fight for King George VI.

This "atrocity" propaganda seems to have been initially successful, even among educated Africans. A typical example is a poem written by Francis Chandwe, a teacher at Katondwe Mission, and published in *Mutende* in October 1939. Titled "The Boom beyond the Seas," the poem is worth quoting in full:

The boom of German artillery,
And the explosion of bombs,
Beyond the seas, has caused great convulsions to the world.
The flight of planes over Poland,
And the showering of bullets over the Poles,
The odium, and the abject poverty,
And misery that will follow is unspeakable.
The cataclysm of this catastrophe,
And the kleptomania of the German monarch,
In search of the road to Utopia

Is horribly detrimental to the world.
The destruction of thousands of lives,
The umbra of fear cast over Poland
The sadism, as it were of the ignoramus,
Yet of a far [more] civilised being, is inconceivable.
The evil of the calamity of that ilk,
The world felt indignation,
And the calmness of the British Empire,
The world can not express.
Poland! Poland! Poland!
Though small as you are
Will you yield, knowing the doom and destruction
Of your liberty, autonomy and your Catholicism?
God forbid![32]

As the war progressed, however, government authorities realized that this propaganda could backfire and that increasing emphasis should instead be placed on such positive messages as "togetherness" and "future colonial objectives." Already, government officials were finding it difficult to answer queries from perceptive Africans who wondered whether—given their own colonial record—Britain and the colonial government had the moral right to question German atrocities. It is most probable that this kind of reasoning was a direct response to such propaganda pieces as the aforementioned *Bantu Mirror* article. The irony of this type of propaganda was that, by colonizing Northern Rhodesia, Britain had also "stolen" the country. Early in 1942, for instance, the district commissioner for Mongu reported being challenged by local people, who asked whether Hitler treated his white slaves any better than Europeans treated Africans in Northern Rhodesia.[33]

Early in the war, the information officer warned the colonial government that

> the African agrees strongly with Hitler that neutrals should be invaded and women and children bombed in order to win the war. . . . He must be educated out of this savage outlook and stress is being laid more and more on the true value for which we are fighting. This is an uphill task and it becomes more difficult with every fresh piece of criminal initiative on the part of the Nazis.[34]

Military Labor Recruitment and Mobilization

While the Rhodes-Livingstone Institute, the country's only research institution, wanted to continue with atrocity propaganda in Barotseland in 1943, the government objected. In reply to a proposal for the continued use of anti-German propaganda made by the director of the institute, the chief secretary to the government stated the following:

> In some ways I think I wish your article had appeared 18 months
> ago, for it was at that stage in particular that we had to impress on
> the African how necessary it was to fight Hitler. . . . I still think that
> there is a strain in the African make up which would consider some
> of the Nazi methods sound policy. If you can destroy your enemy's
> house, his wife and family, you are doing something towards
> beating him. In fact such acts are really rather clever.[35]

Despite these reservations, the use of crude anti-German propaganda continued in Northern Rhodesia, as in most parts of Africa. Fear was a strong motivator for those who had knowledge of German imperial goals in the 1914–18 war. For many people living on the western border of Northern Rhodesia, stories about German campaigns against the Herero in German West Africa also abounded because of their geographic proximity.[36]

Still, Britain's gratitude for colonial support in the war effort did become a favorite Colonial Office theme in the effort to maintain pride and a positive public perception of the war among its African colonial subjects. Printed posters distributed in Northern Rhodesia and elsewhere in British Africa thanked the local people for their financial contribution to the imperial war effort. One such poster depicted several fighter planes involved in aerial attacks on German aircraft, ports, and ships. These planes were presented as the result of the generous financial assistance rendered by Northern Rhodesia and other colonies. Titled "YOUR 'HURRICANES' IN ACTION," one of the posters bore the following caption:

> Subscriptions from Northern Rhodesia have bought "Hurricane"
> fighter aircraft for Britain. These planes protect British homes
> and industries from aerial attack and harass enemy shipping and
> transport. When enemy bombers approach Britain, the fighters go
> up to drive them away. Here is a Northern Rhodesia fighter plane
> shooting down an enemy bomber over one of Britain's industrial

towns. Northern Rhodesia fighter planes also take part in offensive sweeps over enemy-occupied territory and cause much damage to shipping and transport and communications with their machine-gun fire. Northern Rhodesia fighters protect Allied merchant ships from hostile aircraft. Many vital cargoes have reached port only because of the watchful presence of fighter planes. Thank you, Northern Rhodesia![37]

Other war gifts acknowledged and publicized by imperial authorities included contributions for mobile canteens; war charities such as the Red Cross, St. John Fund, King George's Fund for Sailors, and Air Raid Relief; a cinema van; and the Duke of Gloucester's Fund for medical aid to Russia.[38] Financial donations made throughout the country were also given regular publicity in *Mutende*. By October 1940, a sum of £37,486 7s had been raised for war charities.[39] The Northern Rhodesian government also lent one million pounds to the British government free of interest as a contribution toward the imperial war effort.[40]

RECRUITMENT FOR THE NORTHERN RHODESIA REGIMENT

There were three periods of military recruitment in Northern Rhodesia: 1939, with the initial expansion of the Northern Rhodesia Regiment (NRR) and its deployment in East Africa; 1940 through late 1942, following the fall of France and the entry of Italy and Japan into the war; and lastly, the provision of reinforcements for the Asian expeditionary force in 1943–44. Once France fell in June 1940, all prospects of an Allied containment of German power in Europe waned, permitting Benito Mussolini to enter the war and resulting in campaigns in the Mediterranean and Middle East. Italy's entry on 10 June 1940 widened the war beyond Europe. Feeling that Italian greatness required domination of the Mediterranean and, therefore, British defeat, Mussolini sought gains from the British Empire and from France, as well as more power in the Balkans.[41] Without the French fleet to help defend the Mediterranean, Britain was now the only active opponent of Nazi Germany. Italian attacks on Egypt and Suez, and in 1941, the entry of German military power into the Mediterranean and North Africa, placed vast new burdens upon a British war machine scarcely capable of ensuring home defense.[42] Italy was able to carry out activities in North Africa because of the huge metropolitan and colonial forces the country maintained in Libya and recently conquered Abyssinia. In East Africa, plans for the defense of British Somaliland, should Italy enter the war, were torn up when French Somaliland and its sizable armed forces signaled their loyalty to the Vichy regime, making Britain's position there untenable.[43]

Besides, from June 1940, the Japanese navy had begun full mobilization in Southeast Asia, although the German failure to invade Britain discouraged ideas of an attack on British colonies that year.[44] Japanese intervention against Britain was deferred for another fifteen months. In the interim, Japan began its expansion into colonial Southeast Asia by invading French Indochina.[45] From December 1941, the Allies' war with Japan threatened the British position in Africa and the Middle East. The greatest crisis of the war arrived with the Japanese attack on the American Pacific Fleet at Pearl Harbor on 7 December 1941.[46] The Japanese also attacked British and American positions in the Western Pacific and East Asia. This dramatic turn of events forced a swift change in the British policy regarding the expansion of the forces in East Africa for fear of a Japanese attack. Following the fall of Singapore and the bombing of Ceylon by the Japanese, the British Eastern Fleet withdrew to Mombasa, thereby bringing East Africa directly into the Japanese theater of war.[47] An all-out imperial war effort was directed toward assuring a wider involvement of soldiers and increased material resources from the colonies at an unprecedented level.

The numbers of Italian forces in Africa dwarfed those of the British Empire: there were 300,000 Italians and colonial troops in Italy's African Empire, as compared to 88,500 British, dominion, and colonial troops in British Africa.[48] The expansion of the NRR must be placed in this context. In 1939, the NRR consisted of only one battalion, but it increased to eight during the conflict. Of the 15,000 Northern Rhodesian Africans who participated in the war, 98 were killed in action, 171 were wounded, and 300 others died of other causes.[49] Between 700 and 800 Europeans from the territory served abroad, 40 of whom lost their lives.[50] The NRR served in East Africa, Madagascar, Somaliland, Ceylon, India, Palestine, and Burma in various capacities.

Of course, no general picture can adequately capture the diverse motives for enlisting in the NRR in wartime. The main method of recruitment was through chiefs and their headmen, who acted as recruiting agents on behalf of colonial authorities. Chiefs were viewed by the colonial state as having considerable influence, and it was believed that their subjects would respond to their appeal for men for the NRR. The chiefs' willingness to collaborate with British authorities must be viewed within the context of colonial power relations.[51] Colonial rule was always a threat to traditional authorities in Africa. Although military enlistments were supposedly the fruits of spontaneous loyalism, in practice, pressure from chiefs counted for more than civic spirit.[52] As David Killingray and Louis Grundlingh have observed, when chiefs served as recruiting agents for the war, the line between voluntary and compulsory service was often very thin.[53] Unlike the High Commission Territories (Bechuanaland, Swaziland, and Lesotho), Northern Rhodesia did not have one or two central monarchs, but many discrete authorities scattered across the country's seven provinces. This meant that the government had to approach several different chiefs in all parts of the country. The main chiefs were the Chitimukulu of the Bemba, the Mpezeni of the Ngoni, the Litunga of the Lozi, and the Kalonga Gawa Undi of the Chewa. These, in turn, had various senior and junior chiefs below them who were helped by numerous headmen at the village level. Within the framework of the customary social and political order, many Africans obeyed the instructions of chiefs to join the army.[54]

Generally, a chief called a meeting of villages under his jurisdiction and provided information and encouragement to potential recruits based on colonial government and military circulars that outlined the terms and conditions of service and procedures for enlistment. At other times, these meetings were attended by personnel from the NRR or civil servants. Some men were caught up in the excitement of the moment in response to the passionate and persuasive call at such meetings. However, it is too simplistic to see the chiefs' orders for men to join the army as a sign of "exploitation." After all, in the precolonial period, it had been their traditional right to summon their people to arms, especially when their interests were threatened, as they were by German aggression during the war.[55] As Ashley Jackson has noted for Bechuanaland, asking for volunteers rather than conscripts created a dilemma: traditionally, a chief did not ask for volunteers; he told people to perform a duty and they were expected to obey.[56] Relations between chiefs and their subjects were nested in a complex of affinity and power far more subtle than the distinction between coerced and free labor. In this way, it can be argued that although compulsion *was* a factor in recruitment, the image of 15,000

Military Labor Recruitment and Mobilization

miserable men being hauled to various theaters of war by their chiefs obfuscates the extent to which Africans themselves were also active agents in the recruitment process for the NRR.

Despite persistent denials from government officials about the existence of compulsion in the recruitment campaign, evidence suggests otherwise. Rumors that chiefs forced their subjects to enlist in the NRR during the second recruitment campaign in 1942–43 were so widespread among Northern Rhodesian men working in Southern Rhodesia that they feared returning home at the end of their employment contracts. An example was Mendulu Tengetetu Banda, of Chief Zingalume's area in Fort Jameson district, who was working in Gatooma district at the time. He feared going back home, because he had heard rumors that labor migrants returning from Southern Rhodesia were being captured by government or chiefs' agents as conscripts for the army. Thus, he wrote the following to his wife Elina:

> Elina Banda I am asking you about the news of home. We heard
> that people are arrested, to be sent to the war. Is that the truth?
> Because people who come from home say if any person who comes
> from this country, Salisbury, as soon as the person gets there he
> is arrested and is taken to war. I am asking you about this. Don't
> deceive me, because I want to come home. Tell me what is going
> on there concerning the war and about the people being arrested.
> I am sending you these words so that you can inquire for me from
> Mazambani and Misale.[57]

For its part, the government denied authorizing the use of compulsion and heaped the blame on what it termed "overzealous chiefs." The chief secretary to the government responded to allegations of forced enlistments in the following terms:

> I have always been most careful to impress on DCs and the
> seconded military officers who are assisting with recruiting, that on
> no account has any compulsion to be used in addresses to the chiefs
> and people. I have repeatedly stated that our army is an army of
> volunteers.[58]

That complaints should emerge during the third phase of the recruitment campaign in 1943 was perhaps unsurprising. In January 1942, a Northern

Rhodesian "pioneer," Colonel "Chirupula" Stephenson, had been appointed as controller of African recruitment. Stephenson's ruthlessness and his use of crude methods such as the burning down of huts to force people to pay taxes in the early part of the twentieth century are well documented.[59] His appointment by the government was probably not coincidental and was designed to ensure that, by whatever means necessary, as many people as possible were enlisted.

The army sent recruitment teams into hundreds of villages. Posters were put up and pamphlets circulated that stressed the food, order, and cleanliness of army life. The military emphasized that such posters should show servicemen in the best possible light and be of a nature to make the African realize that a soldier's life was full of attractions.[60] Figure 1.1 shows a prominent recruitment poster with a picture of a smartly dressed African serviceman accompanied by the following caption in the Cinyanja language: *Munthu uyu ali msikari. King George afuna Asikari ena. Kodi muli olimba, anyamata, ndi acimwamuna? Ngati muli tero, lowani usikari* (This man is a soldier. King George is looking for more soldiers. Are you strong, male and youthful? If so, enrol in the army).[61] Another poster featuring a sharply dressed soldier is shown in figure 1.2. It bore the following slogan, also written in Cinyanja: *Kampanje kalila, Shamwale! Lowani usikari!* (The trumpet has been sounded, my friend! Enlist in the army!).[62] These posters were prepared by the Information Office with guidance from military officials. They were often printed in color to bolster their eye-catching potential. The purpose was to indicate the personal progress associated with becoming a soldier: gaining a uniform, smartness, a weapon to hand, and proven loyalty to the system.[63] Around eight thousand of these posters were distributed in various parts of the country, with varied slogans in the major local languages.[64] *Mutende* also carried various advertisements urging Africans to join the NRR.[65]

In addition to the government's efforts, propaganda campaigns undertaken by the military itself also induced many men to enlist in the NRR. The regional East African Mobile Propaganda Unit, set up in 1942, explained the life and training of soldiers and demonstrated modern weapons throughout the region when on tour. Led by Capt. A. G. Dickson, it toured Northern Rhodesia in 1943. Though the unit's main aim was to intensify public opinion and support of the war effort and get those at home to pay more attention to soldiers, an ancillary result was a rise in enlistments.[66] For example, in

FIGURE 1.1. Recruitment Poster I. *Source:* Livingstone Museum.

FIGURE 1.2. Recruitment Poster II. *Source:* Livingstone Museum.

September 1943, the unit conducted two demonstrations in Fort Jameson district, the heartland of the Ngoni people. As Giacomo Macola has noted, the glorified place of warfare in the Ngoni's precolonial social system was a key sociocultural force which shaped their choice of enlisting in the army in large numbers. Military service, to the Ngoni people, evoked important aspects of their past relating to bravery in martial occupation, travel far from home, and providing sustenance to the community.[67] That the Mobile Propaganda Unit targeted the "martial" Ngoni people during this recruitment drive was no coincidence, as I demonstrate later in this chapter. The Ngoni simply wanted to cling to the promise of perpetuating such notions of honor and masculinity as had informed their group's sociocultural structures in the recent past.[68] Between 7,000 and 9,000 people attended the recruitment shows in 1943.[69] Among the prominent personalities in attendance at these occasions were the paramount chiefs of the Ngoni and Chewa people, Mpezeni and Kalonga Gawa Undi, respectively. Other chiefs were Mkanda, Chikuwe, Sayiri, Madzimawe, and Nzamane. That such an impressive delegation of chiefs was present can hardly be surprising, given their importance in the recruitment process for the army. On display were events ranging from physical training, rifle drill, and unarmed combat to dispatch riding and mortar and Bren gun firing, all of which mesmerized the crowds.[70] Cinema shows conducted in the evening on both days were equally well attended. Ackson Mwale, a government clerk who attended the event in Fort Jameson on 15 September 1943, confirmed the success of the Mobile Propaganda Unit's tour when he remarked: "I happened to take to the show my three-year-old son who, from that time on has kept saying to everyone at home that he wants to be a soldier in the Army! But if this is the impression left on the young mind, what on the grown up men?"[71] Something of a carnival atmosphere was created in rural areas as a result of the activities of this propaganda campaign. The Mobile Propaganda Unit was thus a great advertisement for attracting recruits for the army.

In Barotseland, perhaps due to the province's lukewarm attitude toward the war, the government, through the Rhodes-Livingstone Institute, took the lead in spreading war propaganda. This campaign was led by the institute's then director, Max Gluckman, who had extensive knowledge of the Lozi kingdom, the geographic area, and the local people, owing to the various studies he had undertaken there since the institute's establishment in 1937.

The propaganda campaign hinged on comparing the Second World War with the outbreak and course of a civil war in the Lozi kingdom in the 1870s. Gluckman likened Numwa, the leader of the faction which had rebelled against the Lozi monarch, Lewanika, in the latter part of the nineteenth century, to Adolf Hitler. In one propaganda article, he argued that, "like Hitler, he [Numwa] wished to live on the work of others whom he would make his slaves, he wanted that he should sit and take the riches worked by others without paying them. In Barotseland, he had the same plan as Hitler has, to conquer all people."[72]

While chiefs and propaganda were the main tools used to entice Africans to enlist in the army, other factors may have led Africans to respond positively to the call to arms. African agency in the recruitment process for the NRR was rooted in economic pull and/or push factors—not dissimilar to those pertaining to migratory labor, a common African experience in the country from very early on. Prominent among these was the desire to earn money. Military service offered distinct economic and social rewards that many individual soldiers tacitly accepted as adequate compensation for the personal hardship and loss of individual freedom that came with military discipline. Speaking fifty years after the events, Rightson Kangwa recalled why, as a twenty-two-year-old peasant farmer, he had enlisted in the NRR. "It looked to me as if it was a good job which I had never seen before because I had never heard of the war or what it meant."[73] Basic pay for unmarried men was one shilling sixpence per day, while those with families were paid two shillings three pence. Additionally, the army provided free food, clothing, cigarettes, housing, and medical care. The army offered some of the highest rates for unskilled African labor.

Furthermore, new commercial opportunities and an appetite for material goods, coupled with the rising cost of bridewealth, led to increased interest in money and wage labor that drove some men to join the army. Although army wages were not very attractive to potential recruits in the more prosperous mining and industrial centers of the Northern Rhodesian Copperbelt, these wages were considerably higher than the going civilian rate for manual labor in outlying areas. In 1940, the average rural laborer was paid twelve shillings and sixpence per month, while on the Copperbelt mines, surface and underground miners were paid fifteen shillings and twenty-five shillings, respectively.[74] Justine Master Phiri confirmed that he enlisted in the

NRR because, to him, that was just a job like any other from which he could earn a living. "It was in April, 1940," he recalled, "when I was recruited at Fort Jameson. . . . I felt happy and thought it was a jolly good job."[75] As the war progressed, recruitment fatigue set in, resulting in fewer people enlisting. What sustained the recruitment process was the financial benefit some servicemen derived from the army and sent to their relatives in the villages. As Colonial Information Officer Bradley found out in Lundazi in March 1940, the war no longer seemed to interest the mass of the people. But although the initial excitement over recruitment had disappeared, nothing had done more to calm apprehensions and dispel suspicion than the regular remittances that recruits in the regiment sent home to their families.[76] At the war front, servicemen had fewer avenues for spending their earnings than when they were home on leave, so some of them were able to save part of their earnings, which they remitted home.[77] These remittances cushioned the lives of servicemen's families, enabling the purchase of food and other household requisites, as well as paying for hired labor services.

For some, volunteering was a way of proving that they were "man enough." Gilbert Malama Zulu enlisted at the age of eighteen, eventually becoming a lorry driver, because he believed that at that age he had matured into a brave and powerful man, ready to join the military forces.[78] This type of thinking was exploited by government propagandists, especially after the victories recorded by the NRR in battles against Italian forces in East Africa. Second Lieutenant K. Thompson, of the 1st Battalion NRR, confirmed this in a radio broadcast transmitted from Lusaka:

> I want to talk about some of the things askari [local soldiers] of our First Battalion in Kenya are saying. Their hearts are very strong, and they are very proud for they feel that when there is a war fighting is the work for real men. They know that they fought well, for each has killed many of the enemy, and now they walk with their heads held high, for by their skill in war they have proved their manhood just as their fathers did in the wars before the coming of the white man.[79]

In despising those who had not enlisted, servicemen often claimed that such people were like women, for whom they had gone to fight.[80] One eyewitness and participant in the war was the renowned Zambian author,

Stephen Mpashi. In his famous Bemba-language satire about the conflict, *Cekesoni aingila ubusoja* (Jackson joins the military), Mpashi noted that one reason young men enlisted during the war was because they wanted to prove their virility. One day, when the villagers were enjoying their local brew, the young men were alerted to go and hide so that they should not be enlisted as soldiers for the Second World War. Having imbibed the traditional brew, Cekesoni initially went into hiding with his friend. But while there, he rejected the idea of shirking combat as being unmanly and unfitting of people who had seen the world. He and his friend had just returned from the Copperbelt, where they had come into contact with people of different races and handled difficult assignments working underground. Therefore, they now felt they could not be fearful of fighting. The two young men then convinced each other that instead of hiding from the messenger hunting for them, they should send word to the governor that Cekesoni and his friend were waiting to enlist, which they did the following day, together with others whom Cekesoni had been able to influence.[81]

Soldiers who went home on leave were encouraged by military and civil establishments to bring back recruits when they returned from their places of origin. As was the case with all military units throughout the empire that were sent to serve in distant theaters of war, serious efforts were made to keep East African soldiers in touch with their home communities, in order to make them more efficient and to limit the disruption of African life that could result from their prolonged absence.[82] Leave, where permissible, was granted for a period of twenty working days to be spent in the serviceman's village of origin, exclusive of days required for travel to and from the village. It was during this period that some servicemen were able to convince their friends or relatives who had remained in the villages to enlist in the army. In Namwala district in late 1942, for instance, the district commissioner noted that Ila servicemen who had returned home on leave from Madagascar and Ceylon were full of tales to tell their friends and relatives, which had beneficial effects on local African opinion and morale regarding the war.[83] The arrival on leave of several askari from East Africa and Madagascar also caused great interest in Sesheke district, resulting in the recruitment of six men,[84] while in Kasama, the district commissioner reported in 1940 that "the [r]anks have returned [from Somaliland] full of the 'defeat' they inflicted on the Italians and how inferior the Italian askari were to them. This has had a stimulating effect on recruiting and over 240 recruits have been attested in less than a month."[85]

It was clear that the well-groomed appearance of askari on leave had a substantial effect on the recruitment of more servicemen.[86] "If they are decently clothed they are, I think," the Secretary for Native Affairs reported in 1943, "more inclined to behave themselves properly, and their appearance might act as an incentive to others to join the army."[87] The items carried by Northern Rhodesian askari on home leave were the following: a hat or tarbush, boots, puttees and hose tops, two pairs of socks, two pairs of shorts, two shirts, a blanket, two shirts merduff (T-shirts), jersey, haversack, greatcoat, razor, mosquito net, blouse.[88] To ensure that this display of material prosperity had its desired effect on recruitment, government officials liaised with military officials to make certain that these conditions were followed to the letter for all servicemen proceeding on leave. The successes in the recruitment process recorded by servicemen on leave prompted the controller of African recruitment to authorize district commissioners to extend the leave, by not more than one month, of serving askari who showed promise as recruiting agents.[89]

Another example of African agency in the recruitment process is provided by men who joined the army because they envied their friends who were already serving in the NRR. They regarded colleagues who had joined earlier with respect. Military service was viewed as a "manly" occupation. The NRR was male dominated, as no African women served in the army during the entire war period. Despite this, African women contributed immensely to the recruitment drive and sustenance of servicemen once in the military. This is yet another way in which gender relations played a key role in militarism during the Second World War in Africa. Women provided a range of material and ideological support to the military. They sewed warm clothing, raised money for items such as cigarettes, and took care of children in the absence of men. On an ideological level, as has been observed elsewhere, they socialized men into a militarized version of masculinity by encouraging their husbands to join the military.[90] Carrying a gun marked a man as a privileged government servant, and some recruits believed that women were attracted to the uniforms they wore. They also believed that serving askari had large sums of disposable income and were preferred by young women.[91] The experience of askari earned them a high level of deference and respect in their home societies, which colleagues also aspired to enjoy once they enlisted.

Some Africans enlisted with a view to acquiring life-changing skills, such as the ability to drive. Others, such as Samson Muliango, were encouraged by their employers to sign up so that they could develop their skills. When interviewed in 1989, Muliango explained that

> it all started in 1939, I used to work for Mr Ivor Windsor Simons. . . . During my time with Capt. Simons he taught me driving around his farm but [I] never obtained a driving permit. After the war broke out in 1939 Capt. Simons . . . told me that he wanted me to join the war, I agreed and I was so thrilled by this suggestion. In October 1939, he took me to the Army Headquarters where I was recruited.[92]

Prominent recruitment posters advertised training courses for African drivers and tailors. These posters were designed by the military and showed African servicemen on the job. The human element was studiously emphasized in the development of these posters. For example, a photograph of an African serviceman *driving* a military vehicle was considered more interesting than one showing a mere fleet of lorries.[93] Enticed by the skills depicted on the posters in various localities, some men enlisted with a view to becoming military drivers or attaining another trade.

Some veterans cited Northern Rhodesian patriotism as their primary motive for joining the army. One ex-serviceman recalled that "it was in September 1939 when we heard the news that the war has broken out in Europe and that Britain and her allied forces are fighting against the Germans and Italians in Europe and in the far east against the Japanese."[94] For this reason, he enlisted in the army. Men such as these enlisted to fight for an imperial "mother country" they had never seen, thousands of kilometers away from their homes. Another ex-serviceman from Kasama district pointed out that he enlisted because of his desire to help the imperial country defeat the Axis powers: "The fighting that broke out spread to all colonies of the British, as well as our country, then called Northern Rhodesia. . . . Thus in my area, recruitment of soldiers was conducted by a Mr. Whitemore, then DC of Kasama. . . . That is how I came to be recruited."[95] To such men, Britain symbolized their own country, despite their never having been there physically. Consequently, the mother country's conflict was regarded as their own.

In explaining his reason for enlisting, another veteran said he did so to fight against "the much, then, hated Germans and their supporters."[96] Despite strict instructions that recruiters should not make deceptive promises or misrepresent the terms and conditions of service, evidence reveals that some ingenious recruiting agents deliberately made false promises to entice Africans to enlist. Some people were, therefore, under the impression that they would be exempted from paying poll tax and would receive huge tracts of land and sums of money at the end of the war. Oral evidence attests to this. "During the recruitment," ex-serviceman Samson Muliango claimed, "the Northern Rhodesia Government promised us all as rewards farms and lots of money if only we fought for the British Army during the reign of King George VI."[97] Another veteran, Chama Mutemi Kadansa, also acknowledged that bogus promises were made to entice people to join the NRR: "Our British officers were seriously promising that after the war a lot of money would be paid to surviving soldiers as reward, and they would be given farms and good jobs. So, we were all very happy and anxious to get to the battle-fields and start fighting."[98] Such "promises" led to inflated and fanciful expectations among some potential recruits and those who had already been enlisted. As will be seen in chapter 6, the failure to fulfill these "promises" would create significant discontent during the demobilization process.

Military service offered opportunities for adventure to some young men, prompting them to enlist. They saw the wartime army as providing them a chance to see the world beyond the village. In an interview, ex-serviceman Joseph Chinama Mulenga, who enlisted at the age of nineteen, said that "the coming or outbreak of the Second World War accorded some of we [*sic*] Africans to indeed have the opportunity to travel overseas or abroad, for the first time."[99] Another veteran explained: "None of us recruits had experienced war before, so we were so anxious to go to war."[100] For Rabson Chombola, his enlistment in the NRR was simply a result of his feeling that "it was a good job going to [a] foreign country."[101] These men left home and familiar surroundings, met different people, traveled to East Africa, Madagascar, the Levant, Burma, and India, saw new sights, and underwent a range of novel experiences. Thus, enlisting in the army was an opportunity for adventure, to escape the repetitive existence and precincts of village life.

Requirements for enlistment in the NRR stipulated that potential servicemen had to meet the following physical criteria:

Military Labor Recruitment and Mobilization

1. Age: 18–40 years.
2. Height: 5 feet 3 inches minimum.
3. Weight: 115 pounds minimum.
4. Chest: 32 inches fully expanded minimum.
5. Teeth: a reasonable dental standard.
6. Hearing: good in both ears.
7. Vision: 6/24 (meters) in both eyes or 6/12 in the better eye and 6/36 in the weaker.[102]

In the early phase of the war, there was a high rejection rate of recruits on medical grounds, but when the army urgently needed men, it lowered the standard of health and operated on the assumption that a period of army feeding, medical attention, and exercise would in time raise recruits to the necessary physical standard.[103]

The successful candidates were then transported by lorry to Lusaka for training at the Infantry Training Centre (ITC) as part of the "Pool." There, candidates were given lectures and talks by senior army officers. The syllabus of lectures given to the recruits included the following:

1. Initial Lecture: why recruits had gone to the ITC and what was expected of them. The avenues open to them in the various army branches were also made known to the men.
2. Regimental history.
3. Standing Orders.
4. Hygiene.
5. Discipline.
6. How to write and address their letters, and censorship in place.
7. Living quarters and rations.
8. Pay, promotion, leave.
9. Method of making complaints and domestic troubles.
10. Weekly talks on the war.[104]

Recruits spent up to three weeks in the Pool, waiting for sufficient numbers to form a junior training company.[105] During this period, the recruit learned a great deal in the "nursery," so that by the time the junior company was formed, he would have accustomed himself to the military environment and would start training with confidence.[106] Men raised in Fort Jameson district underwent orientation and attestation at the local Civil Recruitment Depot. Because of this preliminary training, they tended to spend less time at the Infantry Training Centre in Lusaka. At the end of the training, an attestation form was completed detailing the soldier's name, ethnic group, village of origin, chiefdom, next of kin, weight, height, and physical appearance.

Throughout training, emphasis was placed on the importance of discipline in the army. It was expected that the recruits would show their military superiors the same allegiance they owed to their traditional authorities by law and custom. The army had traditions and duties no less compelling than those at home.[107] The chief secretary noted that discipline was of paramount importance because " military service and all its implications, which the raw native finds so difficulty [sic] to understand, reflect a duty to his own people rather than an imposition from outside his tribe."[108] Upon completion of their training, the men returned home to bid their farewells, but also to show their civilian peers what army life was all about.

"MARTIAL RACE" THEORY IN THE NORTHERN RHODESIA REGIMENT AND RESISTANCE TO RECRUITMENT

During the Second World War, colonial recruiters sought men who were "martial," just as they had done during the 1914–18 war. The British imported Indian "martial race" paradigms into Africa and, along with other colonial powers, identified certain ethnic groups as "martial." The ideology of martial races was developed after the Sepoy Mutiny of 1857, and again in the 1880s, in an effort to recruit better soldiers who could withstand the threat of Russian expansion on India's northwest frontier.[109] In addition, it was meant to ensure that all those who were recruited to the army remained loyal in order to prevent future rebellions. After the mutiny of 1857, British officers concluded that prosperity made the commercial and urban classes of India unfit to be soldiers. As a result, recruiters developed a detailed system of ethnographic classification that identified certain ethnic groups, religions, and castes with the specific biological and cultural attributes of a martial race.[110] These included Nepalese Gurkhas, Punjabi Sikhs, and Muslims from the northern and frontier provinces.

Some of the groups considered martial on the African continent included the Ngoni of Central Africa, the Zulu in South Africa, the Yao in Nyasaland, the Nubi of Northwestern Uganda and Southern Sudan, and the

Tukolor, Malinke, Wolof, Hausa, and Bambara in West Africa. In Northern Rhodesia, the Ngoni/Chewa, Bemba, and Ila were commonly regarded by colonial authorities as martial groups. Members of these groups thus came to dominate the military forces of Northern Rhodesia.[111] In 1938, the Bemba numbered 37.5 percent, the Ngoni 12 percent, the Ila 18.5 percent, and the Chewa 7 percent of the NRR. The remaining 25 percent of troops consisted of other ethnic groups in the country. In relation to their total population, the Ila, Ngoni, and Chewa were more highly represented than other ethnic groups.[112] This was in line with the prewar recruitment policy, whereby those ethnic groups had dominated the police force. In part, the martial nature of these ethnic groups—one which made them well suited for military service in the eyes of colonial authorities—was a result of their precolonial trajectories and early experiences of colonial rule. They were perceived as knowing how to handle firearms and being aware of the rigors of military life. Military masculinity recurs as the primary manifestation of heroic honor—of men's efforts to gain and defend respect before, during, and after colonialism. Military masculinity is related to heroic, often martial, ideals of defending masculine honor from the effects of colonial rule and its economic demands.[113] The Ngoni of Fort Jameson district, for example, had the advantage of having the clear marks of a martial race because of their stubborn resistance to foreign conquest in the late 1890s. The Ngoni had fought running battles against the British, eventually being defeated in 1898.[114] Given their precolonial war-centered social system and normative universe, it is not surprising that the Ngoni came to be conceived as Northern Rhodesia's prime martial race.[115]

At least in theory, the Ngoni were of Zulu stock, being descendants of the soldiers of Shaka, the "African Napoleon," whose *impis* (Zulu warriors) had been the scourge of southern Africa in the first half of the nineteenth century.[116] It was clearly not coincidental that the main recruiting depot for askari during the Second World War was set up at Fort Jameson, in the heartland of the land of the Ngoni, whom recruiters were especially keen to reach. This being the case, it is hardly surprising that "non-martial" ethnic groups, such as the Chewa, Nsenga, and Kunda, who had not resisted British colonization but lived near the Ngoni, also featured prominently among recruits. For such groups, military service was a source of livelihood like any other, of which they took advantage.

In wartime, however, to fill their quotas, military and government officers accepted all the physically able volunteers they could get. That is to say that the doctrines and prejudices underpinning peacetime recruitment were flexible and could be relaxed in wartime if there were not enough members of martial groups to fill the ranks.[117] It is certainly possible that some Africans—such as the Nsenga and Kunda—deliberately identified themselves with universally recognized "martial" groups to access employment in the NRR. If this was indeed the case, then Northern Rhodesia, too, witnessed what Cynthia Enloe has termed the "Gurkha syndrome," that is, the strategic adoption of martial identities on the part of disadvantaged rural groups with a view to accessing military employment and related economic benefits.[118] In sum, martial race theory was not purely a colonial imposition, but, at times, it was negotiated and subverted by some ingenious individuals. In the same vein, in French West Africa, Lieutenant-Colonel Charles Mangin, a veteran of the conquest of the region, argued using racial reasoning that many West Africans were natural soldiers.[119] Other colonial officials objected to this, but also drew on racial arguments. Both sides of the debate shared racial ideas about the relative physical strength and warlike tendencies of sub-Saharan Africans.[120] In recruiting such African servicemen in the 1940s, Mangin thus made direct appeals for them to enlist based on the kinds of benefits they would receive at the end of the war.

Although there was no effective, large-scale resistance to the war effort in Northern Rhodesia, some people made it known from the outset that they did not want to participate in the fighting. There were several reasons for avoiding military enlistment in Northern Rhodesia. Some people feared being killed in action fighting in what they regarded as a European war. Lessons had been learned from the First World War. As in the rest of East and Central Africa, recruitment into the army during the Second World War was met with mixed feelings because of the bad memory people had of the dreaded Carrier Corps used in East Africa during the First World War. The Tonga people of Mazabuka district (whose "womanly" fears have been discussed above) remembered the part played by Africans in the 1914–18 war and were unwilling to serve as carriers again.[121] During that recruitment campaign, the military had developed a sullied reputation among many people.[122] Furthermore, recruitment for the Second World War was hampered by a deeply ingrained hostility in some places that stemmed from

48

broken promises at the end of the Great War. There was the belief among Africans that men had been needlessly sacrificed, wages not fully paid, and obligations not properly met.[123] Complaints of this nature, for instance, were made to government officials during the recruitment campaign in Lundazi district in 1940. The DC concerned had found it difficult to come up with a convincing reply.[124]

It does seem that while economic motives served as a pull factor in the recruitment process, they also acted as a deterrent to those who were already prosperous. This, at any rate, is how some officials explained the apathy they witnessed among Tonga peasants. The Tonga were agriculturalists, cattlemen, and traders, and lucrative markets during this period made them relatively prosperous, thereby lessening the attractiveness of the army as a means to earn a living.[125] This tendency was not new, if it is true that Tonga peasants were already renowned for refusing to offer their labor to settler European farmers in their vicinity due to their own thriving agricultural economy.[126] While equating the German attack on Poland to their own suffering at the hands of the Lozi in the nineteenth century, Tonga peasants could still not understand why the government wanted so many recruits for the NRR if the war was confined to Europe. Thus, in September 1939, a group of local peasants explicitly told the Mazabuka district commissioner that they could not enlist in the army because they believed that there was no trouble in the country to warrant such a move.[127] It was for this reason that, in the last quarter of the same year, only three men were enlisted in Mazabuka.[128]

For other Africans, too, the war was simply too far removed to be of any real concern. Such people remained apathetic and indifferent toward the war. Reports from various parts of the country confirmed this lack of enthusiasm, especially in the hinterland. In such places, people hardly talked about the war, but when they did speak about it, their apathetic and even hostile attitude was very evident. During a meeting in Kalabo in 1941, for example, the DC's efforts to engage in discussions about the war were greeted with such a wall of silence that the hapless official felt "as if one were addressing an assembly of deaf mutes on conditions in Mars."[129] The government attributed the apathy of Barotse Province (to which Kalabo district belonged) to lack of leadership, itself the result of having a sickly paramount chief in Yeta III and of the death of his prime minister in late 1940.[130] A close examination of the situation, however, reveals that the province was experiencing a critical shortage of labor due to continuing migrations to the South African mines—mines which paid better wages than could be obtained from the army. An estimated monthly average of 4,000 to 6,000 men traversed the Mongu-Mulobezi labor route on their way to South Africa in 1941.[131] The government suspended recruitment by the Witwatersrand Native Labour Association for the Rand in 1943, but reversed the policy the following year after protestations by South African capital.[132]

To avoid joining the army, in the early recruitment campaigns, some Africans hid in the bush. "I found that young men ran away from a village as I entered it owing to the fear of being compelled to join the regiment," complained the DC for Fort Jameson in mid-1940.[133] In the same vein, during the official opening of the Chewa National School in 1940, it was observed that young men were conspicuously missing at the event:

> The native spectators consisted almost entirely of old men and boys. The reason there were no able-bodied men present was because the people expected the Provincial Commissioner to announce that now the children can be looked after in the fine school building there is no reason for the men to remain at home, and all would be sent to the Regiment.[134]

It was further reported that rumors were widespread throughout the district that all the able-bodied men were being arrested and forced into the regiment. These rumors were more prevalent the further one went from Fort Jameson.[135]

Others simply crossed over into neighboring territories to avoid being made to join the army. In Chief Kathumba's area in Fort Jameson, men were known to abscond temporarily to Portuguese East Africa.[136] This technique had been an effective tool for evading tax payments in the country since the imposition of taxation at the start of the twentieth century.[137] In Kalabo district, a middle-aged woman was fined £2 or two months' imprisonment with hard labor in June 1941 for spreading rumors about conscription. She was reported to have visited two villages informing people that recruiters would be in the area to forcibly recruit them to go to war. The entire adult male population in about fifty villages, as well as some women, decamped into the bush or over the border into Angola and only returned a couple of weeks later.[138] Similarly, some men in French West Africa also evaded the prospect of being conscripted by the *chefs de canton* (district chiefs) by hiding, dissimulating, or fleeing to neighboring colonies.[139]

For other men, recruitment drives provided the incentive to migrate elsewhere in search of jobs. Government officials complained that the recruitment of men for the war effort was being hindered by the continued movement of able-bodied men to neighboring territories. In Lundazi district in late 1940, complaints were common that whenever recruiters went looking for potential recruits for the NRR, the latter immediately left for Southern Rhodesia.[140] Although some recruits were enlisted, there was neither evident enthusiasm for the war nor any anxiety about its possible outcome one way or the other. The DC further lamented that the habit of working abroad was firmly established in the area, and men simply did what they had been doing for decades by traveling south for jobs.[141]

David Killingray has argued that the absence of up to 30 percent of the male adult population for war service in parts of Northern Rhodesia had a negative effect on food production in rural areas.[142] Such observations have also been made with regard to colonial Botswana, where it was concluded that the absence of adult males from their villages due to military service had serious socioeconomic effects, such as reduced agricultural production, desolate houses and villages, and juvenile delinquency.[143] My research, however, shows a different trend. The network of kin relations through the extended family system took care of the wives and families of the men who had gone to the war front. Moreover, in keeping with the experience of male labor migration to the mines and European settler farms with which people had long been familiar, servicemen sent regular remittances to their families; these funds helped cushion the effects of their absence.[144] In Fort Jameson district, for example, it was reported in 1941 that money from servicemen was plentiful, with crowds of men and women gathering at government offices and the post office with their Post Office Savings Books to withdraw remittances from the large number of men serving in the armed forces.[145] This scenario was replicated in several other places.[146] Monies received by wives and family members were utilized in the hiring of extra labor to help with cultivation in the villages and the building of new houses. At this level, too, the experience of warfare had an impact on gender relations. The war produced, maintained, and recalibrated differences between men and women. In particular, the absence of men from their homes resulted in women gaining greater power and autonomy within the household, similar to the situation Decker found in her study of Idi Amin's Uganda.[147]

One African group which openly opposed the colony's participation in the Allied war effort was the pacifist Watch Tower (or Watchtower) sect. Some Watch Tower adherents proclaimed that the hostilities which had arisen in Europe were the result of God punishing European oppressors. The hotbed for this kind of predication was the Eastern Province, due to its proximity to Nyasaland, where the movement had existed since the early twentieth century. But the activities of this millenarian movement were reported throughout the country.[148] Due to the nearness of Nyasaland, Watch Tower elements would cross over into Northern Rhodesia to spread an antiwar message which local officials characterized as seditious. In mid-1940, a Watch Tower disciple from Nyasaland toured the Fort Jameson district, urging Africans not to contribute to the war effort, which—he alleged—was contrived for the benefit of capitalists.[149] Members of this sect were accused by government officials of preaching subversive doctrines "deliberately calculated to destroy morale and hamper the war effort" and that "their talk was the talk of madmen . . . their doctrines a hotchpotch of the scriptures with cunning interpretations."[150]

Ashley Jackson has observed that this sect in Northern Rhodesia was "by nature underground, unofficial and non-European."[151] This is not entirely correct, as the movement also had European members. Like their African counterparts, the sect's European members (known as Jehovah's Witnesses) also regarded the war as sinful and devilish. The leader of the Jehovah's Witnesses in Northern Rhodesia was Llewelyn Phillips, who was based at the sect's headquarters in Lusaka. Phillips and other European members of the Jehovah's Witnesses vehemently objected to their participation in the war as conscientious objectors. This was in line with Section 9 (3a) of the Compulsory Military Service Ordinance, which allowed any person who conscientiously objected to military service to apply in writing to the governor. Phillips thus wrote to Governor Maybin:

> I have consecrated my life to the service of Jehovah, the Most High God. I have devoted my time and energy entirely to His Kingdom under Christ. I am engaged in serving that Kingdom, therefore, I cannot take part in any military or non-combatant service, and I

cannot conscientiously fight. The Bible forbids the Christian taking human life. Mark 10:19 and Genesis 9:6.[152]

This was not an isolated case. Other Jehovah's Witnesses also made their protestations known to the government based on the same line of reasoning.[153] In June 1942, Phillips preached outside the mine compound at Luanshya, prophesying that any person who was not a Jehovah's Witness would die before the war ended.[154] In total twelve Europeans applied as conscientious objectors under the provisions of the law. Three of these were approved, eight were rejected, and one was found to be mentally unbalanced. As a general rule, the government rejected pleas made by Afrikaner applicants because it considered the reasons they had advanced to be flimsy. Of the eight rejected applicants, three were punished and sentenced to imprisonment: one for one month, another for four months, and the third for two terms of imprisonment of one month and six months.[155]

There was also a marked anti-British sentiment in the country propagated by Afrikaner settlers who had migrated from South Africa. The majority of these were found in the Lusaka and Broken Hill areas and the mining centers of the Copperbelt. Some of these settlers were of German descent and their sympathies lay with the Axis. This group not only showed antipathy toward the South African government for siding with the Allied nations but also disliked attempts made by Northern Rhodesia to aid the Allied war effort. Afrikaner anti-British sentiment in the country was expressed over the course of weekend "parties" held at specific farms. On these occasions, guests reportedly listened to German broadcasts and discussed the war on lines sympathetic to the Axis.[156] So opposed to the Allied effort was this group that when two of their colleagues were sentenced to imprisonment for refusing to enlist in the Defence Force, they were cheered by leading members of the Lusaka Afrikaner community as they proceeded to jail.[157] Three others were sentenced to seven days' imprisonment with hard labor in Luanshya in February 1942 for similar anti-Allied war propaganda, while four newcomers from South Africa applied for exit permits as soon as they were approached to enlist in the Home Guard.[158]

The English-speaking community in the country was highly suspicious of the activities of their Afrikaner counterparts. They were surprised at the apparent ease and rapidity with which sensitive information about Northern

Rhodesia became known to Zeesen, the German propaganda broadcasting station. It was speculated that such information was being relayed by some members of the underground Ossewabrandwag living in Lusaka.[159] This organization represented antiwar Afrikaner opinion. It had the same cultural-political agenda espoused by its parent organization in South Africa, which appealed strongly to Afrikaners to eschew another war on behalf of the British Empire. In another instance, a member of the Ossewabrandwag at Broken Hill hoisted the Swastika at St. George's Church, a predominantly English church.[160] This caused much annoyance to members of the English settler community. Although the culprit was fined £10 for the offense and was eventually deported from the country, the English-speaking community felt that the fine was too lenient. In Lusaka district, farming activities on Afrikaner farms came to a standstill in February 1942 as soon as a leading member of the Ossewabrandwag was arrested by security personnel for spreading antiwar propaganda.[161]

The main conclusion to which our discussion leads is that the recruitment and mobilization of labor for the NRR during the Second World War were influenced by a complex combination of factors. Chiefly institutions and propaganda were undoubtedly the major tools utilized to recruit thousands of Africans into the army. This, however, does not account for the enlistment of all men. I have noted that, under close scrutiny, a more complex picture emerges than that of government leaders simply ordering chiefs to recruit men for military service. Africans themselves were active agents in the recruitment process. At least some Africans saw military service as a form of employment and/or an adventure, as a way to prove one's manhood, to acquire a trade or to respond to peer pressure; others were enticed by military uniforms, as well as the desire to help defend the imperial "mother country" from Axis warfare. In addition, I have argued that the absence of male labor due to war service did not fully disrupt the local people's way of life. This was because, in the absence of male relatives serving in the army, those left behind devised coping strategies. Of course, recruitment for war service was not free from tensions, partly due to opposition from Jehovah's Witnesses and the Watch Tower sect, which discouraged people from enlisting in the military on religious grounds. In addition, members of the Afrikaner community covertly and overtly supported the Axis and thus carried out propaganda activities contrary to the aims of the host colonial state. The next chapter examines the promotion of commodity production in rural Northern Rhodesia, another significant aspect of the Allied war effort which impinged directly on the availability of manpower.

2

Southeast Asia, a Desperate Britain, and the Revival of African Rural Industries

THE SECOND WORLD WAR ACTED AS A MOMENTOUS FORCE FOR economic change in Northern Rhodesia, in much the same way as in many other African colonies. The sustained effort to intensify the extraction of raw materials was an obvious and direct effect of the conflict. Yet, as Raymond Dumett once remarked, despite the impetus given to natural resource exploitation in Africa, this dimension of the conflict is treated only cursorily in most general accounts of the war's impact on the continent.[1] The war in the Pacific against Japan had a direct effect on natural resource mobilization in Northern Rhodesia. Like Nigeria—compelled to revive the production of starch since the war made it difficult for Britain to obtain this commodity from its traditional suppliers, Java and Brazil[2]—Northern Rhodesia, too, embarked on a drive to locate substitute natural products to supplement increasingly scarce industrial ones. This drive lies at the heart of this chapter.

Malaya, the Dutch East Indies, Java, Borneo, and the Philippines, which supplied many of the raw materials needed by Britain and other Allied nations, were overrun by the invading Japanese between December 1941 and March 1942. The victories recorded by Japan gave the invaders control of much-needed raw materials such as tin, jute, iron, rubber, oils, and fats. The Allies' defeat in Southeast Asia would affect the livelihoods of African communities through increased demands for raw materials.[3] The lack of imported raw materials was compounded by the unavailability of merchant shipping space devoted to carrying civilian articles from regions of surplus to areas of deficit, such as the colonies. For example, in just one week, between 20 and 27 June 1940, Axis powers sank as many as 135,699 tons of merchant shipping.[4] This had a telling effect on Northern Rhodesia, resulting in attempts to produce such raw materials as rubber, beeswax, iron tools, string, and rope, which had become difficult to obtain from abroad due to war conditions. Many people responded by energizing these extractive industries.

In this chapter, I examine developments in industry and commerce in rural wartime Northern Rhodesia, thereby broadening scholarly understandings of the political economy of the Second World War. I provide some insights into how war in the metropole can have direct consequences on society in far-flung rural areas on the imperial periphery. Ordinary villagers in the hinterland of colonial Zambia obeyed instructions from London, passed on to them by colonial administrators, to produce such commodities as rubber, beeswax, iron, and string badly needed for the successful execution of the war. As Judith Byfield has noted, without Africa's resources, especially after 1942, Britain and the USA would not have been able to produce the technology or provide the transportation their armies required.[5] The production of rubber, beeswax, iron, string, and rope in Northern Rhodesia reveals the extent to which both the imperial and the colonial governments were prepared to go in their search for resources, as well as the nature of African responses to new opportunities and the unpredictability of the market in export commodities in times of war. However, the production of these commodities faced numerous problems, the major one being the unfavorable prices offered by the British government. It can safely be argued that these African resources sustained the Allied war effort, especially after 1942, but that their mobilization came at a great cost.[6]

RUBBER

Rubber production in Zambia predated the onset of the Second World War.[7] Various species of rubber plant grew wild in certain parts of the country.[8] Wild rubber was derived mainly from the vines of *Landolphia*, of which several species existed in the country, especially in the Northern, Kaonde-Lunda, and Western Provinces, together with the northern parts of the Central Province. The roots of *Carpodinus gracilis*, native to the Kalahari sand areas of Barotseland, also produced rubber. The extraction of root rubber was more laborious than tapping vines for latex, as it involved removing the bark, pulverizing it, and, finally, washing it, sometimes accompanied by further beating.[9] Prior to European colonization at the end of the nineteenth century, wild rubber was used locally on a small scale in the manufacture of such goods as drums, drumsticks, and balls for children's games.[10] It was also an important precolonial trade item, sold from the western part of the country to Portuguese, Ovimbundu, and Luso-African traders from the Bihe Plateau, Catumbela, and Benguela, in Angola.[11]

When the Second World War broke out, rubber's main use was in manufacturing tires for military vehicles and airplanes as well as footwear for military personnel. After satisfying military needs, the remainder was apportioned to civilian use for similar purposes. On the eve of the war, the main sources of rubber on the world market were the plantations of Southeast Asia and, specifically, the Allied-controlled colonies of Indonesia, Java, Malaya, the Philippines, and Borneo. In February 1942, the Allies' fears of facing a shortage of raw materials as soon as the war broke out in the Pacific turned to reality when Japanese forces defeated the Allied territories in the region, triggering a major worldwide shortage not only of rubber but also of essential fats and oils.[12] The late entry of Japan into the war and the rapid fall of Southeast Asia exposed the lack of Allied contingency planning with regard to the supply of raw materials. Acknowledging that Britain had lost 90 percent of rubber production, British Under-Secretary of State for the Colonies Harold Macmillan pointed to the danger of "further interference with our sources of supply. We need to increase colonial production for war purposes on an immense scale. Everywhere we must increase."[13] The single most important source of rubber left to Allied powers was in Ceylon, which produced about eighty thousand tons per year against worldwide requirements of one million tons.[14] This meant that smaller suppliers of rubber in Africa, India, and South America also needed to be mobilized.

It was in this context that the imperial government urged colonial states, including Northern Rhodesia, to develop commercial rubber production as a war measure. Similar attempts also began to resuscitate the old para and ceara rubber plantations in West Africa and the East African colonies of Kenya, Uganda, Tanganyika, Nyasaland, and Madagascar, as well as in Ceylon.[15] Meanwhile, in South Africa, rubber was tapped from the *Euphorbia* tree.[16] As mentioned above, natural rubber production in parts of Northern

Rhodesia had a long history.[17] In the period before the First World War, in the western districts of the country, tax had even been paid in the form of crude rubber balls.[18] Thus, policy makers assumed that, having been an indigenous industry at the turn of the twentieth century, rubber making could now be revived as part of the war effort. Local officials in Northern Rhodesia were initially enthusiastic, anticipating the benefits the industry would bring to state coffers as well as the creation of employment for local people from whom the state could collect taxes.[19] They were quick to suggest that production could be expanded through the immediate purchase of suitable machinery to produce thousands of tons per annum, the use of compulsion to ensure that many African peasant farmers took up rubber production, and the provision of trade goods to entice the local people to engage in rubber collection rather than growing food crops.[20]

On 18 April 1942, the government of Northern Rhodesia sent the first rubber samples to two firms in South Africa: Dunlop South Africa Limited and the South African Rubber Manufacturing Company Limited, both based in Durban. After an analysis of the samples, it was noted that the majority fell into "the medium or top grade." The Rhokana Corporation also dispatched samples of rubber found on their premises in Nkana (Kitwe) to their holding company, Anglo American Corporation in Johannesburg. These were analyzed by another laboratory, J. H. Vivian and Company Limited. On 22 April 1942, the results were sent to Nkana and revealed that while the rubber was dirty and contained impurities, it was of medium quality.[21] The purpose of these inquiries was to determine the real potential of the rubber available in Northern Rhodesia and to devise processes acceptable to the collectors that would result in the largest possible production of marketable rubber.[22] Since Northern Rhodesia was close to the Union of South Africa, imperial authorities placed it within the buying sphere of the Union government, which had been appointed as the regional official buyer on behalf of the British Ministry of Supply. From a strategic point of view, the British government considered it essential to purchase even mediocre rubber, since it was possible to improve it if better purification methods were adopted.[23]

However, the initial price set by the Ministry of Supply, at between six and eightpence per pound of rubber, was too low to stimulate production.[24] As Director of Agriculture C. J. Lewin argued in the same spring of 1942, "with regard to future developments it must be admitted candidly that at a value of 6*d.* per *lb.* in South Africa for raw material such as that already submitted, the prospects [of a profitable rubber industry] are nil."[25] The low price offered by the Ministry of Supply meant a mere twopence profit per pound to African rubber collectors living in the remotest parts of the country from which the bulk of the deliveries would come. This small return was worthless, considering the amount of labor involved in the production of rubber. Africans found the prices for the grueling work of collecting and preparing rubber less attractive than either wage employment or the sale of foodstuffs, and consequently some of them showed antipathy toward the scheme. So serious was the labor shortage in Balovale district that at one point the provincial commissioner had to instruct the district commissioner to discontinue the recruitment of agricultural labor so that local men could participate in rubber production.[26] Local colonial officials agitated for the introduction of labor compulsion in the rubber industry, provided that remuneration to producers roughly corresponded to similar levels earned from normal rural unskilled employment. However, these attempts did not come to fruition. The governor refused to approve mandatory labor because he was of the view that the measure, if implemented, would not guarantee a significant output of rubber since the colony was not a major rubber producer.[27]

Colonial government officials thus recommended that the purchase price paid to African collectors be raised to at least ninepence per pound at all buying centers in the country.[28] If low prices continued to be offered, it was likely that collectors would sell their rubber to traders in either Angola or the Congo, where prices were reported to be about one shilling per pound or where one pound of rubber was exchanged for four yards of calico.[29] It was proposed that, in the case of the best rubber, district and provincial commissioners be permitted to raise the price to one shilling per pound, if the market price over the border areas warranted it.[30]

The Ministry of Supply heeded these complaints, and an announcement to that effect was issued by the government of Northern Rhodesia on 21 July 1942. The first batch of rubber, weighing 14,806 pounds and worth £762 19s. 7d., was dispatched to South Africa on 13 January 1943.[31] The country produced two types of rubber: tapped and bark. The former fetched higher prices than the latter because of its superior quality. Government bought the three grades of tapped rubber at one shilling sixpence, one shilling threepence, and ninepence, while bark rubber was purchased at one shilling threepence, one shilling, and eightpence, respectively, per pound.[32] The rubber trade, nonetheless, continued to experience difficulties linked not only to low purchase prices, but also to the lack of processing machinery, a shortage of labor, inadequate trade goods for barter, and the inconsistent quality of the product.[33]

The shortage of rubber for the Allies came to a head at the beginning of 1943. The considerable stocks of crude rubber which had been set aside before the war were nearing exhaustion, yet military requirements continued to rise.[34] Although the US government had begun to develop alternative sources of rubber, synthetic rubber would not be ready until the beginning of 1944. This state of affairs threatened the production of tires and other military requirements, leading the British Secretary of State to declare a state of emergency for the period between July 1943 and June 1944.[35] This declaration aimed at increasing the resources devoted to the collection and processing of rubber in the colonies endowed with the commodity. It was estimated that, by the latter date, many civilian vehicles would also need tire replacements.[36] Besides, once supplies of synthetic rubber came on stream, a certain percentage of crude rubber would still be necessary for admixture with the synthetic rubber in order to manufacture satisfactory products. To maintain the supply of even this small percentage of natural rubber would require unrelenting efforts to maximize production. As the Ministry of Supply observed, the output of even the smallest producing territory would be vital to averting the threatened check to the United Nations' war effort.[37]

Even before the state of emergency was declared by the secretary of state, government officials in Northern Rhodesia on their own initiative undertook extensive tours of rubber-producing areas with a view to stimulating rubber production. These tours were led by C .G. Trapnell, an ecologist from the Department of Agriculture. Director of Agriculture C. J. Lewin, however, was pessimistic about the whole exercise, because in his view the most effective way to stimulate production was to raise the prices offered to producers. "What effect his [C. G. Trapnell's] tours will have in the absence of any increase in prices I cannot say but we should indeed be failing in a clear duty if we did not take all possible steps to increase rubber production whatever work may have to be scrapped or deferred in consequence," Lewin noted.[38] Nevertheless, this measure did have a positive impact on rubber production in the country. Production levels did increase in the territory and the

Colonial Office was satisfied with the progress recorded. The Ministry of Supply noted this in a minute to the governor in early 1945:

> among the outstanding increases in production is that of Northern Rhodesia which shows, according to the Colonial Office records, an increase in export figures from 34½ tons in 1943 to 107 tons in 1944. . . . This increase, which was achieved in spite of the inability of the Ministry of Supply to agree to a further rise in prices, is very satisfactory, and I should be glad if you would convey the thanks of the Rubber Controller to those responsible for the collection of rubber in your Territory.[39]

As the war drew to a close in the latter part of 1945, colonial administrations anticipated that wartime production of rubber would be curtailed. However, this was not the case, as the Ministry of Supply issued new instructions to continue with rubber production even after the cessation of hostilities. This was because it would take time to restore prewar production levels in the recently reconquered Southeast Asian territories.[40] The Ministry of Supply was anxious that African colonies should maintain existing production and purchase arrangements at least up to June 1946, after which a review of the situation would be carried out. The government in Northern Rhodesia did not take kindly to this suggestion. The director of agriculture, for one, found it

> difficult to believe that it is now necessary or desirable to continue with hopelessly uneconomic production of relatively low grade rubber in this Territory. . . . The price paid to native collectors, although fantastic by pre-war standards, is equivalent, on an average, of less than 6d. per working day. As a consequence the bulk of the rubber has been produced under pressure and this has given an already overburdened Provincial Administration more additional work. While there was the incentive of urgent war needs this additional work could be justified—but not now.[41]

Consequently, the colonial government sought permission from the Colonial Office to discontinue rubber production. Whitehall agreed to this, and on 6 October 1945 the government of Northern Rhodesia announced that consignments of rubber would no longer be accepted at Mazabuka from

31 December.[42] Deliveries continued, however, as traders still had rubber in their possession at the time the announcement to close the market was made. The last batch of rubber from Northern Rhodesia to South Africa was dispatched on 2 April 1946. In total, Northern Rhodesia sold rubber with a net weight of about 500,000 pounds and worth over £40,000 to the Ministry of Supply between 1943 and 1946.[43]

IRON SMELTING

The ephemeral—if somewhat romantic—attempt to revive African iron smelting was another indication of the pressures brought to bear on rural Zambia by the conflict. Food production during the war was affected by a serious shortage of agricultural implements. Writing about this state of affairs in 1954, anthropologist Elizabeth Colson noted that it was often difficult for Tonga peasant farmers to get hoes, axes, nails, and hinges.[44] In wartime, about 40 percent of Tonga families were in the subsistence category, of which about 85 percent owned no implements at all.[45] The shortage of hoes and plows had arisen as a result of the worldwide shortage of steel and iron and the difficulty of transporting these raw materials to the colonies due to limited merchant shipping space and their importance in weapons production. So acute had the situation become on the Tonga plateau that families frequently had to wait until friends or relatives had finished their plowing before they could borrow a plow and plant their crop.[46] With replacements and repairs difficult or impossible to secure, peasants became dependent upon farming equipment which had already seen significant wear and tear.

While steel and iron resources were available in Europe and the United States, these materials were mainly devoted to the manufacture of war products, as opposed to civilian articles. During the war, the problem of shipping was so acute that material from overseas could take as long as twelve or even eighteen months to be delivered.[47] The priority of the Allied nations was to deliver military hardware and supplies to the battlefront. So critical had the shortage of steel and iron become that a consignment of as many as ten thousand hoes imported into Northern Rhodesia by the African Lakes Corporation, Booth (North) Ltd, and Thoms Stores was sold within ten days of arrival in August 1941.[48]

The problem worsened further when the major source of Northern Rhodesian hoes, the Union of South Africa, banned their export in 1942 due to a pressing need to reserve the available iron and steel for local consumption. This predicament caused the exporter, Plows (PTY) Limited, to lament that

> everything possible that can be done at our end has been done. We have turned two tons of steel into Hoes, and have a further supply of steel ready to be turned into Hoes, but since the strict control of iron and steel in the Union during the last few weeks, we cannot take a chance on proceeding with the making of Hoes, only to find that, when complete and ready for shipment, they cannot leave our factory.[49]

The South African government's refusal to allow exports of steel tools was nonnegotiable. Fearing the loss of its business, Plows suggested establishing a factory in Northern Rhodesia to bypass the controls imposed on steel exports by the Union. However, such an undertaking was not feasible, due to the lack of local steel resources in Northern Rhodesia. The company, therefore, decided to maintain the status quo until such time as Pretoria lifted the export ban.[50]

The major source of imported farming equipment for the northern parts of Northern Rhodesia was Tanganyika. In 1942, the government of Tanganyika removed the export ban on hoes to Northern Rhodesia, provided local demand was met. But since the demand for hoes turned out to be insatiable in Tanganyika as well, exports to Northern Rhodesia were not sanctioned. This difficult situation prompted the Abercorn district commissioner to wonder whether "in the meantime perhaps it might be possible to get hold of native blacksmiths and make use of old scrap iron? If we would make ourselves self-supporting in hoes or at any rate cease to import from overseas, it would be a direct contribution to our war effort."[51]

The DC's idea had legs, especially since the iron-smelting industry in Northern Rhodesia enjoyed a long history dating back to the precolonial era. Thus it was that the Northern Rhodesian government took it upon itself to revive the iron-smelting industry in the country so that hoes and axes, so vital in African food production, could be manufactured locally and sold to peasant farmers. The chief secretary felt that "if we are to make ourselves self reliant and independent of importation of food stuffs for our native population, it is absolutely imperative that some interest be given to the production of native hoes and axes in this Territory immediately."[52]

Southeast Asia, a Desperate Britain, and the Revival of African Rural Industries

So desperate was the situation that the board of the British South Africa Company (BSACo), which owned mineral rights in much of the western part of the country, allowed local people to mine and process iron without the payment of royalties on the ore mined. The board agreed that Africans could work iron or iron ore from any deposits in the country, other than those in areas covered by special grants or registered mining locations.[53] This concession referred primarily to land in the Balovale district. The BSACo further emphasized that the iron ore mined would be used solely for the purpose of manufacturing hoes and other implements for use in Northern Rhodesia by Africans either in their village or agricultural life.[54]

The government set up schemes in traditional iron-smelting districts: Lundazi, Serenje, Kawambwa, Mkushi, Balovale, and Abercorn. To foster this industry, the government, through the newly created Native Development Board, offered subsidies to African blacksmiths to produce as many iron tools as they could.[55] The board had been founded with assistance from the Colonial Development and Welfare Act (CDWA) of 1940. Through this law, Britain envisaged spending £50 million on development and welfare in the colonies over the next ten years. Section 1 of the act authorized the secretary of state for the colonies to "make schemes for any purpose likely to promote the development of resources of any colony or welfare of its people".[56] In March 1942, the Native Development Board set aside £500 to stimulate African production of hoes and axes to meet such local demand as could not be met through imports.[57] This money was to be used by officials to purchase iron tools from African smiths for resale to peasant farmers. The board noted that "if output were left to the blacksmiths, many would hesitate to increase their normal rate; but if District Commissioners were given money to buy hoes and axes for resale to Natives, the necessary stimulus would be provided."[58] Tools were bought at the going local price, up to a maximum of three shillings per hoe and one shilling and threepence for an axe. Once purchased, the tools were held in stock by district commissioners for sale to peasant farmers at the same price.[59]

It was soon realized, however, that the Northern Rhodesian iron-smelting industry could not be revived without capital expenditure on such items as bellows and the erection of kilns, which were beyond the means of individual smiths. The provincial commissioner for the Northern Province observed that while Kawambwa was the most promising district for iron production in the country, the smelting industry could not be revived unless the requirements of smiths were also considered. Capital for building kilns would be needed.[60] The Native Development Board approved a grant of fifty pounds to the district commissioner of Kawambwa for this purpose.[61] Colonial government officials estimated that between five hundred and six hundred hoes could be produced in the Kawambwa district alone, if additional smiths were trained and some form of mechanical hammer installed.[62] In this district, five smiths who had previous experience in smelting operations were recruited. They erected five furnaces on a site adjacent to a hill containing a very large deposit of iron ore, using funds from the above-mentioned grant.[63] In other districts, apart from setting up new furnaces, additional capital was required to engage the services of an expert smelter to teach this art to others. In Abercorn, it was estimated that wages for such an undertaking would cost thirty shillings, while seven shillings and sixpence was required for the smiths' food.[64] In Chinsali district, the budget for training new smiths was put at five shillings. In the Balovale district, the erection of furnaces for smelting iron ore cost twenty-seven pounds.[65]

The earliest beneficiaries of government subsidies were Kawambwa, Mkushi, Mwinilunga, and Balovale districts. From the twenty pounds allocated to Mkushi district in 1942, the DC bought 40 hoes and 111 axes from local smiths at a total cost of eight pounds and eleven shillings.[66] In the Balovale district, 120 hoes bought from local smiths by the DC in September 1942 were immediately snapped up by local farmers.[67] In neighboring Mwinilunga, 53 hoes were purchased by the DC from smiths in the same month.[68] A total of 97 axes were purchased from local smiths by the DC in Ndola in August 1942.[69]

Despite these promising beginnings, the revival of the iron industry came up against serious obstacles. The first one had to do with the lack of trained manpower to smelt the raw material. To an extent, this was itself a consequence of the war and the shortage of manpower it had generated. In September 1942, for example, it was noted that "the old iron industry depended on communal labour of a village or group of villagers. It is proving very difficult—in fact impossible to revive this communal working of the people."[70] No doubt, this was also an indication that people were aware of the economic value of their labor in relation to the low prices at which the iron tools they produced were being bought. Many Africans thus preferred to work on the Copperbelt or outside the territory, where wages were much higher than could be earned smelting iron.

Additionally, high production costs made the industry an uneconomic proposition. Commenting on the development of the iron industry, the DC for Kawambwa explained that "it is regarded as purely a war measure to alleviate shortage of hoes in which case it can be subsidised but not as a measure intended to develop the industry permanently."[71] In that district, the cost of producing one hoe was pegged at five shillings. Similarly, when carrying out an experiment to produce hoes locally, the DC for Lundazi discovered that each manufactured hoe cost six shillings and one and a half pence.[72] While acknowledging that the hoes made in Lundazi district were "very good," the provincial commissioner also believed that, given "the present cost of labour, it would not be safe to sell these hoes at less than 6/ 3d. each."[73] At this price, the product was regarded as too expensive compared to the prewar price of three shillings. In line with this, after a mere few months of experimentation, the government agreed that efforts to revive the smelting industry and the manufacture of hoes by means of grants from the Native Development Board had proven disappointing, owing primarily to high costs of production.[74]

However, while admitting there was "little prospect of maintaining this native industry after the war in an area where there are other sources of revenue," it was also resolved that "in view of the present acute shortage of hoes . . . payment should be made from Government funds as Special War Expenditure."[75] The government agreed to subsidize locally produced hoes at the rate of two shillings per hoe. In a circular to the relevant provincial commissioners, the chief secretary to the government directed that "in view of the present acute shortage of hoes it has therefore been decided as a temporary measure, that the difference between the price of 3/ and the actual cost of manufacture should be made up by means of a subsidy paid by Government."[76]

The government began paying a subsidy of two shillings per hoe in 1943, following the allocation of five hundred pounds for that purpose.[77] Among the first districts to benefit from state assistance was Abercorn, which received ten pounds and spent it on subsidizing the cost of one hundred hoes.[78] Kawambwa district was given one hundred pounds, from which they subsidized 221 hoes and 17 axes.[79] In the Balovale district, while waiting for his district allocation from the special subsidy fund set up by government, the district commissioner used other sources of money to purchase iron tools. He feared that "we cannot afford to damp the enthusiasm of local smiths which took so much to arouse."[80] As it took a while before the industry got on its feet, the shortage of farming equipment for African cultivators persisted in some parts of the country.

The resumption of exports from the Union of South Africa toward the end of 1943 changed the government's approach to the question once more. This followed a direct approach to the South African Ministry of External Affairs, requesting cooperation and the special allocation of raw materials used in the manufacture of hoes necessary for food production in Northern Rhodesia.[81] As a result, 250 tons of steel was acquired from the United States for use in the manufacture of 150,000 hoes for Northern Rhodesia in the Union of South Africa.[82] By September 1943, 88,000 hoes, made from steel specially allocated to Northern Rhodesia, had been ordered from the Union by various traders, and each was sold at the retail price of two shillings and sixpence.[83] Given the new circumstances, the government concluded that "the necessity of subsiding the manufacture of native made hoes in order to keep the selling price down . . . no longer arises."[84]

Following the end of the war, the government was reluctant to continue supporting the iron-smelting industry through subsidies. This was borne out by the nonallocation of funding for subsidies in the 1945 national budget. In evading its responsibility, the government assigned the task of providing subsidies for the iron industry to "Native Treasuries." But, as the provincial commissioner for the Northern Province pointed out, it was "unfair to expect the [African] Treasury to bear loss on an industry which was re-started at the urgent request of Government."[85] In addition, local chiefs in Kawambwa district, for example, totally refused to subsidize the iron industry, as they claimed their local treasury was already overburdened with other priority areas. The government did not budge, and interest in the artisanal iron-smelting sector faded away as quickly as it had arisen during the war period.

BEESWAX

The other local industry rejuvenated in wartime was the production of beeswax. As Thaddeus Sunseri has noted, the products of the natural environment, particularly those of the forests, such as timber, copal, beeswax, paper pulp, textiles, cellulose, fodder, and charcoal, have often escaped the attention of scholars; yet their production boomed during the war.[86] Like the iron-smelting industry discussed above, beeswax production was not new to Northern Rhodesia. The commodity was perhaps the earliest nonhuman export commodity, along with ivory, from the western parts of Northern Rhodesia during the precolonial period. Wax was secreted by the African honeybee (*Apis mellifera ssp. adonsonii*) and was indirectly a product of the food of the bee, that is, of honey. To produce one pound of wax, bees consumed about ten pounds of honey.[87] Much of the honey collected by African peasants was used locally for brewing mead.[88] As long as no external demand existed, African peasant farmers threw most of the honeycombs away. Traditionally, local people such as the Luvale used beeswax for making *likishi* masks, the maintenance of musical instruments, and to mend wooden products such as dugout canoes.[89]

In the period just before the war, beeswax worth £9,788 was exported from Northern Rhodesia to Southern Rhodesia, South Africa, and Britain.[90] In the metropole, wax was used in the manufacture of various types of polish, waxed paper and cartons, medicines, candles, and cosmetics. In this regard, it can be argued that African resources helped maintain Britain's national economy both during and after the war.[91] African forests were considered an indispensable component of the Allied war effort, and so British officials intervened massively in the forestry industry in the colonies.[92] As with all other commodities required in Britain for war industries, the secretary of state sent instructions urging the increased production of beeswax in the colonies following the fall of the Allied-controlled possessions in Southeast Asia in early 1942.[93]

Messrs Mann and Bishops Limited of London were the first firm to inquire about Northern Rhodesian beeswax. Writing about beeswax to Barclays Bank, in Lusaka, the company stated that

> it has been proved that this commodity is an essential War necessity, and we are asked to endeavour to increase and encourage shipments from all colonies. You will of course know that the Ministry of Supply are now the only buyers of this commodity and it has been agreed with them that business be carried on as in the past, the Broker offering them all and every parcel that is available for shipment or that is shipped to this country.[94]

Although the Ministry of Supply bought beeswax per ton at a maximum of 220 shillings cost, insurance, and freight (c-i-f) London, Messrs Mann and Bishops Limited now suggested that the buying price should be 200 shillings c-i-f London for the same weight.[95]

While negotiations regarding the price of beeswax took place directly between firms connected with war production in the United Kingdom and traders in Northern Rhodesia, the colonial state was anxious to assist by ensuring that as much beeswax and cash as possible found its way into the hands of local traders.[96] This was done by banning the export of wax to neighboring countries like Angola through the nonissuance of export licenses. This policy was a form of economic warfare, whose ultimate rationale was to prevent the commodity from finding its way to Britain's enemies via Portugal.[97] In South Africa, stringent measures were taken to control the use of wax in wartime. Under Regulation 5 of Proclamation 20 of 1942, the Union of South Africa's controller of soap and oils ordered that all firms or persons holding beeswax in excess of fifty pounds declare such items to the government. Anyone who contravened this law was liable to a fine of two hundred pounds or imprisonment for a period not exceeding one year, or both.[98]

In order to set up a wartime beeswax industry, the government instructed the Department of Agriculture to investigate the sector "and report on the present situation of this industry in the various areas with recommendations as to the areas in which development should be continued." The report was to include "information regarding the quality of honey being produced and an estimate of the value of honey being sold."[99] A nationwide tour was undertaken by the assistant director of agriculture between 15 May and 9 August 1940. Messrs Wilson and Mansfield, who handled the bulk of the Northern Rhodesian wax reaching the London market, observed that beeswax from all over the empire was wanted in the mother country. While many other commodities imported into the United Kingdom required licenses, this was not the case with beeswax—a clear demonstration that the imperial government was anxious to have as much beeswax as possible brought into the country.[100] Wax from Northern Rhodesia also benefited from the relaxation of a 10 percent import duty that had previously been enforced within the sterling area.[101] Wax from Northern Rhodesia was in high demand in London because it possessed the indefinable quality of "brightness" associated with the better qualities that came from Tanganyika.[102]

Southeast Asia, a Desperate Britain, and the Revival of African Rural Industries

The war profoundly altered the production and marketing of beeswax from Northern Rhodesia due to a sharp increase in demand, which, in turn, led to an increase in price. The production of raw materials from African forests reached unprecedented levels during the war period.[103] The price of beeswax rose so rapidly that whereas "in June 1939 Northern Rhodesian wax was selling on the London market at £98 per ton[,] a consignment which reached London shortly after the outbreak of war was sold for £140 per ton and in June 1940 the price of Northern Rhodesian wax was about £160 per ton."[104] However, the government observed that, while shipment had not so far presented any particular difficulty, the absence of direct shipping facilities from the port of Lobito, in Angola, could, in future, seriously hamper the marketing of supplies from far-flung places such as Mwinilunga and Balovale.[105]

By 1941, wax production had become attractive to many peasants in the Mankoya district. The only hindrance to growth in the wax trade was the long distance that separated the district from the line of rail. This meant that producers usually accepted the low prices offered by traders rather than undertake the long journey on foot to the nearest markets in Livingstone or Mulobezi. Many individuals possessed between one hundred and two hundred beehives, from which they derived an income of about five or six pounds annually.[106] Mankoya was unique in that practically the whole of the wax trade was in the hands of African middlemen, and not European traders. In 1940, the district had sixty-seven licensed beeswax hawkers.[107] Wax was bought in the villages by these itinerant African hawkers for cash or cloth, with an invariable "present" of salt also given to the seller. Although much of this wax was sold in the vicinity of Mulobezi and Livingstone districts, a considerable quantity was carried over the border for sale in Angola under the auspices of a Portuguese trading concern, Rhodesiangola, which began operations in November 1939.[108]

Balovale district had the oldest tradition of producing beeswax from hives. Between 1938 and January 1940, two demonstrators were employed by the Department of Agriculture, in addition to two assistants. Their job was to increase production and improve the quality of the product. In the first half of 1940, 7,130 pounds of beeswax were sold and more was expected, considering the good season predicted.[109] Much of this wax was sold to Portuguese traders at Lumbala and Kazambo. Wax was sold at eightpence per pound for the clean variety, while ordinary ball wax fetched sixpence per pound.[110] This difference in price aimed at encouraging peasants to produce cleaner wax. The desired effects were not long in coming, for in 1940 the Department of Agriculture reported that "many of the producers have now learned to make clean wax and there is reason to hope that if tuition and the present discriminating prices continue for a little longer the practice may become universal."[111] Local leaders also encouraged their subjects to engage in wax production and to increase nectar supplies by controlling the burning of forests in order not to disturb bee sanctuaries. In Senanga district, only 885 pounds was sold in 1938, but by mid-1940 over 2,000 pounds had been traded.[112] The only wax trader in the district, A. Harrington, offered "reasonably attractive" prices of between four and five and a half pence per pound for impure and cleaner wax, respectively.[113]

State intervention in this industry included development funds and loans to forestry establishments for use in mobilizing technology and labor.[114] Through the Native Development Board, the state offered subsidies to wax producers for paying instructors and demonstrators and for purchasing uniforms and various other materials used in wax production. The object of the financial support given by the government was to support the industry for a period of at least three years in order to set it in motion. In 1941 the board put aside £818 for the development of the wax trade. Of this amount, £310 was reserved for the five main wax-producing districts: Mwinilunga, Kasempa, Mankoya, Balovale, and Senanga.[115]

The colonial government asked London to authorize the release from duty of military personnel who could help in the production of beeswax. Such a release had occurred in the case of rubber for B. P. Rudge, who returned to Balovale district to aid in latex collection. Rudge also took up the trade in beeswax. At the same time, colonial authorities proposed to order between fifteen thousand and twenty thousand trade goods on government account through lend-lease arrangements in hopes of boosting wax production by enticing Africans to exchange their produce for imported articles such as cloth, blankets, and cooking utensils.[116] This proposal, though, did not go ahead due to ongoing difficulties in the procurement of trade goods for the more viable rubber scheme.

Because his department was already overburdened by the requirements of rubber production, the director of agriculture was reluctant to sanction any action which might result in the government buying, controlling, or

Southeast Asia, a Desperate Britain, and the Revival of African Rural Industries

standardizing the quality of beeswax. It was pointed out that the case of rubber was different, because there had been no existing trade in the commodity at the time the war started. This had meant that the government had to step in to aid the industry. Conversely, beeswax traders already had overseas markets at the outbreak of hostilities in Europe.[117] This position was supported by the secretary for native affairs, who argued that, "in a country where the boosting of native production is a new departure [in Government policy], save as a hobby for the enthusiastic few, it is natural that the efforts of the Agricultural Department should be entirely absorbed in the drives for rubber and foodstuffs and that they should be reluctant to take on anything else.[118] As a result, unlike the more strategic rubber, beeswax was traded without direct government involvement. But because the beeswax industry did not fall under any government institution, traders faced challenges in the course of their business. The primary problem was limited shipping capacity at the ports of Lobito and Beira, which, in turn, resulted in delayed shipment and payments from importers. The main exporter of beeswax in the Balovale district suggested that the government needed to intervene in the trade by providing advance payments so that beeswax peasant producers would not get discouraged due to delayed payments.[119] The government agreed to help with two-thirds advances covering the total value of the beeswax exported, on condition that receipted rail notes be provided.[120]

As in the case of iron, the flourishing of the beeswax industry was short-lived. By the beginning of 1943, the market for beeswax in Britain had become so saturated that prices began to drop. In the Balovale district, for example, the buying price declined from one shilling and twopence to eightpence per pound, and traders found it difficult to dispose of their stocks.[121] This marked the beginning of the end of the deliberate promotion of beeswax production in Northern Rhodesia during the war period.

STRING AND ROPE

In the aftermath of the Japanese conquest of the Philippines and Indonesia, the major sources of the sisal used in the making of string, rope, and sacks for the Allied powers, attempts were also made to look for fiber substitutes. Northern Rhodesia was able to help in this regard because it had a history of indigenous rope making. Like beeswax, this, too, was a forestry industry. In the early 1930s, European traders such as the Renaud Brothers and William

Freshwater, a missionary with the London Missionary Society, bought string made from *chitatula* roots or the *kaboke* plant in Mporokoso district in the Northern Province, most of which they used for fishing nets.[122] In fact, many varieties of trees, shrubs, and vines in the country's evergreen forests yielded excellent fibers. In the Barotse Province, two species of the bowstring hemp type (*Sansevieria*), locally known as *lukushye* and *musokozebe*, had been used to manufacture rope and string since time immemorial because they were "as strong and durable as any" and resembled sisal. The untreated type of lukushye string was sold at about four shillings and sixpence per five pounds, while the treated variety of the same weight fetched six shillings.[123] The major hindrance to the promotion of the industry before the outbreak of the war was that the market was limited to local consumers.[124] Apart from varieties growing wild in the forests, some European farmers also grew sunhemp (*Crotalaria juncea*), which they used as green manure. However, the stem of sunhemp also yielded good "soft" fiber.[125] The disadvantage of using sunhemp for the manufacture of string was that it required a lot of water and machinery for processing; its bulky nature, moreover, rendered the establishment of a central factory impracticable, due to the crops being grown on widely scattered farms.[126]

Wartime manufacture of rope in the country began as soon as instructions were sent from the secretary of state for the colonies to the chief secretary, Lusaka, in early 1942. The secretary of state for the colonies pointed out that, "concerning the inclusion of a proportion of sisal in ropes hitherto supplied with a pure manila content, I have the honour to inform you that, owing to the effect of the present situation in the Philippines on future supplies of manila, it is now necessary to increase still further the use of sisal in the manufacture of ropes."[127] The chief secretary noted that "it is of great importance that string and rope should be produced locally in order to save the necessity of importing it from outside the country."[128] He then remarked that "the least we can do is to be self-supporting in as many things as possible and I believe the native can play a big part in this."[129] The use of local people in schemes involving CDWA grants was in line with the instructions issued by the colonial secretary to colonial governors on 10 September 1940. The circular emphasized that such schemes should be restricted to those that could be carried out with local human and material resources and which would not prove detrimental to the war effort.[130] By June 1942, Northern Rhodesian importers were already facing difficulties in sourcing string from abroad. The North-Western Rhodesia Cooperative Society, for instance, had ordered five thousand pounds of string from Calcutta, India, through their agents, A. J. Butler of Bulawayo. As long as six months later, however, they still had not received the consignment.[131] Another firm, E. W. Tarry's, also complained that although there was a big demand for binder twine, they were unable to procure supplies from their usual sources.[132] The intended market for the locally produced rope and string included government departments, mission stations, and shops in rural areas, while on the line of rail the major buyers were the government printers and the postal office headquarters.

A local European trader in the Abercorn district was the first to send string samples to the government on 22 May 1942. They were manufactured from sisal on his estate by an African employee who produced nine feet of the washed (plaited) type and fourteen feet of unwashed string at a wage rate of sixpence per day.[133] Sail twine was used for sewing sacks and thatching, while binder twine was utilized in the reaping of wheat. The market price of the two string samples was eightpence and sixpence.[134] Other samples received by the government came from the Luano Valley, near Broken Hill.[135] By mid-1942 the government printer reported that he had been able to obtain good-quality string in Pemba and Mazabuka Districts in the Southern Province, and he urged the director of civil supplies to place an order.

True hemp (*Cannabis sativa*), known in Northern Rhodesia as Indian hemp or dagga, was also suggested as a crop that could be used in the manufacture of string during wartime. Its advantage was that the plant grew wild. Unlike other fibrous plants, such as sisal, which took between three and four years to ripen, *Cannabis sativa* grew quickly and matured in one season. These features were ideal for its promotion in wartime. Fears were raised, however, about the deliberate growing of dagga, even for fibrous use. The acting chief secretary observed that "the danger of large-scale native production lies, of course, in the spread of dagga smoking, but if the war need is vital this risk may have to be taken and as many safeguards devised as possible to avoid it."[136] In wartime, Britain did not care where raw materials came from so long as what was needed was made available. Fearing that dagga would be abused by African farmers, the colonial government decided to allow only Polish and Italian evacuees to grow the crop for processing into string.[137] As this type of fiber was soft in nature, it was used in the manufacture of sacks only.

The government also engaged the assistance of magistrates and the police to retain all hemp seeds confiscated for planting in new areas.[138] Additionally, the Department of African Education was asked to issue instructions to African schools to use part of the one-hour handicraft class to teach pupils string making and sack weaving.[139] Acknowledging that the only difficulty in executing this project would be the lack of instructors, the director of African education responded favorably to this suggestion as a war measure, and hoped that the industry could continue even after the war, provided that the local products could survive foreign competition.[140] Instructors were trained at the Jeanes School in Mazabuka so that they could in turn pass on their knowledge of spinning, weaving, and the making of looms to their pupils. The government also wanted to use prisoners to grow and process hemp into fiber. For obvious reasons, this suggestion was not well received in prison administration circles. The commissioner of police, indeed, was "not in favour of the introduction of hemp into the prisons. The introduction of unauthorised articles into prisons is already a problem which requires constant check to keep it under control."[141] But this aside, prisoners were employed in the essential work of food production.

In an effort to promote the local manufacture of string, the government offered subsidies to African producers through the Native Development Board, just as they did with other industries. An account, called the "Advances—String Purchases Account," was opened to enable district commissioners to buy string and twine from Africans on behalf of Messrs Tarry and Company and the Farmers' Cooperative Society.[142] Grants of up to ten pounds were issued for the purchase of string samples in various districts for onward transmission to the two approved trading firms. The director of agriculture also sent samples of good fibers to the Union of South Africa for commercial evaluation.[143]

But not everything was rosy in the production of string. One challenge faced by this industry was the shortage of labor willing to produce the raw material required in its manufacture. Lack of manpower was a marked phenomenon in the Luano Valley, one of the areas producing some of the best string in the territory. The provincial commissioner for Central Province, under whose jurisdiction the area fell, noted that "the difficulty in supplying string and ropes from Luano Valley to Cooperative Society and Tarry has arisen owing to these people being comfortably off through the sale of tobacco etc., and being near a labour market they are not really interested in this proposition although the price is 1/ - [one shilling] per lb for their string."[144]

Due to these difficulties, the colonial state thought the best way of implementing the string project was by employing people to work the "cactus plant" as a commercial concern under the auspices of the Mkushi district commissioner. They would be paid a monthly wage. Approval was granted on condition that the cost of production should not exceed one shilling for each pound of string manufactured.[145] Ten workers were employed on the project under the supervision of a senior messenger, but the average monthly weight of string made by each worker was found to be only just over three pounds.[146] The project was discontinued because it was uneconomical: as the wages paid to each worker amounted to seventeen shillings and sixpence, this meant that the cost of manufacturing one pound of string totaled five shillings and eightpence at a time when the government's recommended rate was one shilling per pound.[147] The situation in Mkushi was comparable to that in other parts of the country. The case was the same in the Abercorn and Sesheke districts. At Abercorn, for example, Hausser was unable to supply string to the local post office at eightpence per pound because, at that rate, workers producing the string could earn only a paltry three-quarter pence per day.[148]

The war affected the lives of the rural areas of Northern Rhodesia through the imperial government's decision to revive the extraction of select raw materials required for the Allied war effort. Apart from exporting rubber and beeswax products to Britain, Northern Rhodesia also revamped such indigenous African industries as iron smelting and string making with a view to becoming self-sufficient at a time when these items were difficult to obtain from abroad. Ultimately, however, all these efforts were hampered by a fundamental contradiction. In its wartime propaganda (see chapter 1), the British government had undertaken to buy African produce at competitive rates if the colonies supported the war against Germany. Yet the evidence surveyed in this chapter shows that Britain actually bought African produce at below-market prices. While imperial officials claimed that low prices were meant to stifle a surge in inflationary pressure, colonial officials on the ground tended to agitate for fairer deals on behalf of "their" African producers. This situation exposes divergent points of view between the metropole and colonial governments regarding the price structure of commodities. The changing character of British policies, of course, can be attributed to the fact that issues of "fairness" in wartime became blurred due to desperation and the desire to secure victory. In this way, unconventional—if not unethical—methods became legitimate strategies for British survival. In the next chapter I deal with more economic challenges the people of Northern Rhodesia contended with during the war: commodity shortages, profiteering, hoarding, the black market, and hyperinflation.

3

War and the Economics of the Home Front

"THE INDIVIDUAL ISSUE OF SOAP, AS A RESULT OF LIMITED SUP-
plies, is so small that it would not be possible to increase the ration
of soap to persons engaged in certain classes of employment without causing serious hardship to the ordinary consumer," lamented the government's
chief secretary in the Legislative Assembly when asked to update the country
on the state of consumer goods shortages in 1947. He went on to say that
"in certain industries special issues of soap are made to employers to enable
their staff to avail themselves of washing facilities before they leave work."[1]
The words of the chief secretary illuminate some of the economic hardships
Northern Rhodesia's Africans endured both during and after the war due
to problems in the supply chain of consumer commodities and the general
contraction in world trade occasioned by the conflict.

War has momentous economic effects on society. Positive developments
might include the increased production of metals directly related to the execution of the war, the rise in employment levels in munitions factories, and
the development of the construction sector when the fighting ends. But war
can also bring about negative economic effects such as the shortage of consumer goods, hyperinflation, the black market, and the rationing of goods.
During the Second World War, similar consequences befell the economies of
the Allied nations and were extended to their colonies all over the world due
to the close links between the European metropoles and their peripheries.
Ordinary Zambian men, women, and children came to bear the brunt of

these economic hardships occasioned by a war whose causes many of them could hardly fathom. These effects lasted for the entire duration of the hostilities and remained visible several years after.

Besides prompting attempts to revive the production of local commodities (see chapter 2), the war also resulted in a general scarcity of consumer goods—a scarcity which necessitated the imposition of austerity measures, such as the rationing of soap noted above. The rationing of consumer goods was just one of the many measures adopted by the colonial administration to cope with pressures on the Northern Rhodesian home front. Shortages of commodities, hoarding, inflation, profiteering, and the black market all meant that the economic cost of the war affected the lives of ordinary people far from the actual fighting. This trend persisted in the postwar period owing to a continued shortage of consumer goods and to the changes in the imperial economic system occasioned by the sterling convertibility crisis of 1947. These challenges compelled the government to abandon its laissez-faire policy to address the economic woes affecting the country. As elsewhere in Africa, the war ushered in unprecedented levels of state intervention in the economies of the colonies.[2] This chapter considers the reasons behind this intervention, as well as its modalities and mixed results.

THE CAUSES OF COMMODITY SHORTAGES

Due to the war, Northern Rhodesia experienced a shortage of such consumer goods as clothing, cutlery, food, and soap. So severe did the situation become in some places that police reported a rise in break-ins and the theft of domestic items, as wartime shortages made mundane items harder to obtain than in peacetime.[3] One of the reasons for this state of affairs was that the country depended on imports for most of its needs. The main exporters of consumer goods to Northern Rhodesia were the United Kingdom, Southern Rhodesia, and South Africa. However, in wartime, the metropolitan economy could not maintain its previous levels of exports to the colonies. A recurrent problem was the shortage of labor, resulting in a drastic fall in production for the civilian market.[4] Britain mobilized civilians more fully than any other combatant country. In June 1944, when 22 percent of the country's labor force was in the armed services, 33 percent was in civilian war work.[5] As much of Britain's industrial capacity was diverted toward war production, the volume of the goods offloaded in Africa was severely reduced, and often the quality,

War and the Economics of the Home Front

as well.[6] The prosecution of total war meant that the manufacture of goods not regarded as priorities stopped. Most raw materials were used in the interests of the imperial war economy. Northern Rhodesia was one of those colonies that bore the brunt of reduced exports from the metropole and elsewhere in the empire.

Additionally, there was a worldwide shortage of raw materials needed to produce goods in the metropole. The shortage of soap experienced in colonies such as Northern Rhodesia was a consequence of Britain's territorial losses in Southeast Asia, from which the empire obtained the bulk of its fats and oils.[7] The Japanese conquest of Southeast Asia was the root cause of supply challenges, as it "severed the shipment routes of food and primary products previously destined for Allied and colonial territories alike."[8] Moreover, such raw materials as still reached the shores of Britain were immediately earmarked for war purposes or local consumption.[9] Worse still was that the purchase of materials in non-sterling areas presented great difficulties, as imperial sterling balances had to be conserved. In 1941, Colonial Secretary Lord Moyne sent a circular to all colonial governors urging the accumulation of sterling balances for future use.[10] The colonies were asked to limit import demands in order to conserve the sterling area's hard currency and ease Britain's balance of payments.[11] As Michael Cowen and Nicholas Westcott have demonstrated, the enforced change in the pattern of international trade in conjunction with the centralization of sterling determined a change in market conditions for raw material production.[12]

Even when manufactured goods for overseas shipment were available, Axis submarine warfare represented another ever-present threat. As John Hargreaves noted, the dislocation of prewar trade patterns, shipping shortages, and maritime blockades weakened whole sectors of Africa's commercial economy.[13] A single ship sunk by the Axis could contain enough goods to satisfy Northern Rhodesia's requirements for several months, and such losses actually occurred more than once during 1943.[14] The concentration of convoys in the North Atlantic route following the fall of France in June 1940 also led to a shortage of shipping. The proportion of British ships using this route to procure supplies from American sources rose from one-third to over a half during 1940.[15] This had a threefold impact on Africa's trade with the rest of Empire. First, supplies of dollars for colonial imports were reduced; British exports to the colonies also shrank because as many as possible were diverted to dollar markets, particularly in Latin America. All of this greatly limited the markets and shipping available for colonial exports.[16] It was in this context that import licensing was introduced in all British African colonies. Speaking in Cairo in 1941, Oliver Lyttleton, the future secretary of state, stressed the urgent need to "[cut] down demands for imports in the most dramatic manner. . . . Whenever something we could do without is shipped the hour of victory is postponed."[17] This policy created severe supply challenges for the colonies in the postwar period.[18]

Once the Allied armies expanded their conquest to new territories, these too had to be supplied with goods. These supplies were drawn from existing production, so that it proved impossible to increase quotas for Northern Rhodesia or other British African colonies for a considerable period.[19] After the war ended, Europe and the newly liberated territories still had to be restocked before others could be considered. As *The Times* had earlier reported, "there is little prospect of any expansion of supplies for export, and if . . . goods have to be sent to some market recently made accessible again to Lancashire firms, such as Madagascar, it is virtually certain that some other market will have to suffer proportionately."[20]

Before the war, the wholesale business of Northern Rhodesia was almost entirely carried out by merchants in Southern Rhodesia and South Africa with distribution franchises over the entire country. Northern Rhodesia and Southern Rhodesia were "geographically contiguous" and "economically integrated."[21] But, following the outbreak of the conflict, both Southern Rhodesia and South Africa introduced export control measures aimed at protecting their local consumers, and Northern Rhodesia was, as it were, left with the scraps.[22] The introduction of an import quota system for civilian requirements in the colonies provided for direct imports from the UK to Northern Rhodesia. In the case of official quotas, however, Northern Rhodesia was coupled with Southern Rhodesia for the joint allocation of commodities.[23] But not all goods so allotted reached Northern Rhodesia.

In early 1944 a special Supply Mission led by Northern Rhodesia's financial secretary, Keith Tucker, held discussions with officials of the Colonial Office, the Board of Trade, the Export Licensing Department, the Cotton Board, and the Shipping Control Office, as well as the London and Manchester Chambers of Commerce. The top priority of this mission was to find ways of increasing the supply of consumer goods to Northern Rhodesia,

War and the Economics of the Home Front

particularly textiles. The annual prewar import quota of cotton goods for the colony was about 9–10 million yards. Supplies had come from Britain and India through normal commercial channels, and partly by indirect importation through wholesalers in Southern Rhodesia.[24] In the twelve months from July 1942 to June 1943, for example, the UK supplied 2,270,000 yards of cotton piece goods, of which 1,301,000 yards were shipped directly and 969,000 imported through Southern Rhodesia.[25] The actual UK quota allocated to Northern Rhodesia for the same period was equivalent to 5,216,000 yards, thereby leaving a shortfall in delivery of 2,946,000 yards.[26] The Indian quota for the same period was equivalent to 2,062,000 yards, but actual receipts amounted to 2,793,000 yards. Thus, although the UK deficiency was partly made good by Indian supplies, the net deficiency still amounted to 2,215,000 yards.[27]

Why the UK quota allocation of cotton piece goods for Northern Rhodesia failed to reach the country, whereas Indian supplies exceeded their quota allocation, is difficult to explain. The UK joint Rhodesia quota was based on 60 percent of prewar imports. The figures for Northern Rhodesia are indicated in table 3.1.

From the above figures it can be deduced that Northern Rhodesia received only 69 percent of its cotton piece goods war quota, leaving a net deficiency in the combined UK and India quota of 31 percent. Northern Rhodesia also received from Southern Rhodesia only 38 percent of the indirect export quota, yet 95 percent of the direct quota allocation arrived in the country. Northern Rhodesia thus received a greater share of the allocations through direct imports than through Southern Rhodesian merchants. One thing that became clear as a result of the supply mission's visit in 1944 was that commodities were in short supply owing to the disruption in trade activities arising from the war conditions.[28]

OTHER ECONOMIC CHALLENGES AND GOVERNMENT RESPONSE

The shortage of commodities was not the only problem besetting Northern Rhodesia's domestic economy during the war. The colony also had to contend with a rising rate of inflation. Increased incomes from rubber sales, remittances from servicemen, and a growing African peasant agricultural sector were not matched by increased imports.[29] As David Killingray and Richard Rathbone have demonstrated, a great deal of money in wartime chased a

TABLE 3.1. Northern Rhodesia supply position of cotton piece goods, 1944

	Tons	% of quota	Tons	%
(a) Prewar imports			3,250	100
War quota			1,950	60
Northern Rhodesian share				
Direct imports	300	15		
Imports via Southern Rhodesia	300	15		
(b) United Kingdom 1942/43 quota			521	100
Direct export	281	54		
Via Southern Rhodesia	240	46		
Received by Northern Rhodesia			227	44
Direct export	130	46		
Via Southern Rhodesia	97	40		
(c) UK quota deficiency			294	56
Direct export	151	54		
Via Southern Rhodesia	143	60		
(d) India quota			206	100
Direct export	112	54		
Via Southern Rhodesia	94	46		
Received by Northern Rhodesia			297	135
Direct export	247	221		
Via Southern Rhodesia	32	34		
(e) India surplus			73	35
Direct export	+135	121		
Via Southern Rhodesia	−62	66		
(f) Total UK + India quota			727	100
UK	521	72		
India	206	28		
Received by Northern Rhodesia			506	69
From UK	227	31		
From India	279	135		
Net deficiency			221	31

Source: NRG, *Northern Rhodesia Supply Mission to the United Kingdom, 1944* (Lusaka: Government Printer, 1944), 5–6.

severely restricted supply of goods in Britain's African colonies.[30] The "knock on" effect of inflation in the consumer goods sector was quickly felt in the food sector, and so the period between 1942 and 1947 witnessed increases in the general cost of living for Africans.[31] In an attempt to stop this, the government decided to curb the amount of cash in circulation by encouraging people to save as much money as possible in the Post Office Savings Bank (POSB). Interest from the POSB was at a rate of 2.5 percent per annum. By 31 December 1946, when these interest-bearing savings were withdrawn, there were 13,679 depositors with deposits totaling £342,258.[32] Among the depositors were African members serving in the armed forces, to whom the scheme had been extended.[33] Through this scheme, consumer demand for hard-to-come-by manufactured articles was curbed.

The state also issued war bonds to encourage people to invest for the future, the auditor general noting that wartime was a period for investment and not consumption.[34] The government issued these bonds as debt securities to finance military operations and other expenditures during the war period. Colonial authorities made an appeal for investment in war bonds to patriotic citizens to lend the government money at a rate of return below the market value. The accountant general issued the bonds at par for five pounds and multiples of five pounds. Individual holdings were limited to £1000, repayable in ten years at the rate of 101 percent. The bonds were cashable at any time, on six months' notice, and at a shorter notice in an emergency, but with loss of interest. A total net issue at the end of December 1945 amounted to £202,000 and was withdrawn in October 1946.[35] This measure helped mop up surplus cash from circulation, thereby limiting inflationary pressure.

In addition, the government issued War Savings Certificates to attract war finance from a previously unreached section of the population, that is, people who were not used to investing money. The certificate took the form of an engraved sheet bearing on its face the name and address of the investor or owner and was sold at fifteen shillings each—small enough for the majority to afford. War Savings Certificates had been introduced as soon as war broke out. Intended to contribute to the United Kingdom's war expenses, they were devised along the same lines as those issued in the metropole. Certificates were issued under the Income Tax War Provisions Ordinance. Individual holdings were limited to 500 units, the total authorized issue being 414,634 units, amounting to 425,000 over the whole period. The balance of certificates available for issue at 30 September 1946 amounted to 42,706 units, but repayments had for some time exceeded sales. The closing date for the issuance of war certificates was 30 April 1948.[36]

Throughout the war, the colonial administration was concerned about profiteering among traders. The most alarming records of profiteering came from rural areas. Indian traders who dominated retail trade in the countryside took advantage of the war to raise the prices of their merchandise, albeit using unconventional methods, such as the refusal to display prices or altering prices depending on the clientele.[37] Throughout the war and its immediate aftermath, government bureaucrats received various complaints against Indian traders in parts of the Southern Province. Such unscrupulous traders included Changanlal and Company, based at Macha; the Nayee Brothers of Chilumbe, in Chief Mapanza's area; and Narayan and Company on Musali Farm, in Choma. Shortly after the war, and following complaints from the general public about the nondisplay of prices on goods, the district commissioner for Mazabuka toured Indian-owned shops. His visit, however, proved fruitless, since, as he reported, "it was obvious that word of my coming had gone before me. The villagers consider the prices in these stores exorbitant."[38] The nondisplay of prices by traders was a violation of the Emergency Powers Control of Prices and Hoarding Regulations of 1942 (amended in 1945), which, beginning on 1 September 1942, had made the display of maximum prices mandatory. The Changanlal stores at Macha Village had no list of maximum prices. But the stores were warned of the government official's impending visit and "something like a bargain sale was in progress" by the time the DC toured the area, finding that prices "bore no relation to the usual ones."[39]

Another widespread tactic used by traders was to make the sale of sought-after goods dependent on the purchase of other articles which were either expensive or not in great demand. This is what happened to Bennet Musongo of Broken Hill, who, on 22 March 1945, went to buy a bicycle tire and tube but was told by the shopkeeper he could only do so on condition that he also bought a shirt and a blanket.[40] Of all the tactics used by evasive traders, conditional selling was the most difficult to deal with by price control inspectors because most transactions of this nature were personal and between the two parties concerned. It was one man's word against another's. Traders, as a rule, were careful not to put anything of this sort into writing, and neither

War and the Economics of the Home Front

buyer nor seller cared to have witnesses when negotiating.[41] Ashley Jackson noted a similar tendency in Bechuanaland, where traders used the "good fors" system, which obliged a customer to purchase an unwanted item in order to obtain a scarcer commodity.[42] In other instances, especially in the case of bread, the weight of goods being sold was reduced, yet the price remained constant.[43] Other common offenses included the nonissuance of receipts and the failure to mark goods as prescribed by law.

Unscrupulous merchants also abounded in the urban centers. The problem of profiteering became one of the focal points of the newly established African Provincial Councils in the postwar period. For instance, the African Provincial Council for the Western Province complained in 1947 that "we do not know the exact prices in the Indian stores but prices are much clearer in the European stores."[44] Between June and September 1947, 110 prosecutions concerning price control regulations were recorded in various parts of the country; nearly 50 percent of these concerned overcharging.[45] Indian traders proved extremely difficult to trap.[46] That Indian traders used underhand trading methods does not mean that they were the only ones to do so. For example, the only two merchants in the European trade at Mufulira were both prosecuted for making excessive profits in June 1941. The general public commended these prosecutions.[47]

In responding to scarcity and other war-related problems, the British government increased its control over and intervention in production and exchange to ensure that all available resources were used to prosecute the war.[48] Control measures were also established over supplies, shipping, the use of local labor, and the purchase of commodities from the colonies. Similar policies were adopted in British colonial Africa, and Northern Rhodesia was no exception. In addressing the resultant problem of scarcity, the Northern Rhodesian colonial government adopted its own policies. The rationing of commodities (including soap, butter, whisky, milk, bread, and petrol) started in early 1940 and remained in place until the end of 1943. In this regard, mine authorities on the Copperbelt reported that "people had cooperated extraordinarily well."[49] Compulsory rationing was only introduced the following year. The new regulations introduced in 1944 required that, within thirty days of their publication, every European residing within the scheduled area register himself/herself and the members of his/her household with one retailer for specified goods.[50] In line with entrenched racial practices, rationing through registration did not apply to Africans. The colonial government was more concerned with protecting the interests of the European community, whose access to goods it wanted to safeguard through rationing, than those of local Africans. Instead, bulk allocations of soap representing half the available supplies were made available to traders for sale to Africans. In short, Africans, unlike members of the European community, did not register to receive commodities such as soap and butter that were in short supply. No African could purchase or receive a rationed commodity on behalf of a European unless he was in possession of a letter of identification signed by the European customer concerned.[51] Contravention of these laws made one liable to a fine not exceeding two hundred pounds, imprisonment for a period not exceeding one year, or both.[52] While coupons were utilized to ration commodities in the UK, this system was not implemented in Northern Rhodesia because of the shortage of paper, additional work for the retailer, and general inconvenience to the public.[53]

The government resorted to rationing to ensure that all people had at least some soap and butter, stocks of which had reached low levels in the country. The root cause of soap rationing was the worldwide shortage of fats and oils and the subsequent rise in the price of these raw materials. For instance, the price of palm oil increased from £65 12s. per ton free-on-rail-Sakania [border with the Congo] in December 1946 to £120 per ton in August 1947; palm kernel oil increased from £78 per ton prior to December 1946 to £110 per ton in August 1947.[54] Due to the increase in cost of these raw materials, the price of a case of Sunlight soap rose from 38 shillings to 50 shillings.[55] *Mutende* newspaper carried a propaganda campaign urging Africans to save soap by drying it in the sun after use, never leaving it in water, washing all their laundry at once, and using ashes for washing dishes and pots, as well as by manufacturing their own soaps using caustic soda and animal fat.[56] The shortage of soap affected women more than it did men because the former were invariably expected to look after their homesteads. Since women bore the brunt of shortages, there was an obviously gendered dimension to the economic crisis.

The necessity of rationing butter also resulted from the worldwide shortage of fats and the severe restrictions on supplies already in force in Southern Rhodesia and East Africa. In a period when control was paramount, colonial officials had to devise new strategies and policies to secure the resources necessary for the war while keeping the lid on social and economic unrest.[57] Following the fall of the British-controlled sources of oils and fats in the Far East in early 1942, the director of civil supplies in Northern Rhodesia instructed all traders and retailers of butter to restrict the sale of the commodity to their customers to 75 percent of their normal monthly purchases.[58] In 1944, the British Ministry of Food diverted to the East Africa Command 150 tons of Northern Rhodesia's normal imports of butter from South Africa. This caused the butter ration for white settlers to fall from 14¼ to 8 ounces per head per week.[59] No such mechanism was instituted for Africans, although the government had pledged earlier in the war to meet the needs of the local population.[60]

When distributing and rationing scarce commodities, maize was the most difficult to allocate, because it was not a luxury item like butter, whisky, sugar, soap, or fuel. The scarcity of maize brought the war home to many Africans who had no substitute to fall back on and who had to pay any price that retailers set. The importance of maize put the government on the defensive; since it could not suggest that people should stop or reduce their consumption, it had to attempt to solve the problem. Maize was a priority. The primary strategy was to encourage a rapid increase in domestic production and ensure a fair distribution across the country. Consumption of nonessentials could wait until the end of the war when they were expected to be plentiful on the market, but not maize.

The shortage of commodities led to the emergence of a black market and smuggling in the colony.[61] An aggravating factor during wartime was the sense of uncertainty, which led to a vicious spiral of panic buying and rocketing prices. The Northern Rhodesian government found it necessary to regulate the prices of commodities and the ordinary commercial processes of distributing goods during the war.[62] No sooner had the war broken out than the imperial government imposed controls to protect the sterling area against a drain on its dollar and gold reserves by restricting all imports from non-sterling countries. But the shortage of goods continued even after the end of the war because of restrictions on dollar-imports. Supplies did not improve much after the war, as the world was plagued by fundamental imbalances in production. The situation was exacerbated by the August 1947 convertibility crisis and eventual devaluation of the pound sterling in September 1949.[63] This entailed an even stricter implementation of price control. In view of the devaluation of sterling in the UK, the removal of import controls was postponed, as its colonies were required to contribute to the preservation of dollar earnings by reducing imports from the non-sterling area.[64]

To protect consumers from exploitative traders taking advantage of shortages by hiking the prices of goods, the government introduced price control in 1942. It remained in force until the early 1950s. The Northern Rhodesia General Defence Regulations no. 301 of 1942 authorized the controller of prices to regulate prices from time to time. Other ordinances were enacted to fix the prices of soap, butter, blankets, and maize meal. Through the Emergency Powers (Control of Prices and Hoarding) Amendments Regulations 1941, Government Notice no. 301 of 1941, the price controller had powers to implement price control measures such as the display of prices.[65]

There were two other methods of controlling prices besides the display of prices. One was by assigning a fixed price to given commodities. The other was known as the "factor system," which was designed to limit retail profits to prewar levels. This was influenced by whether the article had increased in cost since the start of the war.[66] The system depended on the records kept by traders, and these proved difficult to check. The factor system aimed to control profit margins on goods that had increased in cost by means of a table of factors which reduced the prewar percentages permitted in accordance with the increase in cost. For instance, if an article had increased in cost by 100 percent, the permitted percentage was the prewar margin multiplied by 0.70. If a trader had previously made a 50 percent profit, he (or she) would, under this system, be allowed to make 35 percent.[67] Naturally, most traders were hostile to this policy, as they felt they were being asked to sell at a loss. For this reason, the system was discontinued in late 1947.

There were only five full-time members of the Price Control Office (i.e., the price controller, the assistant price controller, the inspector of weights and measures, and two clerks). As a result, the department had to rely on district administrative officers and European members of the Northern Rhodesia Police who were appointed as inspectors of price control for the whole territory in accordance with General Notice no. 60 of 1945.[68] Twenty African constables and an assistant superintendent of police undertook special duties in connection with price control. Since the government could not flood the market with scarce goods, enforcing price control was dependent on the cooperation of traders and consumers, but this was not easy to secure, since profiteering was undoubtedly the objective of at least some traders.

Due to loopholes in the system, and also to the lightness of the sentences imposed when infringements were proved, the workings of price control were widely criticized both by newspapers and in the Legislative Council.[69] In July 1942, a European trader in Broken Hill, a Mr. Jablonski, was convicted of profiteering after making a 288 percent profit on three cases of glass and 378 percent on three dozen sheets of glass.[70] The profit in 1939 for these items had been approximately 100 percent. The accused was fined £5 and ordered to refund £16 13s. excess profit to the purchaser. The excess profit over 1939 was 188 percent and 278 percent, respectively.[71] This was a very light punishment by any standards. Stiffer penalties needed to be imposed on those who contravened the sanctions, but this was rarely the case.[72] Traders like Jablonski went unchecked most of the time because the price control inspectorate was too small. In Britain, conversely, tough penalties were imposed on price control offenders. These included the instant revocation of a trader's license, fining "a sum equal to the amount by which a black marketer benefitted from the transaction and 14 days" penal servitude.[73]

The Northern Rhodesian government used its emergency powers to control sky-rocketing prices of maize meal compounded by the hoarding activities of unscrupulous traders. The Maize Meal (Wholesale Prices) Order of 1942, effective 26 November 1942, ruled that no wholesaler was authorized to sell maize meal at a price greater than the maximum prices prescribed by the order in the towns along the rail line. Apart from ensuring that maize meal was available on the market at the right price, this measure was also intended to prevent a rise in wartime inflationary pressure on the economy. The highest price for a two hundred–pound bag was pegged at seventeen shillings and sixpence for Livingstone, in the south, while the lowest official price—sixteen shillings—was applied to the midlands.[74] Failure to adhere to the approved price schedule was deemed an offense in terms of Regulation 17 of the Emergency Powers (Control of Prices and Hoarding) Regulations, 1942. An offender under this law was liable, on conviction, to a fine not exceeding two hundred pounds or to imprisonment for a period not exceeding two years or both.[75]

Partly to address these problems, as argued by Cowen and Westcott, the colonial government abandoned its prewar laissez-faire economic policy and adopted an interventionist one.[76] In cases where wage adjustments were made conditional on the movement of the price index, administrative action was taken with a view to preventing the cost of living from rising. This took the form of subsidies to millers, as was the case with maize, when an additional subsidy was introduced in 1948 to prevent a further rise in the price of mealie meal.[77] Following a recommendation by a commission of inquiry into the cost of living, government subsidized maize meal, as it was felt that the use of public funds for this purpose was amply justified in the general interest.[78] The price of mealie meal along the line of rail was pegged at fifteen shillings, down from nineteen shillings and sixpence per bag at an estimated cost of £150,000 per annum.[79] As maize was already being subsidized by £240,000 per annum, the total cost of the subsidy on this essential food item was £390,000 yearly.[80] Additionally, effective from 1 January 1948, duty on blankets, clothes, enamelware, and bicycles was suspended at an estimated loss of £163,000 per year.[81] This helped prevent further rises in the retail prices of these items.

The above factors contributed to a general rise in the cost of living in the country. Imported goods from abroad became not only scarce but expensive, too. Rampant smuggling, profiteering, and hoarding contributed to the problem. According to Killingray and Rathbone, black markets thrived throughout wartime Africa.[82] In Northern Rhodesia, smuggling was particularly prevalent at the Mokambo border post on the Copperbelt, where traders obtained commodities from the black market in the Belgian Congo.[83] The shortage of consumer goods and resulting rise in the cost of living are best exemplified by an observation made by the labor officer at Mufulira, who reported in mid-1943 that,

> whereas before the war an African who went into a store with £1 to spend could buy . . . a good blanket for 5/ [5 shillings], a 2 pocket shirt for 3/, a pair of shorts for 4/, a [sic] 4 yards of print for his wife for 4/ and a blouse for 1/6-, still leaving himself 2/6 to spend . . . Nowadays an African in similar circumstances would be lucky if he could get a blanket for his £1. And to buy the other articles enumerated would cost him probably another £1 and even then the quality would be greatly inferior to pre-war standards.[84]

Compounding the dire supply situation was the fact that non-sterling imports fell drastically during the war. In 1938 the value of non-sterling goods entering Northern Rhodesia was 22 percent of total imports; this fell to 15 percent in 1945 and 12 percent in 1946.[85] As a result of these shortages, European employees recruited by the mines from South Africa had to bring their own utensils such as pots, pans, bedsheets, cups, and crockery, as these were hard to find on the Copperbelt by 1943.[86]

In the immediate postwar period, the high price of goods experienced in the country was primarily due to the foreign exchange difficulties experienced by the sterling area. Inflationary pressures caused by the global shortage of commodities, pent-up demand, and a general import dependence on the United States resulted in a rise in the cost of living in the colonies. Although Washington eventually wrote off almost the entire wartime Lend-Lease account, the combined dollar deficit of Britain and the sterling area was over $4 billion in 1947.[87] The deficit in the dollar trade of the entire sterling area increased from $450 million before the war to $1.1 billion in 1948.[88] In 1946, a full-blown Commission of Inquiry into the Cost of Living was appointed by the government, this time due to persistent complaints about the upsurge in the price of commodities from various interest groups.[89] When it submitted its interim report in mid-1947, the commission noted that the increase in the prices of goods had created a serious situation in the territory and that its effects were most pronounced among low wage earners, whose incomes had remained stagnant.[90] Between 1939 and 1946, living costs had soared—for Europeans by 36 percent and for Africans by up to 90 percent.[91]

AFRICAN RESPONSE TO THE HIGH COST OF LIVING

No sooner had war broken out than Africans began to feel the economic crunch due to the rising costs of goods. African miners were the first to openly respond to the high prices of goods by going on strike in March 1940, barely six months after the outbreak of hostilities in Europe. The resultant Forster Commission of Inquiry into this industrial action recommended the payment of two shillings and sixpence as a Cost of Living Allowance (COLA) in order to cushion African miners from the effects of the war on their income. In addition, the government commissioned the Southern Rhodesian government statistician, A. Lynn Saffery, to carry out an investigation into the cost of living for urban Africans in Northern Rhodesia. Saffery's investigation revealed that for a man with two children, the minimum monthly wage requirement was six pounds, which was considerably higher than the average wages paid to African workers.[92] As a result of this, a cost of living index was adopted in the country, as in most British colonies during the war.[93] The index was designed to measure, by means of appropriate weighting, changes in retail prices of goods and services consumed by the particular group to which the index related.[94] As a result, price changes affecting the cost of living of wage earners were subject to control.

The agreed list is illustrated in table 3.2, which shows the comparative costs of commodities as of 30 November 1941, 31 July 1943, and 31 July 1944. In July 1942 the figures were reviewed, and the Chamber of Mines agreed to increase the COLA to five shillings per month. By mid-1943, African miners complained that their allowances were inadequate. By that date, the cost of items on the approved list was 195 shillings, justifying a COLA of three shillings and sixpence, further raised to eight shillings and a quarter penny in July 1944.[95] In 1946, these allowances were upgraded by two shillings and sixpence per month in line with continued price rises.[96] When this change was effected, the chief secretary to the government noted that "the index so arrived at indicates that the African cost of living has nearly doubled since 1939."[97] The government also agreed to grant its African civil servants earning less than two pounds and ten shillings per month the same COLA as that paid to African miners.[98] Most other big employers, such as Zambezi Sawmills, Rhodesia Railways, and the municipalities, also granted COLAs to their employees. African civil servants in receipt of wages and allowances not exceeding fifty shillings per month also received a COLA of five shillings per month, while those whose wages and allowances lay between fifty shillings and seventy shillings per month received two shillings and sixpence.[99]

Aside from the miners' strike, the general urban working class also put up a most remarkable response to these hardships. Unlike their counterparts in rural areas, the urban dwellers were completely dependent on their wages for a living and were thus the hardest hit by the rising cost of living. They resorted to boycotting Indian-owned shops to show their disgruntlement with the high price of goods. The boycott strategy reached its head at Luanshya in 1946. Unhappy with government measures put in place to contain the rising cost of living, Africans there formed a "Boycott Control Committee." A representative of this committee only known as Musumala put it to Sir Stewart Gore-Browne, the member of the Legislative Council deputized to represent African interests, that Indian traders cheated Africans through conditional

TABLE 3.2. Cost of living index for Africans, 1939–44

Commodity	Qty	1939 £	s.	d.	10 Nov 1941 £	s.	d.	31 July 1943 £	s.	d.	31 July 1944 £	s.	d.
Trousers	2		14			17	6	1	7		1	7	
Shorts	2		7			9	6		15		1		
Shirts	3		14	3		15	9	1	2	3	1	1	
Vests	1		1	6		1	3		2			2	6
Socks	1			9			9		1			1	6
Shoes	1		5			5	3		4	9		5	6
Dishes	5		2	6		5		*				2	6
Basins	1		1	9		3		*				1	9
Mug and cup	2		1			1	6	*				1	
Saucepans	3		18			28	6	*			1	4	
Sieves	1			9		1			1			1	
Spoons	1			3			6			6		1	
Knife	1			6		1			1			1	6
Soap	18 pcs			9			9		13	6			9
Blankets	2½**		12			18		1	10		2	5	
Blouses	2		3			3	6		3	6		10	
Print cloth	9 yards		10			11	3	1		3	1		3
Dresses	3		12	9		14	3	1	7		1	2	6
Cotton	2 reels			9			9		1	3		1	
Needles	1 pkt			3			3			6			3
Matches	3 pkts		2	3		2			2			2	
Padlock	1			9		1			2			2	
Candles	24		2	3		2	6		2	4		2	
Total per annum		6	-	-	7	11	-	8	16	10	11	4	3
Total per month			10	0		10	7		16	3		18	8½

Source: NAZ SEC1/1362, Note for Executive Council on Cost-of-Living Allowances ca. 1945.

*Data not available.

**The quantity of blankets refers to the average of the number most people acquired.

sales, selling underweight or under measure goods, and varying prices at will.[100] The protesters demanded that "Indians must go" and that "the sooner all the Indians go back to India the better."[101] As a result of this boycott, business activities in the town's second-class trading area ceased within a few days. The boycott lasted from March until June. It ended only after a mass meeting addressed by nominated members of the Legislative Council representing African interests at which the audience was informed of the impending Cost of Living Commission of Inquiry which was to visit the Western Province the following month. Although the problem at Luanshya fizzled out in mid-1946, another six-week boycott of Indian-owned shops took place at Broken Hill the following year.[102]

In this chapter, I examined the impact of the Second World War on the Northern Rhodesian economy. The colony experienced shortages of consumer goods, profiteering, hoarding, inflation, and the black market. To address some of these challenges, the government instituted austerity measures such as rationing and price control, albeit with limited success. The scarcity of consumer goods prompted by the war illuminates a structural weakness of the Northern Rhodesian economy: its dependence on external markets for basic needs. Since the war disrupted external sources of supply, the country suffered from the British war campaign. The other conclusion regards the management of scarcity. It was easy for the government to appeal to people to reduce the consumption of imported commodities which were not regarded as necessities. No appeal could, however, work with respect to food items like maize meal. And so the government resorted to subsidies to cushion livelihoods for low-income groups. The economic challenges faced by the country persisted many years after the end of the war owing to the devaluation of sterling in 1949. The experiences of demand management and state regulation provided important lessons for postwar economic development. The replacement of the free market with a centralized economy, with a good degree of state regulation aimed at maximizing economic growth, will be further discussed in chapter 5, which examines wartime imperial interventions in the colony's highly strategic mining industry.

4

Strangers in Our Midst

The Dilemma of Hosting Polish War Refugees

F OR MANY POLES, THE INVOLUNTARY ODYSSEY FROM THE LAND OF
their birth began in the early hours of the morning with a simple knock
on the door. On one cold winter morning in February 1940, Soviet NKVD
(secret police) agents and armed forces started forcing Polish families at gun-
point to pack a few personal possessions and assembled them at nearby train
stations for conveyance to an unknown destination. The exiles began their
arduous journeys in horrendous conditions, locked up in cattle wagons,
struggling for survival. This nightmare arose as a result of the Soviet assault
on Poland at the beginning of the Second World War. Several hundred thousand Polish residents of the annexed territory became targets of the mass
expulsions carried out in the eastern parts of Poland by Soviet troops. Three
years later, via a difficult and circuitous route, some of these men, women,
and children arrived in Northern Rhodesia—an unknown, remote place few
of them had ever heard about. To the European community, the Poles were
total strangers in their midst.[1] It was under these circumstances that these
new immigrants would proceed to make Northern Rhodesia their home for
the duration of the war and, for some, their permanent home even after hostilities had ceased in Europe.

Warfare results in devastation that extends far beyond the killing of soldiers. One of its common by-products is the displacement of people, some

of whom may not even be belligerents themselves. The battlefield conflicts of the Second World War went hand in hand with a huge refugee crisis—one which did not leave Northern Rhodesia untouched. Following the unexpected abandonment of the policy of appeasement in early 1939, Britain undertook to protect Poland against Axis threats. When the war eventually broke out in September of that year, Britain took responsibility for sheltering the Polish government in London, as well as attempting to look after the welfare of its citizens. As a British colony, Northern Rhodesia—its restrictive immigration policy notwithstanding—was obliged to accept Polish refugees in compliance with the wishes of imperial authorities. In examining how local colonial authorities grappled with the problems involved in balancing the needs of the local settler community and those of Central European evacuees, I address issues of empire-wide racial hierarchy based on colonial pseudoscientific theories.

The fear of having undesirable European nationals settling in Northern Rhodesia was not new. Since at least the end of the nineteenth century, the British Empire, not least in South Africa, had been engrossed with the problem of "poor whites." Poverty in the British Empire was regarded as a "problem" only insofar as it involved white people, and authorities endeavored to prevent the emergence of a class of white colonial citizens whose lifestyle would be characterized by poverty.[2] One strategy adopted by many colonial regimes to prevent the emergence of white poverty was to restrict immigration to specific settler groups. To maintain a "high class" of white immigrants, colonial authorities required them to exhibit evidence of financial independence or to possess reasonable education and skills. Preference was also given to English-speaking whites over other nationalities. Thus, only a few Lithuanians, Latvians, Austrians, Palestinians, German Jews, Afrikaners, and Asians had been allowed to settle in Northern Rhodesia in the early twentieth century.[3] For instance, in the period just before the outbreak of the Second World War, there was an uproar among European settlers when news circulated that Jewish refugees escaping Nazi persecution would be settled in Northern Rhodesia. Local white settlers feared that the Jewish refugees would include elderly people, liable to become a burden on the taxpayer, as well as young ones, whose presence would result in the depression of wages for European workers due to competition.[4] In nearby Southern Rhodesia and South Africa, the immigration policy was even more restrictive, as colonial authorities strove to avoid the emergence of a class of white citizens living in squalor.

The chapter begins by exploring the reasons for, and the course of, the migration of Polish nationals to Northern Rhodesia during the war, as well as the response of local government officials and, conversely, of the settler community to them. The next section sketches life in the refugee camps that were established at Fort Jameson, Lusaka, Bwana Mkubwa, and Abercorn. For Northern Rhodesian colonial authorities, hosting the Poles was not an easy task, as they faced such pressing issues as crime in the camps, prostitution, intracommunity conflicts, and sanitation. When the war came to an end, the Northern Rhodesian government had to deal with the challenge of repatriating the Polish evacuees and resettling those who opted to stay behind.

IMMIGRATION POLICY AND THE POLES' FLIGHT
TO NORTHERN RHODESIA

In the period before the war, the colonial government had adopted a very cautious immigration policy aimed at encouraging English-speaking subjects, as opposed to non-English speakers. The prewar immigration strategy was designed to prevent Britons from being swamped, politically and economically, by aliens. This trend continued during the war period. The "alien" European population in the colony during the interwar period was never large. Up to 1938, it varied from 7 percent to 9 percent of the total white population, or about 2,785.[5] When a scheme was mooted by British authorities in early 1938 to settle some five hundred German Jewish families in Mwinilunga district, local settlers complained that the refugees would flood the labor market or compete in trade with already established white settlers.[6] The most pronounced opposition to Jewish immigrants was aired by Sir Leopold Moore, the leader of the elected members in the Northern Rhodesia legislative council, during the official opening of the Mazoe Valley Agricultural Show at Bindura, in Southern Rhodesia, on 31 July 1938. Clearly expressing his anti-Semitic views, Moore alleged that if displaced German Jews were settled in Northern Rhodesia, the colony would become "an annexe of Palestine," and further wondered "why 500 British families could not be brought out to Northern Rhodesia."[7] He also argued that "they do not speak our language. . . . They would send members to the [Legislative] Assembly—and the debates would be carried on in Yiddish."[8] A serious bone of contention was that the resettlement of foreigners on such a scale would alter the homogeneous character of the population of Northern Rhodesia and also create an undesirable minority problem.[9] Partly because of the strength of this local opposition, a mere 197 German immigrants had entered Northern Rhodesia on an individual basis between March 1933 and 30 September 1938.[10] No sooner had the war broken out in 1939 than some of these refugees were rounded up due to security concerns that they were Axis spies. Sixty-four German and other Axis aliens were sent to Southern Rhodesia for internment. By January 1940, their number had risen to 120.[11]

Despite the British guarantee of protection to Poland, German troops marched across the Polish frontier on 1 September 1939. Two days later, Britain entered the fighting, followed in six hours by her ally, France. The unqualified terms of the guarantee inadvertently made Britain responsible for the welfare of Polish nationals for the duration of the war. By 1942 German troops were advancing on Soviet territory and the outcome of the war was far from clear. The Allied forces were in dire need of any support available, and the Polish soldiers were a welcome reinforcement. To have these soldiers on their side, it was important to take care of their relatives.[12] The hosting of Polish refugees by Northern Rhodesia was a direct outcome both of the prewar guarantee and of British military strategy.

There were two waves of Polish refugee settlement in Northern Rhodesia during the Second World War. The first, known as the Cyprus Group, arrived in early 1941. This group had settled in Cyprus for some time before leaving for Africa. Its members hailed mainly from urban areas, and many of them were of middle-class background. This party of 350 refugees consisted of 131 men, 145 women, and 74 children, who left Cyprus by ship on 21 July 1941. They were led by Stefan Fiedler Alberti, the Polish consul general in Nicosia.[13] About one-third were, in official parlance, "very reasonable people."[14] On 3 August, they arrived at Durban, where they stayed for a day pending medical examinations before proceeding north by train to Livingstone. The majority were assigned accommodation in Livingstone, while others went to the neighboring towns of Monze, Mazabuka, Kafue, and Lusaka.[15] The second group began to arrive in 1942, followed by further contingents throughout the war period, so that by the end of 1943 a total of nearly 3,500 more Poles had arrived. They were referred to as the MERRA (Middle East

Relief and Refugee Administration) Group because their arrival in Northern Rhodesia had been preceded by stays in refugee camps in the Middle Eastern territories of Palestine and Iran. This group emerged following realignment of refugees in camps in the region. Polish refugees who arrived in the Middle East from Soviet control, and were capable of military service, were separated from the civilian population and transferred to Iran and Palestine, where they were trained to eventually fight alongside the British in North Africa and Italy. The civilians, on the other hand, were taken to more permanent camps in the vicinity of Teheran while international efforts were being made to find them a more stable home elsewhere.[16] The group included an indeterminate number of Polish Jews. Many of its members hailed from the countryside, and many of them were women and children. They were accommodated in camps set up in Abercorn, Lusaka, Fort Jameson, and Bwana Mkubwa.[17]

The camp at Fort Jameson (now Chipata) was one of the first to be set up, in late 1941; it was also the smallest, with a capacity of 200. The Lusaka camp was set up on land belonging to Mrs. E. Marrapodi on Plot No. 90A. Its initial capacity was 500, but this was gradually extended. By 1943, it housed 1,145 inhabitants.[18] The camp at Bwana Mkubwa was the largest of the four. It stood on a piece of land measuring some 3,000 hectares. By mid-1943, there were 1,100 refugees housed in the camp.[19] The Abercorn camp was the last to be built, in late 1942, and was occupied in July of the following year. It had 600 refugees at its peak in 1943. All four camps except the one at Lusaka were established in rural districts.

From the very beginning of their settlement in Northern Rhodesia, non-British immigrants suffered from the hostility of local white settlers. According to Major Mckee, the officer-in-charge of war evacuees, "it was evident from statements made by the general public in the press and verbally, that the allocation of foreign refugees . . . would not be well received, while at the same time it was made clear to me . . . that there would be little objection to the reception . . . of refugees if they were Britishers."[20] Criticism of the Poles in certain quarters of the local white community emerged as early as May 1942. Some settlers raised concern over the perceived generosity accorded to the refugees by the colonial government. Remarks such as "it is better to be a Pole than a British subject" (a reference to the alleged "comforts" afforded to the refugees by the host government) became commonplace.[21] Other settlers looked at these refugees as scroungers, willing to get as much as they could from their hosts without giving anything in return.

These sentiments were sometimes shared by government officials. Some administrators, for instance, alleged that the life of ostensible luxury the refugees had lived in Cyprus before arriving in Northern Rhodesia had had a bad influence on their psychical countenance.[22] Officials accused the members of this party of being "full of requests—for better shelter, better sustenance, schooling for their children, and so on."[23] Making allowance for their refugee status, and their dislike of living off charity in a foreign country, colonial authorities still found the Poles, as people in a difficult predicament, hard to deal with. For example, Stewart Gore-Browne, who succeeded Major Mckee as director of war evacuees in early 1942, complained that "they get free issues of clothing from Red X [the Red Cross] and if they think their neighbour's issue is better than their own they will tear up their own clothes or throw them at the donor's head."[24] For this, Gore-Browne regarded his job as "a thankless and wearing task,"[25] and warned that "the attitude of the population of Northern Rhodesia towards these evacuees is also deteriorating. . . . This is inevitable in the circumstances."[26]

In the same vein, due to the racist classification of migrants which was prevalent in the colonial environment, employment opportunities were few and far between for the refugees. As the colonial policy on European immigration favored those who were either highly skilled or wealthy, to secure a job for a Polish refugee was a hard undertaking. Although some colonial administrators tried to find jobs for some of the evacuees, these efforts were received with scorn from certain British settlers who felt that doing so would deprive British citizens of their rightful dues. For instance, members of the Legislative Council (MLCs) raised objections when word spread that a Pole, instead of a British subject, was to be employed on a government-sponsored antimalaria program. Tellingly, the MLCs disapproved of having a Pole employed even though the British national who was earmarked for the position was over eighty years of age and unable to perform his duties efficiently![27] As in neighboring Southern Rhodesia, local colonial authorities and members of the settler community viewed the Poles as an inferior type of European who took up menial jobs reserved for the African population, and thought that they would not be able to compete with the latter in a free employment market.[28]

Strangers in Our Midst: The Dilemma of Hosting Polish War Refugees

HOUSING, SANITATION, AND CONSUMER GOODS SHORTAGES

The type of lodgings organized by the hosting government for the Poles suggests that they were always meant to be temporary dwellers in Northern Rhodesia. Housing for Poles in the camps consisted of simple brick huts. Attesting to the rudimentary, low-status nature of their living conditions, the roofs of these huts were thatched with elephant grass. In many respects, their way of life can be said to have been not far off from that of most Africans. The Lusaka camp was completely fenced off. By June 1943, Polish and African security guards were engaged to patrol the camp's perimeter in order to discourage any "unauthorised persons" from having access to it.[29] By "unauthorised persons," colonial authorities most likely meant the Africans who lived nearby. This reference to intruders, in fact, served to conceal strong local British prejudices against the Central Europeans, with whom they did not want to mingle. On complaints from certain quarters that it was not fair to keep Polish refugees "caged," the government emphasized that the object of the fence was to keep potential intruders out, not to keep the refugees in, as they were regarded as British allies and not prisoners. The reality on the ground, however, was that the authorities wanted to ensure as little contact as possible between the alien refugees and the local British settler community.[30]

Poor sanitation was a problem recorded in all the camps. Difficulties with the water supply, toilets, and poor ventilation were not uncommon. There was also an outbreak of mental and nervous symptoms in the Lusaka camp in 1942. Apparently, this was due to contamination of the "brekweet" by the vetch *Lathymus sativus* (grass pea) or a related plant.[31] The use of brekweet was thus discontinued. It must also be noted that camp life was characterized by boredom, adverse internment conditions, and the natural desire for freedom, all of which could have been responsible for some of the reported cases of mental health problems.[32] The worst case was probably that of Kirkuc Franciszek. He had committed considerable mischief and felonies within two years of his arrival in Northern Rhodesia. Franciszek served a two-and-a-half-year prison sentence in Salisbury Prison. Upon his release, he was sent back to the Lusaka Polish Camp on 18 September 1945. Soon afterward, however, he was declared a criminal lunatic and transferred to Ingutsheni Mental Hospital in Bulawayo, Southern Rhodesia.[33] There was also an outbreak of tuberculosis (TB) in the Lusaka camp, probably due to congestion. In order to contain the spread of the disease, medical authorities isolated TB patients in ad hoc wards within the camp hospital. No evacuee could enter the TB wards in the camp or be within the fence surrounding these wards, nor could any patient leave the area surrounded by the fence except with the prior authorization of the Polish doctor.[34]

Although the shortage of consumer goods in Northern Rhodesia was the result of war conditions, some British settlers put the blame on the refugees. Thus, the Poles perpetually experienced discrimination and were treated with suspicion, hostility, and contempt by local settlers.[35] In the Copperbelt Province, local white settlers attributed the rising levels of theft of jewelry and wristwatches to the presence of the Polish camp at Bwana Mkubwa.[36] The Poles were clearly an easy target to explain commodity shortages in the colony (see chapter 3). As a result of wartime consumer goods shortages and the workings of the rationing system, the Poles were also restricted from making purchases as freely as they would have wanted, just like the other white inhabitants of the country. When the Polish camp at Lusaka was first occupied, protests were made by the town's inhabitants on the ground that the Poles were buying up stocks of goods already in short supply in the various stores.[37] The practice, it was noted by observers, was not confined to European stores only, as the Poles were said to be buying large quantities of food from the African market as well. A similar problem was also reported in the Fort Jameson district. According to J. A. R. Alexander, camp commandant at Fort Jameson, "there is no doubt that the evacuees are causing a shortage for the permanent European residents of Fort Jameson by their private purchase of eggs, vegetables."[38] This was regarded by government officials as being prejudicial to the interests of Africans, who were already finding it hard to buy food and goods for their own use.[39] This state of affairs was attributed to the fact that the refugees had quite substantial quantities of disposal income. Each of the four camps was estimated to generate about £700 per month in the form of wages for work done by Poles in the camps as cooks, cleaners, and carpenters; some of it came in the shape of allowances from relatives in the army and other undisclosed sources.[40] It was also noted by government officials that there were some refugees who had not declared all the money in their possession on arrival in the country, which had equally distorted the normal supply and demand chain in commerce. One such refugee was a Mr. Kirkuc, who had not declared one thousand South African rand at the port of entry.[41] Certainly, this was not an isolated instance.

Rather than solving the supply challenges, the government decided that the solution was to limit what the Poles could buy. Some government officials accused the refugees of being in the habit of "luxury" shopping for things such as bread, tinned foods, brandy, and expensive clothing.[42] Administrative staff in Fort Jameson went to the extent of recommending that the Poles be prohibited from buying goods from all three types of traders in town: European, Indian, and African. However, government officials in Lusaka disagreed, pointing out that the Poles were not internees, and that such drastic curtailment of their liberties could cause trouble. Instead, they recommended that the refugees be prohibited only from entering the African market or residential areas in the district.[43] This was in order to safeguard Africans who were the most vulnerable section of the population insofar as the supply of consumer goods was concerned.

Civil servants and other workers who had limited time at their disposal in which to do their weekly shopping, generally on Friday afternoons and Saturday, also complained that they were hampered by Poles crowding into shops. In February 1944, the director of war evacuees and camps acknowledged that "the general public continues to attribute any shortage of supplies which it has to put up with to the Poles."[44] The same complaint was voiced by settler farmers in the Lusaka area regarding Fridays, when—they alleged—they encountered congestion in the stores due to Polish buyers. Similarly, the shortage of things such as chicken and eggs in Abercorn was attributed to Polish refugees.[45] After rejecting the possibility of confining Polish refugees to their camps on Fridays and Saturdays, some colonial officials suggested that the only solution lay in paying pocket money and wages for the refugees in the form of coupons. The government's final decision was that it would be unpolitic to confine the evacuees because the latter were not war internees. It thus resolved to set up well-stocked canteens and shops within the confines of each camp in order to prevent the Poles from accessing supplies meant for long-term urban residents. This strategy was not entirely successful owing to supply challenges, forcing refugees to devise strategies to beat the system by accessing goods through African intermediaries.

PROSTITUTION AND INTERRACIAL SEXUAL RELATIONSHIPS

Prostitution was seemingly rife among some female refugees, especially in Lusaka and Livingstone, owing to a growing urban population living close to the evacuees. The socioeconomic strains of the war led some of the least well-off female refugees to resort to prostitution.[46] The primary motive for engaging in prostitution was financial. A less convincing reason had to do with the fact that there were more women than men within the refugee population. There were approximately 18,000 Polish refugees in the entire East African region; of these, 48 percent were women, 12.5 percent men, and the remaining 39.5 percent children.[47] There was nothing unique about the levels of prostitution among Polish refugees in Northern Rhodesia, as similar observations were recorded in the nearby territories of Tanganyika and Uganda.[48]

The problem of illicit sex activity by Polish women in Northern Rhodesia reached the ears of members of the general public and government officials soon after their arrival. In the early days of settlement in Livingstone, the Poles alleged that the most prominent prostitutes in their community were Miss Piatkowska and Miss Szynder, who would, under the cover of night, go out to solicit for male clients. Once the authorities got wind of the two ladies' activities, they were removed from the Bon Accord Boarding House in Livingstone in May 1942, on account of what the director of war evacuees and camps classified as "immoral behaviour." Fellow inhabitants of the boardinghouse and the rest of the Polish community in Livingstone endorsed the transfer of said women to Mazabuka because their activities "reflected adversely on them."[49] Nonetheless, the two women refused to leave and resorted to a hunger strike in protest.[50]

The Lusaka Women's Institute, led by Ethel Locke-King, worried that the Polish peasant women housed at the Lusaka camp were providing "clandestine services" for white officers.[51] In this regard, the Women's Institute enlisted men from two military battalions stationed nearby to keep a close eye on the activities of the Poles. The government's official position did not condone prostitution, yet the system ignored regular liaisons between whites and Africans in spite of being aware of the troubles that could follow "miscegenation."[52] In November 1943 at an emergency meeting of the joint committee of the Women's Institute, the Child Welfare Association, and the Girl Guides Association, all of Lusaka, the following resolution was passed:

Strangers in Our Midst: The Dilemma of Hosting Polish War Refugees

> That it has been brought to the notice of these welfare societies that irregularities of conduct on the part of some members of the Polish Camp are bringing discredit to the camp, causing distress to many families therein, and affording a grave example to their children, while the proximity of the camp to the Barracks and the town aggravates this evil.[53]

The committee urged government to take active measures to remedy "this serious menace immediately." These organizations' major fear was "the unfortunate and lasting influence this conduct is having on the African peoples."[54] This suggests that some of the Polish women had African male clients or that, if the situation remained unchecked, it could degenerate into many more sexual relationships between the refugees and local men. According to Kaonga Mazala, who erroneously refers to Polish refugees as prisoners of war, this development became a matter of great concern to European residents. The fact that these women also offered themselves to African men was regarded as degrading and bad for prestige—the ultimate transgression of colonial racial hierarchies.[55]

Interracial sexual relations between African men and white women were greatly abhorred in colonial circles. The Synod of the Methodist Church adopted the resolution of the emergency joint committee and called for adequate action to be taken against all refugees who were involved in selling sex.[56] For its part, the government stated that moves were afoot to create a segregation camp where such "undesirable characters" could be banished.[57] A short time after the emergency meeting, another "authentic report of two flagrant cases involving Africans was received," and government was urged to remove "these undesirable persons from our midst."[58] Europeans in Broken Hill echoed these complaints about the behavior of some female refugees. Members of Roy Welensky's powerful Labour Party of Northern Rhodesia had "a lengthy discussion" about the moral conduct of some of the Polish refugees. Welensky noted that "some of our Members had heard rumours that some of the Polish women were conducting themselves in a most immoral manner. They had reason to believe that the rumours were not without foundation."[59]

In line with the above, the government also tried to prevent "undesirable marriages" between Polish female refugees and residents of Northern

Rhodesia. In conformity with regional norms, the authorities in the country banned interracial marriages between Polish women and African men, or with European males who were known to be of bad character or without a steady source of income.[60] To prevent such unions, all Polish refugees who sought to get married to "respectable members" of the European community in the country had their unions solemnized by the Polish Consular authorities.

Although most Poles who sought refuge in Northern Rhodesia were perceived by government officials to be law-abiding individuals, there were some bad characters among them. Within the first few months of arrival in 1941, cases of bad behavior were reported among the group that was accommodated at the Lusaka Hotel. In that group, three men, Leon Popiel, Tadeusz Rydarowski, and Zukawski, were the major culprits. They were notorious for their arrogant manners vis-à-vis staff and fellow occupants of the hotel. Their odd behavior was noted by the hotel manager, who complained that "during meal hours they will argue with the waiters— Mr Rydarowski caused a disturbance during a lunch hour last week by shouting for a boy [sic] and then banging his fork on the plates—merely because I had asked him to shift to another table."[61] Following incessant complaints leveled against these three characters, the government transferred them to a farm in the Mpima area in Broken Hill district. Two of them, Popiel and Rydarowski, refused to be moved, however.

This incident and the earlier one involving the two prostitutes in Livingstone put the government in an awkward position. It thus resolved to introduce emergency measures which would compel the movement of refugees to specific areas of residence when so ordered by colonial officials. Until then, the only legal tool in the hands of the government was the Restrictions of Aliens Regulations. However, under these regulations, the government could not order a person to move. Law-abiding members of the Polish community took it upon themselves to apologize to their consul-general, M. Zaleski, as well as to the Northern Rhodesian government for the poor behavior exhibited by some of their colleagues. In direct reference to the goings-on at the Lusaka Hotel, they stated:

> We all here are privileged and in a very good position, when compared to . . . Poles deported to Siberia and to Germany. The

Strangers in Our Midst: The Dilemma of Hosting Polish War Refugees

> conditions in which we are living in Northern Rhodesia and
> which enable us to spend the time of war in safety and far from
> the war theatre are excellent. . . . Therefore we must condemn
> all compromising symptoms which are the contradiction of our
> national dignity and which deform our real face.[62]

To address the situation, the government came up with Notice no. 128 of 1942 under emergency powers to compel war evacuees to reside only in areas or premises earmarked by relevant authorities. Any contravention of said provision made a refugee liable to conviction and to a one-year imprisonment or to a fine not exceeding £200, or both.[63]

In spite of such a backing on the statute books, it took nearly two months, even with help from the police, to remove a woman from the Kafue Hotel whose behavior was "causing an open scandal to the entire neighbourhood."[64] It was then that government officials felt the need to do more to make lawbreakers abide by its regulations. Government bureaucrats contemplated the withdrawal of all payments for maintenance to any Polish evacuee who refused to comply with instructions given by the state. It was further suggested that similar punishment be extended to refugees who refused to accept reasonable employment for frivolous reasons.[65] A case in point was a Pole who had refused an employment offer at Zambezi Sawmills at the rate of £30 per month because he thought the climate in Livingstone would not suit him. Another example was an evacuee who had been approached over a £300-per-year government appointment but refused on the grounds that his social standing might suffer if he took the job.[66]

Several hardened criminals were part of a group of Polish refugees that was sent to Northern Rhodesia and other East African territories. These should never have been sent to the African colonies, and a protest was lodged with the authorities in Cairo. Part of the arrangement for sending European refugees to the colonies was that only those who were in good standing with the law would be included. As it turned out, it was Polish refugees with a criminal background who were responsible for the outbreak of a violent riot at Bwana Mkubwa camp on the evening of Saturday, 4 September 1943. Gore-Browne was well aware that Bwana Mkubwa had witnessed "attempted murders" and housed "a 'regular gang of Apaches' which preyed on their own folk."[67] On that fateful evening, five Polish guards on duty were attacked with knives by one Bernard Masiuk during a party in one of the huts in the camp. Eventually, twenty-three individuals were arrested by the police on the charge of unlawful assembly and, in the case of Masiuk, of assault occasioning bodily harm.[68] The root cause of the riot was said by the police to have been discontent at the issuance of fines for various breaches of camp discipline on the previous Friday, a payday.[69] There were also accusations of Polish camp officials, including the British commandant, pocketing the money they obtained from fines. According to the Polish consul-general, however, the cause of the troubles at Bwana Mkubwa went back as far as incidents which had taken place during the relevant refugee group's journey from Persia.[70] What was clear nonetheless was that there were several very bad characters, variously estimated at between ten to twenty, who had been stirring up trouble in the camp. It can safely be argued that boredom in the camps and homesickness tended to cause refugees' behavior to deteriorate. Two of the troublemakers were deported to Southern Rhodesia, and two apiece to Uganda and Tanganyika.[71] Three were convicted of unlawful assembly and imprisoned for a period of one month within Northern Rhodesia.

The other source of conflict between the local settler community and the aliens was the language of communication. The English community disliked the use of Polish in a British colony. Such tension was not new in the country, however, as the English speakers had equally taken great exception to the use of Afrikaans by Afrikaner migrants, many of whom worked on the Copperbelt.[72] An incident reported in the press soon after the first Polish group arrived in the country concerned a local English couple who felt snubbed by a Polish group in the dining room at Mazabuka Hotel. It was reported that the "aliens" simply walked away when asked to translate into English the war news which one of them was reading aloud for the group. The press was agog with serious condemnation of the Polish group at the hotel. Using the pseudonym "Robot," a resident of Nkana wondered, "Is it an insult to innocently ask a foreigner to speak English in a public room in a British hotel in a British colony?" He further went on to tell the government that "in conclusion we would like to be assured that the refugees in Northern Rhodesia are not taking over and running hotels south of the Copperbelt. Rumour has it that the hotel in question is being so run."[73]

By July 1943, some officials in the government had begun to raise concerns about how many more refugees could be taken in. Public officials and private individuals claimed the country had reached the saturation point in accepting refugees. The director of war evacuees and camps noted that "by accepting 4,000 Polish refugees as we have done, we have increased our total European population by about 33%."[74] The major challenge involved in taking in more refugees was the general shortage of food. Eggs, vegetables, cheese, butter, milk, and meat were not readily obtainable in the country, as was the case in the entire region. Furthermore, there was the lack of building materials to expand accommodation facilities for the prospective new arrivals. These challenges were conveyed to the Conference of East African Governors by the Northern Rhodesian government with a suggestion that "if it becomes imperative for us to assist in taking more refugees it would have to be clearly understood that ALL food for them would have to be provided from outside and satisfactory arrangements made for delivery."[75] The supply problem notwithstanding, it must be noted here that the likely real reason for not wanting to accept more refugees was the fear that the English-speaking community would be outnumbered by aliens—a prospect that local public opinion greatly resented. Faced with these concerns, imperial authorities agreed not to dispatch any more Polish refugees to Northern Rhodesia.

END OF WAR AND REPATRIATION

Following the cessation of hostilities in August 1945, official attempts began to be made to repatriate the refugees to Poland. As far back as October 1940, Roy Welensky, the representative for Broken Hill constituency in the Legislative Assembly, had asked government for an assurance that all such aliens would be repatriated home once hostilities ended in Europe. Government had responded that some of the refugees could remain in Northern Rhodesia on compassionate grounds or if they were able to take care of themselves financially.[76] However, the state put no concrete policy directive in place. Thus, Welensky returned to the charge in May 1943. His concerns this time around were echoed by members of the Women's Institute, who—as noted above—were uncomfortable with European men having affairs with Polish women. In July 1945, Welensky asked another question—whether, in view of the changed war situation, the government could outline the steps it had taken to return the evacuees to their country of origin.[77] The government was forced to come up with practical steps for the repatriation of the evacuees due to a sympathetic leader in the *Livingstone Mail*, which described how the US and Australian governments had softened their attitudes toward the resettlement of Polish evacuees.[78]

Following these incessant public and private outbursts, the colonial government, with guidance from London, came up with a policy on how it would proceed with the evacuation of the refugees back to Europe. On 2 December 1946 it enacted a law which gave powers to the governor to expel any recalcitrant evacuee from the territory, though it could not force such persons to go back to Poland. By then, however, the government had become more sympathetic toward the refugees, because of the change in the political situation in Poland, occupied by Soviet forces in 1944. The Polish government in exile in London suffered a final eclipse following the imposition of a Communist regime at home. In 1947 the government enacted Ordinance 5, which amended the 1946 law. The amendment provided for the requirement of a month's notice before a refugee could be repatriated—primarily owing to the changed political environment of Poland. By the amended law, Poles could now be ejected from Northern Rhodesia, provided due notice had been given and that arrangements had been made to ensure their safety.[79]

While the colonial government was now prepared to concede that it had to assimilate some non-British Europeans on humanitarian and other grounds, it was still keen on getting rid of refugees with undesirable characteristics. Addressing the Legislative Council in mid-1947, the governor noted that his government wanted to keep down the rate of European unemployment by giving first opportunities of immigration and settlement to British nationals.[80] In his own crude words, "the majority of the Poles here are of the peasant type and we do not like putting them loose in the Territory. We really fear deterioration of European stock if the Poles become indigenous with no chance of life in a temperate climate."[81] On the other hand, the same governor also stressed that the Poles had been allies with the British during the war period, and that there was no need to abandon them now that the hostilities had ceased. He argued that Northern Rhodesia was not so overpopulated as to make it necessary to restrict settlement rights to those who were already self-supporting. But, most importantly, the colony had an obligation to the empire, as all the colonies and dominions would be asked by London to assimilate as many of the displaced people as possible in the long run. It was noted by advocates of Polish settlement in Northern Rhodesia

Strangers in Our Midst: The Dilemma of Hosting Polish War Refugees

that Britain was burdened by financial and many other challenges due to a long war. In this regard, the government noted that it was to its advantage to keep in its territory people it already knew. Using a metaphor, the governor asked: "Isn't it going to be cheaper and more effective if we now choose the best of the devils we know, rather than wait for a completely unknown breed of underfed and disillusioned devils from destroyed countries in Europe?"[82]

As the war ended, it became clear that some refugees did not want to return, mainly because of fear of the new Communist regime. "It was a hot potato, nobody wanted to touch it," stated Reverend Z. Peszkowski in 2004.[83] In this regard, the British foreign secretary gave assurance that no Pole would return to Poland after the war without his or her consent.[84] A few sought to be repatriated to countries such as the US, Britain, and the dominions. This was not an easy undertaking, and only a handful managed to get there. For example, the Tulasiewicz family left Northern Rhodesia and joined relatives in the US in November 1946.[85]

By early 1948, all evacuees had been removed from the camps at Abercorn and Bwana Mkubwa. They were repatriated via ports in Tanganyika (today's Tanzania) or Kenya. The last camp to be closed was the one at Lusaka. A Committee on the Application for Permanent Residence was formed to examine cases of those who had applied to remain in the country. Of about 1,000 applications received in October 1948, the committee recommended the granting of permanent residence in Northern Rhodesia to 251 Polish evacuees.[86] In considering the various applications made by evacuees, the committee was very anxious to try to ensure that only "valuable" members received favorable consideration. The priority was to favor individuals who could be expected to support themselves and their dependants and who were unlikely to become a charge to public funds.[87] Apart from those who already had steady employment, the committee approved applications from people in possession of artisan qualifications, as the latter were regarded as having a role to play in the industrial development of Northern Rhodesia. Among the most sought-after Polish artisans were bricklayers, carpenters, mechanics, and plumbers. The government agreed to solicit guarantees from prospective employers of such artisans to ensure their livelihoods. Notwithstanding this, a few other applications were approved purely on humanitarian grounds.[88] In October and November 1948, all but one refugee who had not been granted asylum left the colony. The remaining refugee left the Lusaka camp in September 1950, following his transfer to the International Refugee Organisation in Tanganyika.

Northern Rhodesia was obliged to accept Polish refugees in order to abide by the wishes of imperial Britain. This chapter has examined the complex relation that existed between this new group of central Europeans and the hosting white settler community. I have demonstrated that Polish refugees were not well received in the colony because of antipathy from certain sections of the settler community. The negative attitude exhibited by some sections of the English-speaking community toward Polish refugees was in line with the broader policy of the colonial government with respect to the exclusion of non-British migrants into the territory. The settler community feared that, once allowed entry during the war period, the Poles would never leave, thereby distorting the English character of the colony. The Poles were regarded as Europeans of a lower standing compared with British nationals. As such, settlers did not expect the Poles to add value to the colony. This reasoning, it must be emphasized, was yet another instance of that racial and ethnic stereotyping which was so prevalent throughout the British Empire. The local settlers were also afraid of creating a shortage of employment opportunities for their own members if Polish citizens settled in Northern Rhodesia. When they eventually arrived in the colony, Polish refugees thus faced discrimination in terms of accommodation, employment, and language. The settler community also abhorred sexual relations between their members and the Poles and, more so, between Polish women and African men. To compound their difficult situation, the refugees were also accused by the settler community of being behind the wartime shortage of consumer goods, as well as the concomitant rise in crime.

5

The Copper Mining Industry
and the Allied War Effort

NOT MANY PEOPLE WERE STARTLED WHEN EUROPE EXPLODED into war on 1 September 1939—the war had been long in coming. Planning for the conflict had dominated much of the 1930s, as shown by the arms race that had stimulated the global base metal market. The Second World War was thus not only a conflict over territorial expansion but also a competition for important raw materials such as minerals. Control over global natural resources was one of the key ingredients for success. For this reason, world governments intervened in commodity markets and industry affairs as soon as the war broke out. Lawrence Butler has noted that the demands of total war required parallel efforts to maximize the production of African minerals.[1] Britain extended its imperial tentacles to ensure its colonies supplied the vital mineral resources, especially copper, which were crucial to the successful execution of the war effort. In this regard, Britain was fortunate to be able to count on Northern Rhodesia—an important source of the red metal required in munitions production. The principal customers for Northern Rhodesia's copper in 1937 were Britain, which took half, and Germany, which obtained a third of the total production.[2] On the outbreak of war, the British Metals Corporation was taken over by the British government, and henceforth began the bulk purchase of copper, to the total exclusion of enemy territories.

In this chapter I address the impact of the war on Northern Rhodesia's economic mainstay: copper mining. I argue that British control over copper mining in Northern Rhodesia lasted almost continuously from the beginning of the Second World War until many years after its conclusion, due to the desire to benefit from "the most important African supplier of a single base metal for the Allied cause."[3] The importance of copper in the postwar period was prolonged by reconstruction in Europe and the construction of industries in the United States, a global shortage of the metal, sterling's devaluation in 1949 and, then, the increased international demand occasioned by the Korean War in the midst of the Cold War. I also show that activities in the mining sector were, in turn, closely related to the agricultural sector, for mining impinged on food security, without which the production of base metals could be threatened. With approval from London, the colonial state resorted to labor conscription for European settler farmers in order to attain food self-sufficiency for the growing urban population. Furthermore, I demonstrate that as the financial value of this "minor" colony increased in wartime, so, too, did it become more tightly bound to the "mother country" in the postwar period. The colony's new importance owed much to the fact that a fiscally challenged Britain benefited from the dollar earnings of copper exports. But the high cost of doing business in postwar Britain, as well as the decline of the City of London as the world's financial center, compelled the mining companies to shift their domicile to Northern Rhodesia at the turn of the 1950s.

THE IMPORTANCE OF THE COPPER MINING
INDUSTRY IN WARTIME

The demand for total war by the Allied nations called for the extraction of various raw materials from virtually every continent on an unparalleled scale. Despite prewar self-sufficiency in basic ores, such as coal and iron, the Allied powers were compelled to augment existing mineral stocks in nearly all categories through imports from around the world.[4] Northern Rhodesia, known for its copper, an essential metal in the manufacture of ammunition and wires, came to play a pivotal role in the Allied war effort in this regard. Apart from copper, the colony's mines also supplied cobalt, whose main use in wartime was as an alloy in tools requiring high-speed cutting steel.[5] Early in the war, more than half of Britain's copper imports came from North America,

The Copper Mining Industry and the Allied War Effort

TABLE 5.1. Estimated world copper production by country ('000 long tons)

Principal producers	1937	1938	1939	1940	1941	1942	1943	1944	1945	1946
US	745	497	656	797	878	980	995	898	719	539
Canada	234	259	277	293	287	270	257	244	213	166
Mexico	46	41	48	40	51	51	45	43	61	58
Peru	35	37	35	43	36	35	33	32	30	23
Chile	407	346	334	357	461	477	489	490	463	356
Germany	29	30	30	23	22	23	23	21	(a)	15
Spain and Portugal	31	34	25	13	10	12	12	12	9	(b)
Yugoslavia	39	41	41	42	(a)	(a)	(a)	(a)	(a)	(a)
Russia	91	96	105	(a)	(a)	(a)	(a)	(a)	(a)	(a)
Japan	75	76	76	(a)	(a)	(a)	(a)	(a)	(a)	(a)
Belgian Congo	148	122	121	147	160	163	154	163	158	141
Northern Rhodesia	209	212	213	260	231	250	247	220	193	183
South Africa	(b)	11	10	14	19	21	23	22	23	26
World Total	2,231	1,953	2,130	1,999	2,166	2,295	2,292	2,162	1,898	1,621

Source: *The Economist*, 2 August 1947.
(a)   Data not available and excluded from world total.
(b)   Data not available but estimates included in world total.

but by 1945, nearly 68 percent were from Northern Rhodesia, making the territory by far Britain's most important supplier of the base metal.[6] Together with the Belgian Congo, Northern Rhodesia remained a major supplier of the mineral to the Allies throughout the war. As shown by table 5.1, during the war, Northern Rhodesia became the world's fourth-largest producer of copper after the United States, Canada, and Chile. Between 1935 and 1945, the country produced about 2.3 million tons of refined copper to buttress Britain's munitions needs.[7]

Copper, exported in either blister or electrolytic form, was mainly used in the manufacture of brass cartridges and cannon shells. The greater portion of what was exported, however, was in the form of blister. Additionally, thousands of miles of copper wiring were needed for the electrical systems in aircraft, tanks, and warships, while copper tubing was essential for refrigeration units, plumbing, and heat transfer devices.[8] Although Broken Hill mine produced vital quantities of lead, zinc, and vanadium—essential to American and British manufactures of high-speed tools and ultra-strength steel forgings—copper production took center stage.[9] Due to the increased demand of the Allies, the government repeatedly reminded the mines that Northern Rhodesia could make the greatest contribution to the war effort by maintaining and, if possible, increasing the production of copper. Speaking at Broken Hill early in 1940, Governor John Maybin stated that

> the territory has one great asset of vital imperial importance— the base metal industry. It is producing metals which are vitally necessary to the Empire's war effort. In the case of copper it is the only sterling source of supply. We must keep up our production. I have that on the authority of the Secretary of State. The output of our copper mines has been virtually taken over by the Ministry of Supply.[10]

The country's two mining corporates—the Rhodesian Selection Trust (RST) and Rhodesian Anglo American (RAA)—devoted all their energies to satisfying the Allied demand for copper. As belligerent nations had intervened in commodity markets and industrial affairs at the onset of hostilities, free market forces were suspended. During the war, bulk purchasing provided Britain with an assured and steady supply of raw materials at the lowest possible prices.[11] The British government closed the London Metal Exchange (LME), suspended existing sales agreements made by empire producers, and authorized the Ministry of Supply to take over sales and pricing arrangements for copper.[12] The British Metal Corporation, in turn, was contracted by the Ministry of Supply to purchase the whole of the colony's copper output at the fixed price of £62 per long ton throughout the war period,[13] based on the LME price quoted the day before the war broke out.[14] When pressed by the European Mine Workers' Union (MWU) to explain the arrangements entered into with the British government, the colonial government stated that the mines were supplying copper at a price far below the current world price,[15] a message that was reemphasized throughout the war period.[16]

In line with emergency regulations, the Allies considered copper and other base metals as "contraband of war" if they had a military function and were intended for enemy use. In wartime, contraband was classified as either absolute or conditional. Absolute contraband referred to all such minerals which were particularly serviceable to the enemy in war and had a hostile destination.[17] On the other hand, all minerals which were fit for the purposes of war and peace alike, and which had a potential hostile destination, were regarded as conditional contraband, because Axis powers could easily buy such through third parties.[18] Copper belonged to the latter category. This nomenclature was in line with the objectives of economic warfare, which aimed at denying supplies to the enemy and securing them for the Allies.[19] Strict controls over the export of commodities from the colonies were thus instituted. As P. T. Bauer noted, the machinery of export control consisted of three elements: the licensing of exports to direct them to specific destinations; a statutory monopoly in the handling of the main exports; and a system of quotas in the purchase of export produce.[20] Before the war, the most important markets for Northern Rhodesian blister copper were Britain, Germany, and Italy, in that order. Germany absorbed about one-third of the output in each of the last four years before 1939 and Italy one-tenth.[21] Italy also bought large but varying quantities of electrolytic copper. Under war conditions, this trade situation could not continue, as both Germany and Italy belonged to the opposing Axis.

Unlike before the war, export licenses now had to be issued by the comptroller of customs for all consignments of copper. Copies of such licenses were forwarded to the Ministry of Economic Warfare in London to ensure that Axis powers did not benefit from such colonial supplies. Government Notice no. 144 of 1939 (the Export Prohibition Order, 1939) stipulated that electrolytic and blister copper, vanadium oxide, lead, and cobalt alloy could be exported from the territory only with British government approval.[22] In conformity with economic warfare, there were no restrictions on the issuance of licenses with regard to exports destined for Britain, the United States, France, the French colonies, Portugal, Turkey, Egypt, and Iraq. The export of base metals to other non-European countries, except Russia, was at the discretion of the Northern Rhodesian government, with the proviso that difficult cases were to be referred to the secretary of state for consideration.[23]

The copper industry, however, faced several problems which threatened the supply of copper to the Allies. A key moment of tension occurred in March 1940, when the miners went on strike, despite the promulgation of Emergency Regulations prohibiting work stoppages during the war. This led to loss of productivity. On 17 March, about two thousand European miners went on strike at Mufulira and Nkana mines. A few days later, African mine workers followed suit. That the strike occurred six months into the Second World War was not a coincidence, nor was it simply a product of worker militancy against the color bar, as some historians have argued.[24] Instead, economic developments specific to wartime copper production provided the critical preconditions for the strike. These developments, which included a shortage of labor, inflation, a high cost of living, and stagnant copper prices, prompted the Northern Rhodesia Chamber of Mines to resist any wage increases for miners. Mine managements sought to parry the workers' demands by stressing that their profits were taking a hit as a result of virtually all the metal being bought by the Ministry of Supply at a fixed price. Arguing that they were losing much of their profit through taxation, the companies instead asked the Colonial Office to clarify the situation with the MWU. This was a self-serving argument, since the fixed price of £62 per ton still enabled the mining companies to achieve net profits averaging seven pounds and ten shillings per ton for most of the war years.[25] The Rhokana Corporation's profits, for example, had gone up from £615,000 in 1933 to £2,388,000 in 1939.[26]

Another vexing economic problem facing miners was the rising cost of living due to war conditions. This issue was raised with the various mine managements by the miners' union in January 1940. At that time, the European miners' union noted that living costs on the mines had increased by 8½ percent at Mufulira, 12 percent at Nkana, and 13½ percent at Nchanga between September 1939 and January 1940.[27] For their part, mine managements resented the MWU's expectation that the companies should bear the total cost of increases in the standard of living for their employees. They argued that they could not increase the miners' wages because shareholders, too, were making a great sacrifice by selling copper to the Ministry of Supply at a low price.[28] Warnings about a possible strike by miners had been issued by some shareholders in the mining industry early in the war, but the companies took no action. An official of RAA in Johannesburg, C. Wilson, who had visited Broken Hill in December 1939, found that the rise in living costs was already noticeable at that time. In this regard, Wilson had counseled his group's London offices to prepare for a pay increment for miners in order to avoid "unpleasantness" in the future. He had reported that

> it appeared . . . almost inevitable that in due course there will be an agitation among employees for some additional pay to offset the increase in the cost of living . . . In view of the likelihood of it doing so it appears desirable at this stage to make up our minds whether we are prepared to do anything in the way of granting bonuses or increased pay and, if so, how far we should go in this direction.[29]

Although no strike took place at the zinc and lead mine owned by RAA at Broken Hill, conditions there were no different from those obtaining on the Copperbelt in early 1940.

The shortage of skilled European labor resulting from wartime mobilization strengthened the hand of the MWU. The miners, many of whom were young men from the Rand, felt the time was ripe for action on pay. Expecting a postwar slump, and fearing that their chance would vanish along with rising unemployment, they believed that they could not delay taking action.[30] Moreover, added to the existing sources of resentment among the European workforce was discontent over the barring of some of them from leaving their positions on the mines for the war front due to war Emergency Regulations.[31] At the beginning of March 1940, therefore, miners at Mufulira formed a Committee of Action to negotiate on their behalf owing to their loss of confidence in their union. This committee called for an immediate pay raise, improved overtime payments and housing, and a government investigation of silicosis.[32] As no fruitful answer came out of an ultimatum given to the mine management at Mufulira, the workers refused to go to work on 17 March. The strike spread to Nkana mine, but not to Luanshya's Roan Antelope. The strike came to an end on 27 March, when management awarded miners an increase of 5 percent of their basic wages and conceded to other demands.[33]

The African miners' strike of 28 March was a result of the Europeans' strike, which had ended the previous day. It started at Nkana and spread to Mufulira, but, like the European strike, not to Luanshya. This was in spite of the fact that wages and conditions of service at Luanshya were no different from those at Nkana and Mufulira.[34] There are two plausible explanations for this. First, Roan enjoyed comparatively better relations with its rank and file than did the other mines on the Copperbelt in the early stages of the war.[35] Another explanation could be that memories of the bloody occurrences of the 1935 strike at Roan Antelope, in which military personnel had killed six African miners, were still too fresh for the miners there to contemplate undertaking another strike.[36]

African miners were aware that Europeans had gone on strike to secure a pay increase to meet rising costs of living. Having seen that the demands of the organized European workers had been met, they became more insistent in their own demands.[37] They argued that if the European miners had attained their objectives by striking, a strike was the appropriate and, indeed, inevitable course of action for obtaining similar benefits for themselves.[38] Pointing to the example of the successful European strike, one African witness told the Forster Commission, which was set up to investigate the causes of the strike, that "a father . . . had two children. They were hungry and to one food was given, while the other was let without. The one given food went to his brother and said: 'My father has fed me because I refused to work for him.' Then the other said: 'If I do as my brother has done, my father will feed me.'"[39]

The grievance over disparities in the conditions of service between the two racial groups on the mines was elaborated upon in several anonymous notices calling upon African miners to emulate the European strike. Two of these notices, posted in the Nkana compound, were written under the pseudonyms of "I don't know" and "Katwishi" (the Bemba equivalent of "I don't know"). "I don't know," for example, after drawing the attention of his fellow workers to the fact that "the Europeans left their work for the sake of an increase in pay," told them that if the white miners won wage increases as a result of their strike, "then we should work for one week and if we too do not receive an increase in pay then, so be it, let us leave work."[40] "Katwishi," on the other hand, wanted the strike to be total: "I entreat you strongly my friends that we should not differ about leaving work and that we should come to an understanding with each other so that the thing should be done."[41]

The Copper Mining Industry and the Allied War Effort

Apart from low wages, African miners brought out several other grievances during the strike. Among these were housing, rations, overtime allowances, firewood, and welfare matters.[42] The Forster Commission was taken aback by the extent of the African mine workers' grievances. Although similar issues had been raised five years earlier, it soon became clear that the welfare of African mine workers had not seen much improvement. The commission also found that in the years immediately preceding the war, conditions for mine workers had been allowed to deteriorate. An example of this was the overcrowding noted at the Nkana and Kitwe mine compounds.[43] The commission, however, considered that Africans were not yet ready for trade unionism and that the current system of tribal elders should continue. This reasoning was based on racial assumptions aimed at limiting representation of African workers.

The strike on the Copperbelt was not unique to Northern Rhodesia. Wartime inflation was the main causal factor.[44] There is no consensus on the rate of inflation in individual colonies and urban centers, as estimates range from 75 to 400 percent.[45] As demonstrated in chapter 3, war conditions had contributed to a rise in the cost of living in the colony. The war had both intensified colonial grievances and contributed to economic and social conditions which could only generate unrest.[46] There were similar strikes, walkouts, demonstrations, and marches elsewhere in wartime Africa. For instance, railway workers went on strike in Nigeria in support of a Cost of Living Allowance (COLA) in 1941–42. So did their colleagues in the Gold Coast, who went on a work stoppage in 1941 for the implementation of a similar allowance, which they had been promised in 1939. Other strikes were recorded in the mines of Katanga in 1941, while workers at the port of Dar-es-Salaam demonstrated in 1943. Kenya, in particular, experienced a great deal of unrest during the war, as there were massive strikes by railway workers in Mombasa and Nairobi in both 1942 and 1944.[47]

While the cost of living had gone up, the basic minimum wages for African miners were actually lower in real terms in 1940 than they had been in the 1920s. The reason given by the representatives of the mine owners was that in the development days of the Copperbelt, labor was more difficult to obtain than during the war. During the Depression, African wages had been cut, and despite the subsequent rise in living costs and the fact that the mining companies were now making sizable profits, these cuts had not been restored.[48] Wages had gone down from 17 shillings and 6 pence in 1929 to 12 shillings and 6 pence for surface workers in 1940, and from 30 shillings to 22 shillings and 6 pence for underground workers.[49] These wages were equal to annual rates for Africans of about £10 16s. for surface workers and £18 18s. for underground; European miners, for their part, earned an average £506.[50]

In addition, urbanized Africans had, by the outbreak of the war, developed new material wants. A witness before the Forster Commission, Reverend Frank Bedford, explained that "soap, clothing, furniture, better schools, books, things which were luxuries are now becoming necessities. Certain commodities commonly purchased by the African have increased in cost by 40 per cent to 50 per cent. . . . On the other hand, wages have not increased in the same proportion as the rise in the standard of living."[51]

African miners detested the color bar and the racial assumptions upon which it was based.[52] Not unexpectedly, therefore, the low wages paid to African miners, and the great disparity between their own wages and those of white workers, represented the most basic and strongest grievance for all categories of African mine workers. The strike ended on 3 April 1940, following the killing of seventeen miners and the wounding of sixty-five of their colleagues at Nkana by soldiers who had been called in to keep law and order. Despite its bloody ending, the strike was partly successful, as African miners were awarded a wage increase of two shillings and sixpence per month.[53]

Besides encountering workers' militancy, the wartime production of minerals was also hampered by the shortage of vital supplies and modern machinery to replace obsolete and worn-out equipment. Some of the most important items in short supply were repair parts for ball mills, shell plates, crushers, rock drills, and locomotives, as well as reagents, graphite electrodes, coach screws, rivets, bolts, nuts, and smelter bricks.[54] The global shortage of these items affected maintenance schedules and, consequently, levels of production on the mines. In 1945, the general manager of Rhokana Corporation reported that

> by the end of 1940 . . . the general deterioration of plant, particularly the crush plant, had become so serious that it was necessary to reduce production to permit some headway to be made with maintenance and repair work. The production rate was accordingly reduced to an average of 8,100 short tons per

month during 1941, including approximately 1,200 short tons from Nchanga.[55]

The British government's decision to ban the export of machinery in order to preserve it for local consumption led to this state of affairs. A similar policy was adopted by the USA in 1942.

Industry officials, however, engaged with the colonial government to intervene in the supply bottleneck and apply for stocks under Lend-Lease. In peacetime, the mining companies had routinely put out inquiries to different firms and selected the most suitable quotation on their own. Under war conditions, however, this option was no longer available to them. In line with the principles of economic warfare, supplies could only be obtained through the Lend-Lease arrangements stipulated between the US government and the receiving government. But once supplies were purchased, the government used merchants at Ndola as distributors.[56] The government of Northern Rhodesia placed bulk orders for the mines with the British Colonial Supply Mission in Washington, DC, through the United States' War Production Board at unspecified prices.[57] The supplies were consigned to the governor and then delivered to individual mining companies. Under Lend-Lease arrangements, no commission was to be paid to merchants, who had previously received it from their principals. This was to ensure that the mining companies paid fair prices for their supplies.[58] This policy guaranteed reduced costs of production for the mines so that there would be no ripple effect on the price paid for metals bought by the Ministry of Supply.

Through Lend-Lease, the mines were able to obtain regular supplies of unmanufactured and semimanufactured iron and steel; nonferrous metals, ingots or their semimanufactured forms; and finished nonferrous products, including copper starting sheet blanks, bare copper wire, and insulated copper wire. Other imports included ball and roller bearings, graphite electrodes, machine tools, cutting tools and other small tools, hand tools, magnesite bricks, chemical reagents, and Canadian timber.[59] Effective from January 1943, shipping space for transporting bulk supplies was guaranteed by the British Ministry of War Transport. To ensure this measure was carried out smoothly, mining companies were requested by the governor to estimate their annual shipping space for all requirements from the US and Britain.[60] With this support from the metropole, the mines were warned to "take every reasonable precaution to ensure that production shall not be affected by a shortage of supplies."[61]

THE COPPER INDUSTRY IN THE POSTWAR PERIOD

As the war drew to a close, economists, mining magnates, miners, and colonial and imperial officials all predicted a postwar slump arising from the availability of large copper stocks.[62] Lusaka was anxious about the implications of a sudden postwar cut in production, not least the unemployment which would affect the politically influential European miners.[63] The British Ministry of Supply even cut back its purchases of Northern Rhodesian copper in 1944, since it was felt that—by then—the Allies had secured enough supplies. The following year, the Allied powers estimated that the change from a two-front to a one-front war against Japan would lead to a reduction in military copper consumption of about 264,000 tons per annum.[64] Furthermore, the outlook for the mines seemed bleak, as the cost of deep-level mining was increasing, fuel was scarce, and the necessary machinery and railway stock were in short supply.[65] Because of these pessimistic calculations, the mines reduced production from a high of 250,000 tons in 1942 to 183,000 tons in 1946.[66] These fears were not unfounded, since similar trends had been observed after the First World War. This time around, however, stakeholders in the industry were all proven wrong, since, far from falling or even remaining constant, copper production went up significantly in the postwar period.

Indeed, in the aftermath of the Second World War, copper became even more vital to Britain's economic survival. The ravages of war had disrupted the world economy, resulting in a global shortage of foodstuffs and consumer products, inflationary pressures and, most significantly, a general dependence on imports from the United States. Although Washington wrote off almost the entire wartime Lend-Lease account, the combined dollar deficit of Britain and the entire sterling area was over four billion dollars in 1947.[67] This created a crisis in the convertibility of sterling in comparison with a resurgent US dollar. One response to the convertibility crisis of 1947 was to devalue or float sterling, rather than suspend convertibility.[68] Consequently, the currency was devalued by 44 percent against the US dollar in September 1949, to compensate for the shift in the economic fortunes and competitiveness of the UK as opposed to the US.[69] The devaluation of sterling meant that Britain could export more easily, as foreigners could now acquire more pounds sterling with the same amount of their own currency. On the other hand, of course, Britain had to pay more of her depreciated money to acquire goods from abroad.[70] One of these commodities was copper. The copper industry took a new lease on life following the devaluation of sterling. Since the price paid by the British government for the metal had been based on the dollar price, following devaluation, the mining companies persuaded the Ministry of Supply to raise the sterling price accordingly.[71] Between 1949 and 1953, the dollar price for copper rose by almost half.[72]

It was in this context that the Northern Rhodesian copper mines acquired a new importance to Britain. Equally important was that, with the notable exception of royalties, most of the costs on the mines, including wages, transport, and fuel, were sterling driven and thus unaffected by the devaluation.[73] The increased production of vital export commodities in the colonies was crucial to Britain, as it was meant to reduce its dependence on the United States, uphold the international value of sterling, and enable the country to earn dollars.[74] Apart from being vital sources of raw materials for sale, the colonies contributed to the hard currency pool through their dollar earnings. They also held sizable sterling balances in London, which the imperial government could manipulate more freely than was possible elsewhere.[75] "The whole future of the sterling group and its ability to survive," Minister of Economic Affairs Sir Stafford Cripps told an African governors' conference in November 1947, "depends . . . upon a quick and extensive development of our African resources."[76] Emphasizing the urgency of the situation, he exhorted colonial governors to "increase out [of] all recognition the tempo of African development . . . so that within the next two to five years we get a really marked increase of production in . . . anything . . . that will save dollars or sell in a dollar market."[77]

Northern Rhodesia responded accordingly. Blister copper worth £2 million was exported to the United States in 1948, this being the first consignment sold for dollars since the war. The following year the figure rose to £4.8 million.[78] More important than its dollar-earning capacity was the position of copper as a dollar-saver; and still more dollars were saved by the coming into operation of the new electrolytic refinery at Nkana mine in 1951.[79] The refinery was of considerable significance to the sterling area because Britain did not possess sufficient capacity to produce electrolytic copper of higher purity. As a result, it exported scrap copper to the tune of 145,000 tons per year to the US to be refined in exchange for dollars.[80]

The imperatives of postwar reconstruction in Europe and the United States also spurred demand for copper. The war had left devastated areas and industries which needed to be rebuilt. The US and Britain, two principal consumers of copper, required more of the metal—especially for their electrical and automotive industries—than had been thought possible before. In 1947, *The Economist* estimated that as much as 50 percent of all the copper imported by the US and 40 percent imported by Britain was being consumed by the automobile industry, followed by the shipbuilding industry, which accounted for 20 percent of the total.[81] Imperial officials estimated that the resumption of copper purchases by the Ministry of Supply after the war saved Britain the equivalent of some £11 million in dollars annually by 1950.[82] Production, which had fallen to 182,289 long tons in 1946, reached 309,141 long tons in 1951.[83]

The postwar period also witnessed increased demand for copper in other nontraditional spheres, such as architecture and building construction. The use of copper sheet and strip for roofing, flashings, damp-proof course, and rainwater goods made headway—as did the use of copper tube for hot- and cold-water and gas pipes and heating.[84] As a result, the price of blister copper soared from the controlled wartime level of £62 to £137 per long ton by March 1947.[85] The American government's creation of a strategic copper reserve also aided the market's buoyancy, which benefited producers by keeping surplus war stocks from coming back onto the market and adding to available supplies.[86] Furthermore, the demand for copper remained strong and prices buoyant following the end of US price controls in November 1946.[87]

Another factor contributing to the prosperity of the copper mining industry in the period after the war was the outbreak of the Korean War in 1950, which led to increased demand for the metal from defense industries and to the expansion of Western rearmament programs.[88] By 1951, rearmament in Britain and the US had created a serious global deficiency of the metal. This resulted in a sharp rise in the price of copper from £180 to £420 per long ton between 1950 and 1956.[89] This development also encouraged massive investment in expanding the mines on the Copperbelt to maintain and increase output. As Lawrence Butler has demonstrated, spurred by the effects of the

The Copper Mining Industry and the Allied War Effort

Korean War and escalating Cold War, the Americans began to show a willingness to invest in Northern Rhodesia's mining and infrastructure to boost copper production.[90] This coincided with a period when British capacity for overseas investment was increasingly stretched. Thus, the expansion of the Copperbelt came to rely on American capital. With the intensification of the Cold War in the late 1940s, and increased defense spending by a financially handicapped Britain, Washington developed more and more interest in Africa's potential to contribute to strategic stockpiling of commodities vital to the West.[91] The West viewed central Africa through the prism of Cold War calculations, and aimed to forestall Soviet penetration of the industry.[92] The overall effect was a rise in the value of minerals produced in Northern Rhodesia from £50 million in 1950 to £95 million in 1953.[93]

Increased demand for copper by the US for its stockpiling program led to a rise in American interests in Northern Rhodesia's mining industry in the 1950s. This was the rationale for the US government's loan of £3 million to the RST in 1951 (later increased to £5 million) for a new mine at Chibuluma.[94] Butler argues that this development was propelled by a new emphasis on strategic stockpiling, itself a product of the Korean War and intimations of future conflict elsewhere, that is, from cold to hot war.[95] The primary aim was to safeguard the supply of copper, a strategic commodity in the prosecution of the Korean War. Chibuluma was the first mine opened by the RST group in the postwar era. Further US assistance included a grant of £200,000 to Rhokana made in 1953 for the establishment of a cobalt refinery. This culminated in the opening of two new mines at Bancroft (RAA) and Chibuluma (RST) and the extension of Nkana and Mufulira mines, as well as the establishment of the highly profitable open pit at Nchanga.[96]

Concurrent with these developments, the balance of power in the region took a new shape. For some time, the political influence had been shifting from London to members of the European population in central Africa. The end of the war thus had political ramifications for the region, as it revived the idea of a closer union among Northern Rhodesia, Southern Rhodesia, and Nyasaland. This, however, was an imperial and not just a local movement. There were similar federation schemes in East Africa, the West Indies, and Southeast Asia during this period.[97] The issue of amalgamation in central Africa, which had died down during the war, now acquired new vigor and relevance due to the boom in the copper industry. In the meantime, the

129

copper industry made another significant administrative change by moving its head offices from London to Northern Rhodesia. RST moved to Lusaka in 1951, and RAA relocated to Kitwe on the Copperbelt in 1953. They left the City, which had long been losing much of its importance as the heart of global finance.[98] White politicians in Southern Rhodesia wanted to benefit from the prosperous copper mining industry in the north and renewed their efforts aimed at amalgamating the three central African territories.[99] Britain was in favor of federation, as it also feared Afrikaner expansion northward following the Nationalist Party victory in the 1948 election. After much debate, both for and against the Central African Federation, the project came into being in August 1953, the same year in which the LME was reopened and bulk buying of copper by Britain came to an end.

The mines still faced supply challenges in the postwar era. This time around supplies in the most critical bracket were steel mill products such as bars, sheets, plates, structured shapes, pipe, and nails.[100] The shortage was ascribed to the rearmament program and reconstruction in Europe and America. The situation arose at a time the mines such as Nchanga were undergoing extension programs requiring large quantities of steel supplies. The main supplier of steel during this period was the US. The procurement of mine supplies from that country, however, was complicated by the necessity of having to pay for them with US dollars, which were scarce.[101] Naturally, the British government was behind the mines and ensured that the supply of dollars was fully met. To this end, the Colonial Office granted the copper mining companies' full requirements of US$1,813,000 in 1951 and further guaranteed US$2,500,000 for 1952.[102]

Moreover, to alleviate supply problems, the US government created the National Production Authority under the Defense Production Act of 1950. The Department of the Interior became the claimant agency for all mines and concentration plants, and for smelters and refineries of nonferrous metals. It had powers to allocate and issue directions for the use of mining machinery and equipment used in American and foreign facilities.[103] An extension of priority to their suppliers for maintenance, repair, and operating supplies to the extent of a dollar quota per quarter for various materials other than steel, aluminum, and copper was made to Northern Rhodesian mines.[104] The latter were allocated under the Controlled Materials Plan. In this way, mines such as Roan and Nchanga were able to obtain high-priority ratings for the purchase and shipment of needed mining supplies for their expansion activities.

Another obstacle on the path of the mining companies was the ruthless Export Profit Tax (EPT) of 1941. Imposed on orders from London, the EPT stifled reinvestment and improvements in the mining industry.[105] Under existing tax laws, a company whose control and management were based in Britain, but which operated wholly or partly abroad, paid full British taxes on all its profits wherever they were earned.[106] As both RAA and RST were based in the City of London, the British Exchequer received 60 percent of the excess profits made by their Northern Rhodesian subsidiaries under this arrangement. The balance of the profits was taxed at a net rate of four shillings and threepence per pound. For its part, the government of Northern Rhodesia also taxed the total profits at four shillings and threepence per pound.[107] The rationale for the introduction of EPT was clearly to fund the British war effort. This was explicitly stated in debates in the House of Commons: "this heavy taxation collected by the UK from the mineral enterprises in Northern Rhodesia and elsewhere is all being spent for the united war effort. . . . It is a terrific tax at its present rate and with its present incidence, it comes from the wealth created by the Almighty in those overseas countries."[108] Stakeholders in the industry were opposed to this drastic rise in tax expenditures, which they regarded as a "formidable problem,"[109] or, in the words of Ronald Prain, chairman of the RST group, as "punitive taxation."[110]

Whereas in 1937–38 the three main copper-producing mines of Nkana, Roan Antelope, and Mufulira had paid an average of 17 percent of their operating surpluses as tax, this figure rose to 67 percent in 1941.[111] This, in turn, had a negative impact on the mines' development and expansion programs and, importantly, on the rates of dividends paid to shareholders. One of the hardest-hit mines in the RST group was Mufulira.[112] The accounts of Mufulira Copper Mines, the youngest of Northern Rhodesia's mines, clearly show that the weight of the EPT burden was the sole cause of the reduction in dividends declared to shareholders. At its eighteenth annual ordinary meeting of December 1940, directors of Rhokana Corporation expressed unhappiness with the implementation of EPT, which had reduced the company's gross dividend from £217,149 the previous year to £177,668.[113] Consequently, company directors recommended a reduction in the final dividend distributable to shareholders, from 25 percent to 15 percent.[114] Rhokana's 1940 taxation provision, £1,060,000, was £601,000 higher than the previous financial year. This new tax provision marginally reduced the net distributable earnings, from £582,431 to £548,254.[115] The reduction in the Mufulira dividend involved a decline from £422,082 to £343,328 in the profit of the controlling company, RST, for the quarter ending 30 September 1940. Consequently, RST's dividend was lowered from 16⅔ percent to 13⅓ percent.[116]

Concern over EPT came to preoccupy the main stakeholders in the mining industry during this period. Between 1941 and 1947, a net total of £7,092,483 was paid to the British Treasury by RAA and RST mines as EPT.[117] Opposition to EPT came from various stakeholders when they gave evidence to the Royal Commission on Taxation of Profits and Income in June 1952. One of these was the Council of the London Stock Exchange (LSE). The council's main argument was that heavy taxation of the mining companies discouraged investments in stocks on the LSE. Those against EPT felt that mining companies should be treated no differently from other firms with domiciles outside Britain but with British shareholders. The latter firms only paid British taxes on such portion of profits as was remitted to shareholders in the United Kingdom. The rest of the profits were taxed at local rates, which were generally lower than in Britain.[118] The tax burden on the mining companies, referred to by Butler as "a general centrifugal influence,"[119] would be the overriding reason for their transfer of head offices from the City to Northern Rhodesia after 1950.

The liability placed on the copper mines in wartime was not limited to EPT, however. The Northern Rhodesian government also became dependent on the mines for revenue to run its administration. For example, the government added to the burden of taxation with its request that the mines pay in advance a portion of the estimated income tax for the 1941 financial year to ease its cash flow deficit. This practice originated from the Depression, when colonial state coffers had dwindled.[120] As a result, Roan Antelope Copper Mines Limited paid £500,000 to the Treasury in 1940. Of this, £200,000 was an advance against income tax, and £300,000 was an interest-free loan.[121] The colonial government's reliance on the mines as a source of revenue continued into the postwar period. With high receipts from copper sales, income tax paid by the mines to the colonial Treasury rose from 28 percent in 1947 to a high of 57.5 percent in 1952.[122]

The Copper Mining Industry and the Allied War Effort

The British government, however, did provide some relief to the mines for fear that they might not fulfill their contracts with the Ministry of Supply regarding existing plant capacity. Nchanga mine obtained the most significant assistance: a loan of £750,000 to cover half the cost of its expansion program in 1943.[123] Aside from this, the amounts granted were minute, such as the £7,500 given to Roan mine to pay for the partial cost of fifty-two temporary houses for European miners.[124]

AGRICULTURE AND THE MINING INDUSTRY

Mining was also linked to the agricultural sector, because miners had to be fed to keep production going and to prevent industrial action. The size of the African labor force employed in the copper mines rose from 7,200 in 1933 to 24,000 in 1939 and 36,000 in 1943.[125] Added to this was the general increase of the African population on the Copperbelt, as more and more Africans adopted the urban areas as their homes for long periods. These population dynamics led to the growth of bustling towns such as Kitwe, Luanshya, Chingola, and Mufulira at each of the mines.[126] During this period, however, the territory witnessed a decline in food production owing to a number of factors, the principal of which were the drought of 1942, the scarce supplies of chemical fertilizers, and a general lack of labor due to war conditions.[127] In addition, as demonstrated in chapter 2, war conditions led to a shortage of farming implements, which, in turn, negatively affected the capacity of peasant farmers to produce food for the market. This situation forced the country to import much of its maize requirements throughout the war years, and it continued to do so until 1954.[128] In 1941, the Department of Agriculture noted that "the season was one of the most difficult and disastrous yet recorded. Planting was delayed and reduced in extent by alternating periods of deluge and drought. The cessation of effective rain in early February caused much of the unavoidable late planted crop to come to little or nothing."[129]

The quantities of maize produced in the country did not match the rate of consumption, which had increased, especially on the Copperbelt and other urban centers in the line-of-rail provinces. It was estimated that, by 1944, the urban areas alone consumed about 430,000 bags of maize per year each weighing 200 pounds, versus 200,000 in 1941.[130] As consumption increased, so did the fear that it would be difficult, even in favorable seasons, to meet the demand for food from local supplies. In 1942, maize meal

TABLE 5.2. Maize sales in the line-of-rail provinces, 1941–44 (bags)

Year	European Grown (200 lb. per bag)	African Grown (200 lb. per bag)	Total (200 lb. per bag)
1941	120,000	38,000	158,000
1942	146,000	51,000	197,000
1943	144,000	60,000	204,000
1944	212,000	115,000	327,000
1945	273,000	202,000	475,000

Sources: NRG, *Department of Agriculture Annual Report for 1944* (Lusaka: Government Printer, 1945), 5; and NRG, *Department of Agriculture Annual Report for the Year 1958* (Lusaka: Government Printer, 1959), 8.

rations for miners were reduced by as much as a quarter. The government, in turn, praised the miners for accepting this reduction, which it viewed as a necessary sacrifice under war conditions. When he addressed the Legislative Council on this subject, Governor John Waddington stated that

> during recent months, our food position has caused me considerable anxiety and I regret very much that the reduction in maize rations that was effected a few months ago is still in force. This cut on rations has imposed a considerable hardship on African consumers and I wish to express my appreciation of their most helpful attitude in treating the matter as one of the sacrifices to war conditions which has to be cheerfully endured.[131]

This crisis needed to be addressed urgently. Table 5.2 shows the quantities of maize sold on the line of rail during the war period.

Inadequate local production of maize during the war brought metropolitan intervention to ensure adequate food supplies. The imperial government was concerned about the colony's food security, which had a bearing on industrial harmony in the mines. Labor unrest on the mines could disrupt the production of vital base metals. Additionally, as demonstrated above, Britain derived immense financial benefits from a thriving Northern Rhodesian mining industry. London was keen on ensuring that nothing disrupted the colony's copper production and stepped in to scour Africa for possible sources of supply.[132] Emergency imports were sought from neighboring territories, although none were available. There was no surplus in nearby South Africa, and the entire crop of the Belgian Congo had already been bought by the governments of the two Rhodesias in 1942.[133] It was then that the British Ministry of Food agreed to release stocks from other parts of Africa where a surplus existed. In view of the urgent need, the Ministry of Food provided 10,000 tons of maize from its Middle East quota.[134] Britain further helped in the acquisition of 33,600 bags of maize from Argentina in March 1943; 5,600 bags from Southern Rhodesia's purchases in the Belgian Congo; and 5,000 bags of potatoes from South Africa.[135] In April another purchase of 6,720 bags of maize from Angola was made after Britain agreed to sell 1,000 tires to the Portuguese government in exchange.[136]

While maize remained the most important crop for feeding African miners, it was by no means the only one consumed. As part of the war effort, the government promoted the cultivation and consumption of cassava as a substitute crop. This crop was widely grown in the Northern, North-Western, and Luapula Provinces. In 1942, the government even used trucks from Southern Rhodesia and also diverted vehicles of the Department of Public Works to transport cassava from the major producing areas to the Copperbelt to avert starvation.[137] The production of sorghum was also revived because, for the first time, the crop began to be purchased by government agricultural marketing agencies.[138] But these measures proved inadequate to solve the food situation in the country. The government thus resorted to labor conscription for European settler farmers to address this situation.

Forced labor for the military was an accepted practice in wartime, as manpower was required for direct war work. Although the resort to compulsory labor during emergencies was a common and accepted practice in British colonies, large-scale conscription for civil production in wartime, especially for private enterprise, was a new departure in policy.[139] Some officials in Whitehall argued that if conscripted labor for the army was an accepted practice in Britain, then it could equally be utilized in the colonies fighting the war against Nazism. For example, before compulsory service regulations were introduced in Tanganyika and Kenya in July and October 1940, respectively, quotas of recruits for the army had been imposed on areas by district commissioners.[140] As civil conscription for the military was already being used in East Africa, a precedent had been set in raising labor for essential services that could be followed by other colonies. In Tanganyika, about 84,500 people were forced to work on estates, producing sisal, rubber, pyrethrum, and other agricultural products.[141]

The British government insisted that it abhorred forced labor, but in reality, it practised it in its colonies. Although colonial authorities were careful to employ words like "recruitment," Africans in Southern Rhodesia used the word *chibaro*—meaning slave or slave labor in local languages—to refer to recruited laborers.[142] During the war, about 15,000 such men were recruited to work on the construction of airfields for the Empire Air Training Scheme in Southern Rhodesia. But the most deplorable form of forced labor in wartime Africa took place on the tin mines of Jos in Nigeria, where thousands of laborers died due to poor sanitation and working conditions.[143] That Britain used forced labor in wartime showed that the colonial government was not above applying double standards. In peacetime and at the beginning of the war, Britain had denounced French policies of conscripting soldiers in their West African colonies, under both Vichy and Gaullist regimes.[144] In trying to win African support at the start of the war, Britain had used propaganda to denounce Germany as a violent country (see chapter 1). In the event, as the war progressed, Britain, too, was forced to resort to similar practices.

The League of Nations had issued its "Slavery Convention" in 1926, reminding colonial powers to stop the slave trade and slavery, while asking the International Labour Organisation (ILO) to investigate the best means of preventing compulsory labor from developing into conditions analogous to slavery. The League's convention of 1930 strongly condemned forced labor for private purposes and created elaborate regulations for compulsory public works labor, arguing that it should be phased out.[145] Britain was a signatory to this pact. The convention, however, left a loophole, in that colonial powers were permitted to forcibly recruit manpower in time of emergency, including war.[146] As Carolyn Brown has noted, the war brought an intensification of coercive "developmentalist" schemes that featured brutal policies of colonial social engineering.[147] The introduction of forced labor in wartime Africa was similar to the desperate policies adopted by Britain elsewhere in the empire in order to win the war at any cost. In India, for example, wartime imperial policies perpetuated famine conditions in the state of Bengal, leading to the death of about three million local people.[148]

Although the Colonial Office was unhappy about the use of forced labor on privately owned European farms, it was reluctant to stop the practice for fear of antagonizing white farmers in a country where white mine workers, another important constituency, were already hostile to the state. The colonial state wanted to balance the conflicting interests of the various sectors of capital without endangering its own interests or upsetting the social unity necessary for the accumulation of profits. To increase maize production, the Colonial Office allowed use of compulsory labor to prepare land for a two-month period, starting on 21 February 1942. The War Cabinet, in agreeing to an increase in the number of agricultural conscripts, emphasized the great importance attached to the limitation of profit where the use of conscripted labor was allowed for private employment.[149]

No sooner had the war broken out than settler farmers in the agriculturally developed parts of the colony began agitating for a new agricultural policy. This was first voiced by the Midlands Farmers' Association, which was especially critical of state agrarian policies, and, later, by the Mazabuka Farmers' Association. The farmers' groups emphasized that the increase in cash cropping among African peasants reduced the accustomed flow of labor to settlers' farms. Settler farmers argued that their contribution to the war effort through greater food production ought to be matched by an African contribution in the form of enforced farm labor.[150] This campaign was partly engendered by statements on wartime agricultural efforts in Britain and neighboring Southern Rhodesia. Settler farmers hoped that through such a policy, substantial financial assistance from the government would come their way.[151] But at this juncture, government policy opposed any price incentive to maize farmers to boost production or a guaranteed supply of labor and loans free from normal restrictions such as collateral.[152] The governor spelled out the government's wartime agrarian policy in 1939:

> It is essential that production of agricultural produce for internal consumption should be maintained at least at its normal level. Export of crops in large quantities is not an economic proposition, but internal consumption is more likely to increase than to decrease. Some farmers have enlisted in the fighting forces and others wish to go. This is tribute to their spirit, but decrease in

production must not be allowed to follow in consequence of it. In time of war much always depends on agriculture.[153]

This appeal for increased food production, especially maize, was based on the premise that the country would witness increased food consumption levels and that a market for exports readily existed overseas due to war conditions. Farmers, therefore, were urged to remain on their farms and increase levels of production.

The government's main thrust to increase food production was directed at settler commercial farmers, who were called upon to contribute to the war effort by bringing a greater acreage under cultivation. By 1942, the number of mechanized farms was low. The overwhelming majority of farms were undercapitalized, with less than 200 acres under plow, and farmers constantly complained about the lack of labor.[154] In consultation with the Food Production Committee, the government envisaged an increase in the production of maize by 30,000 acres and that of wheat by 5,000 acres. For this to succeed, the government planned to recruit between 2,000 and 3,000 farm laborers in 1942 and raise this figure to 4,000 by 1944.[155]

To attain its objectives, the government exercised its legislative powers to compel Africans to work on settler farms, enacting several laws to coerce African labor. The first such law was the Emergency Powers (Recruitment of Farm Labour) Regulation of 1942. By this law, the controller of labor was empowered to recruit volunteers aged between sixteen and forty-five to work on settler farms for a period of two years, with provision of penal sanctions for desertion, absenteeism, or evasion of duties.[156] Punishment took the form of a fine not exceeding £5 or imprisonment for a period not exceeding three months or both. This law was in line with the wartime Emergency Powers (War Defence) Act Notices no. 139 of 1939 and no. 178 of 1939, which empowered the governor (or any other competent authority) to use force to maintain supplies and services essential to the life of the country. Every recruit under this law was paid wages amounting to ten shillings per thirty-day ticket with food rations for youths who were not liable to tax. Those who were eligible for tax payments were paid twelve shillings and sixpence as well as food rations.[157]

Up to this point, commercial farmers had depended on voluntary African labor to sustain their operations. Africans went to look for work on

The Copper Mining Industry and the Allied War Effort

their own on European farms or were recruited by private entities on behalf of the farmers. This voluntary recruitment of labor, however, had proved ineffective: relatively few people came forward, because working conditions were not competitive. For example, it was estimated in April 1942 that while only 3,000 volunteers could be recruited under the voluntary scheme, compulsion could bring in about 9,000.[158] As elsewhere in colonial Africa, the local people generally regarded forced farm labor as one of the least desirable forms of employment. Worse still, some European settler farmers had earned a reputation for ill-treating farm workers. After frantic appeals to chiefs to persuade their subjects to converge on the farms failed to achieve the desired goal, the government accepted a recommendation from the African Labour Advisory Board (ALAB) that it should directly recruit labor and invoke Emergency Powers for essential food production.[159] This resulted in the enactment of another law, the Emergency Powers (Conscription of Natives for Farm Labour) Regulation, on 21 February 1942.

Shortly afterward, this was followed by the passing of the Emergency Powers (African Labour Corps) Regulations of 1942. Through this law, the government embarked upon the conscription of Africans under military discipline in the form of squads to work under the same conditions as the "volunteer" scheme. This constituted a more permanent standing pool of labor for settler farmers. The first group of 730 conscripts, mainly from Barotseland, arrived in Lusaka and Mazabuka to work on maize and wheat fields between March and June 1942. Other conscripts were obtained from the pool of "loafers" on the Copperbelt.[160] Members of the corps were at first organized into gangs of twenty-five under a corporal. For easy supervision, the number was reduced to fifteen in 1948, and eleven in 1950.[161] The African Labour Corps operated under the charge of an experienced labor recruiter and former farmer around the Lusaka area, Captain J. Brown. Any farmer unable to get labor for food production by other means could hire one or more gangs for a specific task or for a period of two to six weeks. The greatest advantage of the corps was that it brought squads of workers directly to the farm at the most critical periods in the farming cycle: stamping, clearing, sowing, and reaping, or in times of emergency, such as during a locust invasion.[162] Conscription was costly to implement because, in addition to paying wages, the government transported, housed, and provided medical facilities for the workers. Often the system ended up benefiting inefficient producers and bad employers who could not attract free labor. Still, it was only in 1952 that the government discontinued the system.

In April 1942, Governor John Waddington appealed to the Colonial Office again, noting that progress in voluntary recruiting had been "very unsatisfactory." As a result, another 700 males, mostly youths under sixteen years of age, were conscripted in May 1944 and a further 1,000 in January 1945.[163] Waddington was convinced that the only way to get Africans to work was by conscripting them, because they had a lot of cash in hand and no reasonable inducement could make them work on farms in sufficient numbers.[164] When interviewed in 1983, a former conscript, Timothy Siamaimbo of Sichiimbwe village in Pemba district, confirmed the nature of the conscription process. He stated: "That *cibbalo*: He caught us—Bwana Price, the Mazabuka D.C. He came into this village with his messengers. The messengers caught us . . . there were many of them—six on this side, six on that side."[165] Siamambo and his friend Thomas Sichintu were the unfortunate ones captured from their village on that occasion. "The rest ran away—they found us . . . no luck!"[166]

The use of forced labor during the war period supplemented the substantial grants, loans, and extension services made available to settler farmers and marked the epitome of the agrarian reforms initiated during the Depression. The reforms of the 1930s had been aimed at protecting settler farmers from competition from African peasant farmers on the Tonga plateau.[167] During the war, white farmers came to depend on conscripted labor through the Labour Corps system. By 1945 conscripted labor for settler farms had become so entrenched that stopping the system could hurt the territory's food requirements.

Northern Rhodesia played a key role in the provision of base metals for the Allied war effort. As the largest single producer of copper in the sterling area, the country granted the Allies a regular supply of this much-needed raw material for ammunition manufacture. The fact that copper had to be produced at any cost to buttress the British war effort brought about increased colonial and imperial government involvement in the activities of the mining industry. At the end of the war, moreover, the copper mines assumed a new prominence for a hard-up imperial government. Rather than granting political independence to the territory, Britain instead increased its grip on the colony so that dollar earnings from the copper industry could cushion its economy from further shocks. London's calculations, as Peter Cain and Anthony Hopkins have noted, were based primarily upon a heightened awareness of the economic worth of empire during the period of postwar reconstruction.[168] The prosperity recorded in the copper mining industry in the postwar period was the main reason behind the fast-tracked trend toward political unity and the inception of the Central African Federation. Increased mining activities in turn had a bearing on the supply of food needed to feed miners so that copper production remained uninterrupted. To ensure that settler farmers kept up the production of the much-needed food, the colonial government condoned the use of forced labor, recruiting, transporting, and paying Africans to work on settler farms.

6

Demobilization and the
Great Disappointment of War Service

> When I heard the news that the war was over I looked at the
> scar of my two fingers blown off by the Japanese gunners. I
> thought when I reach Africa I would ask my commanding
> officer to remain somewhere in Africa rather than returning
> to my home, I have a lame hand what will my wife and my
> parents say what had happened to me because now I will
> not be able to do manual work as I used to do before I was
> recruited into war.
>
> —Rabson Chombola, Northern Rhodesia Regiment
> veteran[1]

AFTER SIX LONG YEARS OF GALLANT AND BITTER FIGHTING AND
the sacrifice of valuable Allied lives, the Germans were defeated, sur-
rendering unconditionally on 8 May 1945. Three months later, following
Hiroshima and Nagasaki, Japan was subdued as well. The war against the Axis
was over. On Thursday, 21 February 1946, Northern Rhodesia paid just and
due homage to its fighting men. Before thousands of European and African
spectators, the First Battalion of the Northern Rhodesia Regiment trooped
its colors, which had not been unfurled since September 1939, in ceremonial
parade in Lusaka. The men in Burma green stood proudly at attention as the

Demobilization and the Great Disappointment of War Service

governor, in full dress uniform, inspected their ranks. With heads held high, they swung past the saluting base to the music of the 6th Northern Rhodesia Regiment band and the applause of the crowd. Attentively, they listened to the governor when he addressed them in these words: "In a few days you will be returning to civilian life. I hope that you will find happiness and that the knowledge you have gained during your military life will prove of value to you in whatever occupation you may follow."[2]

But, as this chapter demonstrates, African ex-servicemen hardly found happiness, nor did they feel valued. For most of them, the postwar period marked the beginning of another struggle. The views of veteran Rabson Chombola at the beginning of this chapter speak volumes about how African veterans from Northern Rhodesia felt at the end of the hostilities. The aftermath of the hostilities in Europe and the Far East inaugurated a new phase in the lives of the former servicemen—one marked above all by frustration and bitterness. Veterans complained about their delayed repatriation, gratuity amounts, standards of living, health care, educational and employment opportunities, and housing facilities. The plight of Chombola was sadly typical of the experience of many men who suffered permanent physical or mental impairment as a result of military service.[3] Here I argue that even as the Second World War came to an end, it—just like any war—left behind a trail of consequences not only for those directly recruited to fight and their families at home but also for the broader society to which discharged soldiers eventually returned. Owing to war experiences, veterans usually face psychological trauma, stress, injuries, and physical handicaps, as well as a fundamental uncertainty about their return to civilian life. For their part, the soldiers' families commonly suffer from emotional distress due to the absence of household heads and the occasional rise of juvenile delinquency among children and breakdown of marriages. On the larger societal level, a question usually arises regarding the role that veterans should play in the postwar period. In the African context, this question came to focus squarely on the position of servicemen in the politics of nationalism and independence.

In this chapter, I examine how Northern Rhodesian ex-servicemen—like their colleagues in other parts of Africa, Asia, and the Caribbean—coped with home life following the cessation of hostilities. I pay special attention to the main problems they and their home communities faced. On demobilization, the government of Northern Rhodesia expected that most African ex-servicemen would simply slip back into the rural lives they had left behind several years earlier. But as veteran Chombola reminds us, this was easier said than done. The challenges faced by African ex-servicemen often made them restless and discontented. Especially irksome was the differential treatment African veterans received from the Northern Rhodesian government, which paid European ex-servicemen higher gratuity rates and rewarded them with land and employment opportunities.

Despite all of this, the return of nearly 15,000 servicemen failed to have any appreciable impact on the growth of nationalist politics in Northern Rhodesia. This peculiar development calls for an explanation. Departing from older academic arguments, my contention is that African ex-servicemen were much more preoccupied with their immediate personal well-being than with wider issues, including nationalism and the fight for political independence.[4] Of all the conventional ideas about Africa and the Second World War, the view that returning servicemen invariably had a significant and direct political impact upon their home societies is possibly the most debatable.

THE DEMOBILIZATION PROCESS

The end of the war in Europe and the Mediterranean in May 1945 was foreseen, whereas the Japanese surrender on 15 August came abruptly following the American use of two atomic bombs. Although fighting had ended, major logistical problems persisted for the triumphant Allies. A large army of labor was needed for reconstruction after such a long war. Vast supply dumps of war materials had to be secured and then disposed of. There was also the need to reoccupy enemy-held territories and guard prisoners-of-war. Moving men and materials was a complex business involving coordination between various government departments—those of the Colonies, Dominions, and War Transport, plus the War Office, Admiralty, and Middle East Command—as well as the military commanders in the field and colonial administrations in various places.[5]

Postwar colonial demobilization was first discussed by an interdepartmental Committee on the Machinery of Demobilisation set up in January 1941. It consisted of representatives of the service departments, Ministry of Labour, and National Service. These plans were put on hold as the empire's prospects looked bleak due to Japanese successes in the Pacific until early 1942.[6] However, in July 1943, when victory appeared imminent,[7] the

Demobilization and the Great Disappointment of War Service

colonial secretary of state dispatched a circular to the colonies to formulate resettlement plans and set the tone for demobilization throughout the empire.[8] Demobilization was to proceed through the dispersal of groups whose composition depended on age and length of service; it was not to be based on the availability of transport and employment opportunities, as had been the case at the end of the 1914–18 war.[9] The justification for this was the lack of employment opportunities and shipping capacity to absorb everyone at once.

Once instructions on postwar resettlement from London reached the colonies, respective local administrators began to implement them immediately. The demobilization roadmaps drawn by colonial governments impressed Colonial Secretary Oliver Stanley, who in November 1943 praised the official initiatives taken by colonial administrators to establish a machinery that would ensure the speedy return of troops.[10] Although the Northern Rhodesian government gave thought to the organization of demobilization and the resettlement of ex-servicemen, the process was tied to imperial and military demands beyond its control. Colonial administrations were consulted at times, but more often than not they had to conform to plans drawn up by imperial and military authorities. The demobilization of Northern Rhodesian servicemen, like that of their counterparts hailing from other African colonies, faced major difficulties. The first problem was largely an imperial one and concerned the shortage of shipping. Ships had to be in the right place and of the right type for transporting men. Priority, however, was given to demobilizing British troops, on account of their race, of course, but also because their skills and labor were urgently needed to power British industry and reconstruction at home.[11] The men from Northern Rhodesia, like other colonial personnel from Africa, Asia, and the Caribbean, were low on the priority list. This also ensured that their labor could be conveniently used locally, in place of the British troops who were heading home. While no open protests over the delay in repatriation took place among the men of the Northern Rhodesian Regiment, who were very far away from home in the Middle East and Asia, French West African veterans stuck in transit camps in southern France refused orders, demolished buildings for firewood, and beat up bakers and shopkeepers who would not supply them.[12] A mutiny also occurred in the Royal Indian Navy, accompanied by rioting in Karachi, Bombay, and Calcutta in February 1946.[13]

Administrators in Northern Rhodesia agreed to the delayed demobilization of servicemen because of imperial and local logistical challenges. A local committee set up to examine the problems involved in reabsorbing African servicemen acknowledged in 1943 the need for gradual demobilization in order to regulate the reintegration of the men into civilian life as systematically as possible.[14] One major worry concerned the transportation of returnees, should all of them be repatriated within a short period.[15] Another concern had to do with finding employment opportunities for them. The Chamber of Mines stressed the undesirability of any sudden demobilization of large numbers of askari, as this would work against their gradual absorption by the mining companies.[16] In neighboring Nyasaland, it was considered essential that demobilization be gradual, partly to lighten the burden on transport facilities, partly to ease the strain on the Army Pay Corps, and partly to facilitate arrangements for the resettlement of returnees.[17]

By January 1946, five months after the defeat of Japan, less than half of the 15,000 men from Northern Rhodesia had returned home.[18] The 5th Battalion of the NRR, which had been assigned for guard duties in the Middle East as part of the East African Military Labour Corps, left the region in April 1946.[19] The last Northern Rhodesian soldiers were repatriated from India as late as late 1946, long after the war had ended in both Europe and Asia. Soldiers anticipated that demobilization would take a long time, but the explanation given by military authorities in the East Africa Command was not acceptable to those men who wanted to get back home to their families.[20] Men were angered by the repeated delays. The process of demobilizing was desperately slow, and camp life was boring in the extreme. The news that British soldiers were leaving for home clearly demonstrated racial discrimination already felt over disparities in pay and conditions.[21]

The journey back home from the theaters of war in East Africa, India, and the Middle East was likewise lengthy. For some it took as long as three or more months. The 3rd Battalion sailed from Rangoon in HMT *Cameronia* in March 1946. One member of that battalion, Joseph Maliselo, recalled: "After the war it took us about three months to reach home, that is, one month in India, three weeks in Nairobi, Kenya, and about one month in Lusaka before we received our discharge letters."[22] Once soldiers arrived in either Durban

Demobilization and the Great Disappointment of War Service

or Mombasa, they faced a further trip by rail and then road to their homes. As Chama Mutemi Kadansa explained,

> I spent five years in the army. The war came to an end in 1945 while I was in Burma in the town of Rangoon. On our coming back after the war, we boarded ships which brought us to Mombassa [*sic*] in Kenya. We sailed through Ceylone [*sic*], Bombay and landed in Mobassa [*sic*] at long last. From Mombassa [sic] we got on lorries to Nairobi, passing through Iringa, Dodoma, Arusia [*sic*] and Kisumu to Lusaka. We travelled day and night except during meal times. From Lusaka we were taken back to our home districts by war trucks. While in Lusaka, the Governor . . . entertained us with local beer, each of us being given just a tumblerful of it. A cow was also slaughtered to provide meat for the victorious soldiers.[23]

Not all reached home as scheduled. Those who came from remote villages were marooned on the way because of transport problems. For instance, after leaving Lusaka, the journey of a group of ex-servicemen returning to Namwala, in the Southern Province, was delayed in Pemba, where they needed to board other lorries to take them to their villages. But the lorry service from Pemba to Namwala only ran weekly on Tuesdays. This delay caused the askaris to complain that the three-day food rations issued by the military were insufficient to cover the time taken by the journey.[24] This problem was only solved, after repeated complaints from the men, when local administrators engaged Messrs Cavadia and Nephews to run an additional truck service on Fridays and on any other day on which at least twelve ex-servicemen were waiting to be repatriated. Government officials feared that the more time the men spent at Pemba, the more they would wander around in nearby villages and waste their money on beer and women.[25]

Many soldiers returning home had not seen their families for several years. There is an emotional edge to most ex-servicemen's memories. Speaking in 1989, Joseph Chinama Mulenga had the following to say about his return to his village home:

> It was common to see those who had lost their wives to others in the villages, including their children who they had left behind to roam about. This was so because there was a general belief with

fear that those who had gone to war may not return. A few spouses with strong love ties of mind stayed waiting for the day when their beloved, long gone husbands would return. Others through anxiety bore children from other men contrary to tradition.[26]

Returning home was often a difficult time for ex-servicemen. Army life, the exposure to new ideas, and such skills as training, cuisine, health, hygiene, and the experience of warfare had changed soldiers' perspectives and expectations. Wives had changed, grown older, and become detached. More broadly, gender roles, too, had changed, as women had often acquired greater power and autonomy in their household in the absence of their men. Children had also grown up and asserted a greater degree of independence from their parents. Families had suffered from the long years of separation. While visiting servicemen in Madagascar, Harry Franklin, the territory's information officer, reported that the men's most vociferous complaints concerned the misbehavior of wives at home, how they took the askari's money, committed adultery with villagers and, worst of all, in some cases actually married other men.[27] These concerns, of course, were not unique to Northern Rhodesia or even limited to the Second World War, since they had long informed the social life of labor migrants.[28] Some ex-soldiers found their worst fears confirmed, though if such extramarital unions had not produced any children, information about them could remain confined to the shady domain of rumor and suspicion. On this subject, the district commissioner for Broken Hill reported in 1943 that "at present, the average soldier regards villagers with contempt and dislike—largely, I think, because the villagers interfere with their wives."[29] But some servicemen themselves had also been involved in illicit sexual encounters while away, and some of them returned home with venereal infections.[30]

Disillusionment over monetary entitlements, housing, and employment prospects made the business of resuming domestic life even more difficult.[31] Resettlement and reabsorption required men to go back to their homes and, where possible, resume their preenlistment occupations. At the same time, the scheme devised by the colonial state included provision for training and work for about five hundred men in order to utilize the skills they had acquired while in the army. Officials had some idea of the expectations of literate soldiers, but there was a general anxiety that they might be well beyond what could be offered by the strained postwar colonial economy.[32]

Demobilization and the Great Disappointment of War Service

POSTWAR EMPLOYMENT, REWARDS, AND BENEFITS

Apart from having to suffer the patronizing overtones of the speeches by government officials on their return home,[33] African servicemen did not receive the same postwar treatment as their white counterparts. On their discharge from the armed forces, Northern Rhodesian European ex-servicemen reported either in person or in writing to the director of manpower in Broken Hill to seek government's help in securing employment. This applied to both European ex-servicemen who were resuming their former occupations and those who had new employment opportunities waiting for them after the war. The director of manpower was obliged to advise the ex-servicemen on the question of reemployment and to put such applicants in touch with local reinstatement committees. The director of manpower paid the cost of maintenance for discharged soldiers while they waited to be employed as well as the cost of rail fares, incidental traveling expenses, and subsistence allowances during unavoidable periods of unemployment, pending their reabsorption into civilian life.[34] This process was decentralized to districts, where these functions were performed by reinstatement committees set up in Livingstone, Lusaka, Broken Hill, Ndola, Nkana, Luanshya, Mufulira, Chingola, Mazabuka, and Fort Jameson. In each case, the committee was under the chairmanship of the relevant district commissioner.

To formalize reabsorption into civil employment, the Legislative Council passed the Reinstatement in Civil Employment Ordinance in June 1945. This law made provision for the restoration in civil employment of European persons who, after 24 August 1939, were in full-time service in one of the armed forces of the Crown. The law empowered any person to whom the bill applied to make an application to his former employer for reemployment within a period of four weeks upon being released from the army, and to state the date on which one would be available for employment. On receipt of the application, the former employer became liable to reemploy the applicant at the first opportunity for a period of at least twenty-six weeks or as was reasonable and practicable.[35] Where the previous employment, however, was of fifty-two weeks' duration or longer, then the minimum period of reemployment was fifty-two weeks. It was considered unreasonable and impracticable for an employer to reengage an applicant if this could be done only by discharging someone who had been in his employment for a longer period than the applicant, or by refusing to employ some such other person who had applied for reinstatement.[36] In such a case, the employer's liability ceased if the applicant refused the offer of employment.

African servicemen also expected reasonable financial rewards at the end of the war for their contributions to the Allied war effort. As they arrived home, these expectations were seldom met, and many of them grew disillusioned. The promise of reward often features prominently in the reasons for enlistment in the Northern Rhodesia Regiment. Ex-serviceman Kadansa recalled that "our British officers were seriously promising that after the war a lot of money would be paid to surviving soldiers as a reward, and they would be given farms and good jobs. So we were all very happy and anxious to get to the battle-fields and start fighting."[37] Research in other parts of British Africa has shown that this phenomenon was not peculiar to Northern Rhodesia. A similar trend was noted in Botswana, Lesotho, Swaziland, South Africa, Ghana, Nyasaland, Nigeria, Kenya, and Uganda.[38] The fact that African servicemen expected financial and material rewards at the end of the war could be ascribed to deliberate misinformation, vague promises, misunderstandings, and rumors disseminated by recruiting government functionaries, traditional authorities and, in some instances, servicemen themselves. Early in 1945, for instance, "wild rumours as to elaborate houses to be built by government for returning soldiers and other imaginary benefits were circulating freely amongst soldiers on leave" in Mkushi district.[39] The provincial commissioner for the Northern Province, too, observed that the view that the servicemen would be "looked after" by the government in the postwar period was widespread in his area. There were reports that all askari would be pensioned for life and supported by government with grants toward any rehabilitation needs they would have.[40] A continuing complaint of ex-servicemen throughout British colonial Africa was that they did not receive such pensions as had been promised by British authorities. In reality, pensions specific to war service did not exist in the British Army or its colonial appendages.[41]

It is not possible to accurately calculate the amount of money each soldier took back home at the end of the war. Deferred savings (usually one-third of what was earned in the army but sometimes more than that), encouragements to save through the Post Office Savings Bank, and remittances to relatives at home for investment meant that prudent soldiers could count on a decent capital upon demobilization. That was the ideal situation. Most

Demobilization and the Great Disappointment of War Service

soldiers, however, were disappointed at the small amount of money they were paid in return for their absence and hard work.[42] Some soldiers came back with only a few pounds; others had enough to buy a bicycle, sewing machine, or clothing as an indication of their new status. Though money was spent quite quickly, only a minority appear to have squandered it all without tangible gain. Some invested it in cattle, farm implements, and home improvements and paid for brides.[43] When interviewed in 2011, ex-serviceman Simon J. Simwinga said he had saved part of his army pay through remittances sent to his mother. He had then used the money to start life afresh after the war, including marrying his wife.[44]

Soldiers, moreover, quickly realized that, as a result of wartime inflation, the money in their pockets had lost much of its value.[45] As one European member pointed out in the Legislative Council as early as 1941, Africans were suffering from a sharp rise in the cost of living. While the price of their maize had increased by only sixpence, farmers were now having to pay ten shillings for a blanket that had sold at five shillings before the outbreak of the war.[46] Additionally, there were shortages of many basic imported goods in the stores, especially food and clothing. The rate of inflation differed from place to place, with towns along the line of rail being hit harder than rural areas. In the urban centers of the Copperbelt and in Livingstone, Lusaka, and Broken Hill, where imported manufactured goods and foods were marketed, prices had increased by as much as 30 percent or more during the war years.[47] But inflation reached even remote areas and was reflected in the cost of consumer goods, livestock, and bride-price. Returning soldiers put slightly more money into circulation and thus inadvertently contributed further to the inflationary spiral as they competed for scarce goods to buy.

War gratuities had been set aside for African veterans who had served for at least six months before they were released, died, or were honorably discharged from the army. They were paid according to rank, as shown in table 6.1.

In addition, the men were allowed to keep part of the personal attire and equipment they had used in the army. These included one pair of boots or sandals, two pairs of shorts, two pairs of socks, two shirts, one jersey, one blanket, two towels, a coat, a kit bag, a clasp knife, and a spoon.[48] Those who served for at least six months in the army were also paid £2, with which to buy civilian clothing.[49]

TABLE 6.1. Gratuities paid to African servicemen of the Northern Rhodesia Regiment, 1939–45

Rank	Amount per month of service
Private	3 shillings and 6 pence
Corporal	4 shillings
Sergeant	4 shillings and 6 pence
Staff Sergeant	5 shillings
Warrant Officer II	5 shillings and 6 pence
Warrant Officer I	6 shillings

Source: Mutende, no. 198 (August 1945).

On leaving the theaters of war, the men submitted their paybooks to military authorities for the computation of their final deferred pay and gratuity. The nominal rolls containing final pay balances were then sent from Pay Corps Headquarters in Nairobi to the Army Pay Office in Lusaka, where, in conjunction with the local Records Office, they calculated a man's gratuity.[50] These amounts and nominal rolls were in turn sent to the postmaster-general in Livingstone for the preparation of the men's Post Office Savings Bank (POSB) accounts. The POSB books were then sent to dispersal centers in the districts from which the ex-servicemen finally received their dues. The calculation of deferred pay and gratuity included deductions of any fines incurred while serving in the army. An unmarried private earned one shilling sixpence per day, while a married private was paid two shillings threepence per day, of which nine shillings was deducted as deferred pay for both classes of soldiers. The system of deferred pay was widely misunderstood during and after the war, leading to confusion and suspicion.

The scheme of saving through the Post Office was not successful in inducing savings during the war, though it was the only method of handling a man's deferred pay. Typically, soldiers withdrew all their money as soon as they could. In line with imperial paternalism, the administration worried about men squandering their money, but there was very little that could be done to prevent it. The district commissioner for Mkushi noted this problem in February 1946, since out of a total of £1,468.6 paid in service benefits to veterans in his district, only £748 had been deposited in savings bank

Demobilization and the Great Disappointment of War Service

accounts. He reported that "there is a great reluctance to save money and without a considerable amount of persuasion I doubt it if anyone would save a penny of their benefits. . . . I know of one msikari [plural = askari] who deposited a good proportion of his money at Mkushi and then went straight into Broken Hill and withdrew all of it again within a few days."[51] Even those who had saved part of their payments with the Post Office soon went back and withdrew part, if not all, of what they had left behind. This problem was universal. In Mankoya district, government officials went to the extent of trying to limit the amount each returning serviceman could withdraw from the savings bank on arrival at the dispersal center. Reports from other African countries show that the experience was the same, as men withdrew money from their bank accounts almost as soon as they were opened.[52]

The scale of pay and gratuities offers the most easily measurable index of the inequality between African and European soldiers. Unlike African servicemen, European officers and other ranks were entitled to the following "Release Benefits":

1. Six days' pay and ration allowance in the case of General Releases Class "A." Men released under Classes "B" and "C," however, were granted twenty-one days' pay and ration allowance,

2. Overseas service benefits at the rate of one day's pay for each month served "overseas." This required the individual to have served "overseas" for not less than six months. For this purpose, service in British or Italian Somaliland, Abyssinia, or Southeast Asia was regarded as service overseas,

3. £15 for civilian clothes. In addition, certain items and army clothing were retained by the men.[53]

4. War gratuity at the rates given in table 6.2 for every month of service.

These payments were made by the army base paymaster in Lusaka by check to the individual officer and soldier, or to his bank account. Measures were also taken to compensate apprentices who had served in the armed forces before completing their terms of apprenticeship.

Another major demand made by African servicemen both during and after the war concerned the allocation of land on which to establish farms.

TABLE 6.2. Gratuities paid to European servicemen of the Northern Rhodesia Regiment, 1939–45

Rank	Amount per month of service
Private	10 shillings
Lance Corporal	10 shillings
Corporal	12 shillings
Lance Sergeant	12 shillings
Sergeant	14 shillings
Staff Sergeant	16 shillings
Warrant Officer II	18 shillings
Warrant Officer I	20 shillings
Second Lieutenant	25 shillings
Lieutenant	30 shillings
Captain	35 shillings
Major	40 shillings
Lieutenant Colonel	45 shillings
Colonel	50 shillings
Brigadier	55 shillings

Source: NRG, *Notes on Demobilisation: Benefits, Rehabilitation, Procedure, etc., for Persons of Northern Rhodesian Origin Serving in the Armed Forces* (Lusaka: Government Printer, 1945), 2.

This was the preferred occupation for most servicemen when asked what they wanted to do after the war. The district commissioner for Chingola reported in 1943 that, "undoubtedly, the common topic of conversation among askari on post war settlement is land and housing. Many of them have expressed strongly their desire to have a plot of land, for leasehold which they will pay rent to the Government."[54]

While serving in the army, some servicemen began to ask colonial authorities about the possible provision of land in the postwar period. A typical example is that of Private Alfred Hezekiah, who wanted to acquire a farm in Mazabuka district. While serving in the South East Asia Command, Hezekiah wrote: "I have the honour to ask you, the price of the farm [*sic*] and its tax in

Demobilization and the Great Disappointment of War Service

a year according to the N[orthern] R[hodesia] law. I want to buy a farm [on] which I can live with my mother and my wife too."[55] In reply to this request, the chief secretary stated there were no farms yet set aside for African troops.[56] Although the Native Land Tenure Committee had earlier recommended that land in certain parts of the country be reserved for returning African soldiers, the government had refused to do so.[57] Instead, such tracts of land as *were* set aside in parts of Central and Southern Provinces were intended for European ex-servicemen. This was similar to the Kenya land resettlement scheme initiated after the First World War.[58] While the aim of the Kenyan scheme, involving over two million acres of land, had been to boost the number of new white settlers in Kenya, the main intention of the Northern Rhodesian government was rather to draw (or draw back) existing European residents to farming.

On the one hand, a loan scheme was prepared with a view to assisting European farmers who wanted to resume farming operations after having spent time in the armed forces. Loans were administered by a committee chaired by the director of agriculture. Conditions under which loans were granted were as follows:

1. The applicant was required to satisfy the committee that his financial resources were insufficient to enable him to take the necessary measures for getting his farm into production again.
2. The maximum loan granted to an individual was £1,000.
3. Loans were interest-free.
4. Repayment of loans would start after the third year of farming. Thereafter, repayment was at the discretion of the committee, subject to full repayment being completed within a maximum period of fifteen years.
5. Loans granted were for the purchase of equipment, stock, and farming requisites, the payment of labor, the erection of buildings, and repairs to existing ones. Loans granted could not be used for the purchase of new land.[59]

On the other hand, Crown land measuring 3,407 square miles was set aside in the area between Livingstone and Broken Hill districts for the settlement of European ex-servicemen who wanted to go into farming. In order to encourage new settlement by this category of Europeans, the Land Board made advances of initial capital on the following conditions:

1. Applicants were required to have in their possession a minimum capital of £500.
2. The maximum loan granted was £2,500, or such lesser sum as was necessary to bring the applicant's total capital up to £3,000. But where the applicant already possessed capital in excess of £1,500, the maximum loan was £1,500.
3. Interest on unredeemed portions of loans was charged at the rate of 4 percent per annum.
4. Interest on loans was waived for the first three years from the date of issue of the first portion of a loan.[60]

Applications could be made within one year from the date of the applicant's discharge from the army. Additionally, a monthly training allowance was paid to the new farmers at the following rates: unmarried men £5, married men £10 plus £3 for the first and £2 for each subsequent child.[61] Furthermore, to qualify for these benefits, an applicant was required to have either

1. been resident in Northern Rhodesia at the time he joined the Forces, or
2. joined the Forces within three months of having ceased to be resident in Northern Rhodesia, or
3. been resident in Northern Rhodesia for at least eighteen months during the three years immediately prior to joining the Forces.[62]

These schemes were primarily designed for the growing of Turkish tobacco, whose production had fallen in the Middle East and the Balkan states due to war conditions. Northern Rhodesia was one of the alternative suppliers identified by the United States because of its long history of tobacco growing.[63] In 1951, the Land Board demarcated 145 farms measuring 2,000–6,000 acres in the Mkushi farming block; 15 of these were occupied in the same year.[64] There were also many applicants for land from South African ex-servicemen, most of whom were attracted by the possibility of making money quickly from tobacco growing.[65]

African ex-servicemen also faced challenges with medical care when they left the army. As noted by Timothy Parsons, governments invested heavily in the means of waging war, but tended to consider impaired former African

Demobilization and the Great Disappointment of War Service

servicemen as expendable and disposable.[66] Those who were sick, wounded, or maimed due to military service found it very difficult to find work in the postwar period. A few soldiers never recovered from the psychological effects of war, but provisions for their needs were minimal. Physical wounds were relatively easy to identify; mental scars were not—so that some ex-soldiers who were traumatized by their war experiences received neither pensions nor gratuities for such ailments. It seems certain that significant numbers of African servicemen suffered debilitating combat- or disease-induced mental illnesses, such as schizophrenia, hysteria, and psychological trauma, as was observed in Kenya.[67] Maimed soldiers feared that they might not be able to work again. Such men included Chombola, whom we met at the beginning of this chapter. When he made his fears known about returning home as a physically handicapped person, his superior assured him of government support. He reported that

> my Commanding Officer told me do not worry because of this lame, you can see some of your colleagues have lost their arms some their legs and some have died. Do not worry of this lame, when you get home you will be rewarded by the Government. . . . But after [the war] all these promises became a night dream which never came true.[68]

As it happens, physically maimed soldiers did obtain pensions specific to their war service and were in fact the only category of ex-servicemen to be granted such privilege. Physically handicapped ex-soldiers received *ex-gratia* payments from the government, but the amount was insufficient to sustain their livelihoods, considering the high cost of living in the postwar period. Each of them was paid nine shillings and fourpence per month in accordance with government Notices no. 167 of 1940 and no. 254 of 1942. One such beneficiary was Private Levi Ngangula, of Broken Hill district, who was blinded in action in Abyssinia in April 1941. So small was this pension that the District After-Care Committee in Broken Hill provided him with an additional 10 shillings and eightpence each month in order to cushion his suffering.[69]

Viewing African ex-servicemen as cheap and expendable, colonial governments believed their only obligation to them in terms of rehabilitation and compensation was to provide them with the basic means with which to function as patriarchal household heads in subsistence rural societies.[70] They made no special provision for the medical care of disabled African veterans in urban hospitals. As the total number was only thirty-seven, the government felt that there was no need to make special arrangements for the resettlement and rehabilitation of soldiers categorized as medically unfit. Colonial authorities assumed that the ultimate cost of caring for impaired ex-servicemen would be borne by their larger ethnic communities. They expected African women in their home villages to take primary responsibility for mitigating the disabilities of their husbands and kinsmen.[71] By placing the responsibility of care on wives, mothers, and other female kinsmen, postwar efforts reveal the highly gendered nature of African military service, in general, and rehabilitation, in particular. A committee set up to investigate and report on this problem concluded that treatment could be provided within the framework of existing health institutions.[72]

Even at this level, racial disparities were obvious. Unlike Africans, discharged European soldiers with at least twelve months' service were entitled to receive free treatment at Northern Rhodesian government hospitals for any medical or surgical condition for one year from the date of discharge.[73] This concession, however, did not include the cost of transport to and from the hospital, nor did it apply to accidents covered by the Workmen's Compensation Ordinance or other forms of insurance. To qualify for the scheme, an officer or soldier had to submit an application to the director of medical services within six months of discharge from the army, providing evidence that he was eligible for the concession.

Another scheme devised to help European ex-servicemen reintegrate into civil life was educational assistance. This was designed to assist, by means of grants or loans, former military personnel whose university studies had been interrupted by the war or who wished to take up such studies for the first time.[74] Those interested were encouraged to contact the director of European education at Mazabuka in order to collect an application form. A maximum grant of £80 could be supplemented by an interest-free loan not exceeding £150 per annum.[75] All loans paid out were to be repayable over a period of fifteen years, with repayments commencing two years after the completion of the university course undertaken. Consideration was also given to aid applicants who wished to study at any institution of their choice other than a university.

Demobilization and the Great Disappointment of War Service

The greatest headache for the colonial administration, however, was the demand for employment by the newly released African servicemen, many of whom had learned a trade in the army. While the military was responsible for demobilizing the men, the Department of Labour was charged with the responsibility of finding work for some of them. While serving in the army, African servicemen had been warned that there would not be enough jobs available for all of them upon demobilization. This did not reduce their expectations, though. Former servicemen argued that they ought to be rewarded for their wartime service with jobs. The low level of economic development in the country during the war and in the immediate postwar period meant there were simply not enough jobs to meet the demand.[76] The most difficult to satisfy were those who had been recruited from among the literate sections of the population, and those who had acquired trades in the army. Ex-servicemen returned home with high expectations of economic opportunity and social advancement, often to be cruelly disillusioned.[77] Nor were men keen on remaining in the army. When asked to return to military positions in the postwar period, most men of the NRR 2nd, 4th, and 5th Battalions vehemently declined the offer. The chief secretary to the government reported that "roars of laughter greeted the suggestion that anybody might stay in the army."[78] Working for the army was now looked down upon.

Several men who had learned trades in the army hoped to find equivalent jobs in civil life. Signalers looked to the Post Office; pioneers to the Public Works Department; tradesmen such as blacksmiths, carpenters, and drivers to the copper mines and Rhodesia Railways. Skilled and semiskilled ex-servicemen were not interested in settling down in their villages, but wanted jobs in the urban centers. Similarly, in French West Africa, veterans had no desire to return to villages where they would be subordinate to elders and, in many cases, to former masters. They hoped to stay in the cities or go to other places where they could sell their labor.[79] In fact, up to one in every three conscripts in French West Africa never returned to their rural homes.[80] Unlike in the Gold Coast, where ex-servicemen with primary education and a trade generally found satisfactory employment,[81] the situation in Northern Rhodesia was dire. Even ex-soldiers with Class I proficiency, such as drivers, signalers, and medical orderlies, struggled to find suitable jobs. Northern Rhodesia had 1,473 men who had been trained as drivers, 270 as nursing orderlies, and 263 in other trades.[82] The Northern Rhodesian economy lacked

159

the capacity to absorb this large pool of qualified drivers and other trades-men. At the time, there were few secondary industries with openings for the skilled tradesmen who came back from the war. This situation, however, was not unique to Northern Rhodesia. In Nyasaland, for example, it was esti-mated that, upon demobilization in 1945, the colony would have to find jobs for about 4,000 army drivers and other veterans who had built up wartime skills in medical, clerical, and educational roles.[83]

Once demobilized, ex-servicemen hoped to receive income commensu-rate with the new skills and experience they had gained within the ranks. Many had high expectations of what they would be able to do after the war. The majority were dismayed to find that jobs were just not available or, if they were, to be told that they were not well qualified for them. When ex-servicemen refused to accept the jobs they were offered and demanded higher pay than other workers or complained excessively, they soon exhausted pub-lic sympathy and patience.[84] The press accused this class of ex-servicemen of suffering from a superiority complex or being infected with the "Burma Complex."[85] This problem was probably very common, as Timothy Staple-ton observed a similar trend in neighboring Southern Rhodesia.[86]

Returned servicemen developed a dislike for manual labor. Many of them preferred to be employed in supervisory positions, especially those who were literate or skilled. This category was far less willing to return to their prewar work or economic condition. In the Barotse Province, for instance, it was reported in 1946 that "the msikhari [sic] is at the moment mostly inter-ested in an easy job of the capitao [foreman] kind, and would rather loaf in the village than handle a pick and shovel."[87] Opportunities for the types of relatively more prestigious and better-paid work expected by veterans were rare: as Stapleton demonstrates, Africans tended to retain these jobs, and em-ployers did not want to discharge an experienced person to hire an unknown former soldier.[88] The low numbers of ex-servicemen who were reemployed in civilian supervisory, skilled, or semiskilled positions reflected the levels of unemployment among Africans in the country. Owing to the territory-wide implementation of the color-bar policy, especially in the mining industry, the single major employer, not many Africans could be employed in the higher classes.[89]

Other employers argued that ex-servicemen were not employable due to inadequate training in the army. For instance, Major J. E. Kitchin, a

Demobilization and the Great Disappointment of War Service

transporter with Smith and Kitchin Company, thought that the ordinary ex-army driver had not been prepared by his army training to undertake efficiently the duties of a civilian transport driver. His firm could not employ many returned drivers because

> the ex-Army driver, although a good driver and able to carry out routine maintenance on a vehicle was used to driving in convoy or to having ready assistance from a breakdown vehicle and probably from a British N.C.O., should trouble occur. The commercial driver must be self-reliant when it came to repairs to his vehicle, especially when on his own, on the road.[90]

Ex-servicemen who had received occupational training in the army as drivers and artisans found that military standards of proficiency often did not prepare them to carry on the same occupation in civilian life. As Hamilton S. Simelane has noted in his work on Swazi veterans, the army was simply a war machine, and its educational functions were limited to those necessary to accomplish that single task.[91]

Government departments which were expected to give ex-servicemen preference in filling appointments also had reservations about engaging them. The Post Office, for instance, was expected to employ all ex-army signalers. The assumption was that military training had given the servicemen new skills. The postmaster general, however, noted that not all men could be taken on, not only because of insufficient openings for postal clerks in the system, but also because of incompatibility between the military signalers' training and that offered at the Postal Training School in Livingstone. For a start, the postal system employed twenty-five men, representing 25 percent of the total number of Northern Rhodesian Africans who had qualified as signalers in the army. It was noted that the signalers' course offered in Nairobi was designed solely for military requirements, as its syllabus dealt with military signaling procedure, heliograph and flags, and lighting, all of which were useless for Post Office requirements.[92] Furthermore, the signalers' military requirements did not call for training in accounts, counter duties, Post Office procedures, and rules and regulations which formed an indispensable part of a postal clerk's training.[93] There were also reservations in the Department of Health concerning the employment of medical assistants, sanitary assistants, and nursing orderlies who had served in the military. This was due to inadequate training offered by the military. The director of medical services noted that the qualifications of former medical personnel in the army were of very low standard. He could not expect any worthy position in his department to be occupied by former army medical staff unless such officers underwent further training.[94]

Ex-servicemen who did not find work often became destitute. Anwell Siame, who had served in the Northern Rhodesia Regiment as a medical orderly, despaired of finding employment after the war. When interviewed in August 1989, he said, "I wanted to hang myself simply because I had no chance of going back to school, no where to get money to support my family and since I had no education qualifications I had no were [sic] to find employment, so I joined the world of starvation."[95] Such stories proliferated, as gratuities and savings ran out and the probability of finding work shrank by the day.

THE POLITICAL ROLE OF AFRICAN EX-SERVICEMEN

Many early Africanist historians stressed the important role of African ex-servicemen in postwar nationalist politics,[96] but the evidence for this is thin on the ground. This debate emerged particularly strongly in the West African context, where the involvement of ex-servicemen in the Gold Coast disturbances of 1948 was regarded as a key moment in the rise of nationalist sentiment. Recent research presents a different view—that ex-servicemen as a group were no more significant in territorial politics than any other occupational group. Scholars have thus challenged the idea that the impact of returning African soldiers was of great significance for the rise of nationalism.[97] With a few exceptions, military service does not seem to have transformed servicemen in Northern Rhodesia into politically active citizens with a new national, or nationalist, outlook. As one European soldier observed during war service in Asia, the worldview of African soldiers was merely broadened, rather than revolutionized.[98] The same witness, Captain Johnstone, regarded "as fantastic any suggestion that the returned African soldier will clamour for the franchise—he is not in the least interested in such matters." On their return from the war, either through discharge or demobilization, African ex-servicemen did not organize themselves into a political movement calling for the end of colonial rule. Many of them remained politically aloof, seemingly loyal to British colonial rule and valuing the war medals awarded

Demobilization and the Great Disappointment of War Service

to them at the end of the fighting. In a statement about the Gold Coast which might equally apply to Northern Rhodesia, David Killingray observed that "without doubt military service, particularly overseas, helped extend the political and economic understanding of individual soldiers. A number of men undoubtedly returned home with a wider knowledge of the world, and a determination to translate their new perceptions into social and political action. However, military service alone did not mean that the soldiers developed a deeper understanding of politics."[99]

This chapter endorses the above conclusions for Northern Rhodesia. That ex-servicemen from Northern Rhodesia did not participate, collectively at least, in the rise of nationalism in the country cannot be wholly accounted for by pointing to their overall numbers. While this explanation may suffice for colonial Zimbabwe, which contributed a mere 2,000 soldiers,[100] it cannot do for every African colonial territory. This is because even in colonies where the ratio of servicemen to the general population was much higher, their large numbers did not necessarily make them amenable to nationalist politics in the immediate postwar period.[101] Individual self-improvement and development were very much the order of the day. These had to do with the search for jobs, better living standards, and survival in general. Joanna Lewis has made similar observations about Kenya, whose ex-servicemen were also more concerned with everyday issues than with nationalist politics, furthermore, the experience of being in military service often had a conservative effect on individuals.[102] Upon their return, few of the men desired great change or, if they did, did not do much to initiate it. They wanted to be left alone to pursue their lives, imagining prosperous futures within the bounds of traditional avenues of self-enrichment and advancement. It is not obvious that the war made Africans question colonial rule or the rule of chiefs through which it was mediated. As in Bechuanaland, so too for Northern Rhodesia, after up to five years of unbroken military service, most men were simply overjoyed to return to their homes and resume civilian life again.[103]

In Northern Rhodesia, as in Uganda, nationalist politics developed on the home front, and were not a development initiated by the return and subsequent frustration of ex-servicemen. The history of nationalism in the country predates the onset of the war. It stemmed from the formation of welfare societies and trade unions. The first welfare society for Africans in Northern Rhodesia was formed by African mission-educated elites in 1912 at Mwenzo.[104]

During the next few years, a number of welfare societies were formed in other rural districts, although these turned into social clubs without any political aims. Between 1929 and 1931, more welfare societies were formed in several towns along the line of rail. These were more purposeful than the previous ones. Like others before, they were confined to small groups of the educated class, that is, clerks and teachers, among whom Livingstonia Mission graduates were prominent.[105] But the welfare societies made important efforts to protect the interests of ordinary people, and it was easier to do this in towns than in the sparsely populated countryside. According to a leading nationalist and member of the Mwenzo Welfare Society, Kapasa Makasa, discussions in the meetings of the society in the late 1940s and the 1950s centered on the need to sensitize Africans regarding the exploitation they had been subjected to in the First and Second World Wars. As he explained,

> promises that were made when recruiting Africans were never fulfilled. Fortunately, some of the war veterans who had survived the wars attended these meetings. It was easy for us to point to one of the ex-service men at the rally and compare his poverty-riddled existence with his European counterpart. We did not fail to expose the discrimination and slave-like conditions under which the Africans laboured in the two wars. Apart from earning starvation wages as compared to European soldiers, African *askaris* . . . could not be offered employment or any other benefits which their white counterparts enjoyed on their return.[106]

This was how some ex-servicemen joined the struggle for independence in the country. African trade unions emerged after the war, but their history goes as far back as the first mine workers' strike in 1935.[107] The first political party for Africans in Northern Rhodesia was formed in 1948, following the transformation of the Federation of Welfare Societies into the Northern Rhodesia African Congress (NRAC). It was led by Godwin Mbikusita-Lewanika, an aristocrat from Barotseland.

Oral evidence supports the argument that, rather than initiating nationalist politics, ex-servicemen in Northern Rhodesia simply jumped on the already moving bandwagon of the struggle for political independence. On their return home, ex-servicemen found nationalist politics already in motion. As Mulenga put it,

Demobilization and the Great Disappointment of War Service

by and large, we *found* the situation back home, in urban areas different. There *was* a different struggle going on—a political one, which was perceptively new to us war veterans. I, like many others, through understanding certain implications had no choice but to toil [*sic*] the line *to support* the political will. After the good things we had seen abroad; [the] dire need to see change [at home] was aflame [emphasis mine].[108]

This testimony is corroborated by Makasa, who stated that

we [nationalists] reminded them [ex-servicemen] that they were bundled and pushed into these wars just because they were colonial subjects. We made it doubly sure that these points got rubbed into their heads and that they would understand the evils and disadvantages of colonialism. We called upon them to join the political struggle in order to break the chains of colonialism.[109]

Additionally, the impact of the war on the Northern Rhodesian home front was not as great as in parts of East and West Africa. The war did not precipitate widespread discontent in Northern Rhodesia that was later transformed into resistance to colonial rule. Undeniably, the war brought economic and social hardships to ordinary people, as has been demonstrated in previous chapters in this book. But compared to the huge labor demands made on other British colonies such as Nigeria, Sudan, and the Gold Coast, and the scarcity of goods which these territories experienced, the war's impact on Northern Rhodesia was undoubtedly lighter. As Ashley Jackson has suggested, part of the solution to the mystery about why returning ex-servicemen played little part in postwar political developments must lie in the fact that the majority of them, despite numerous grievances, were content enough to return to the life they had lived before the war.[110]

Rather, ex-servicemen directed their frustration toward their traditional leadership. This was primarily because the same authorities had helped recruit many of them for military service and because the government's failure to fulfil the "promises" made to them during enlistment fell on chiefs. Some of the veterans rejected local social structures, although this sometimes took an implicit form. As many ex-servicemen returned to their rural homes, some exercised a significant political role in challenging the authority of chiefs and questioning accepted ideas and practices. "Truculent" behavior by servicemen toward civilians was also reported from early on in the war, and, later, there were also reports of assaults on civilians.[111] Others made more direct attacks on "unprogressive" traditional authorities. Partly as a result of their exemption from the *indigénat*, the harsh penal code applying to France's *sujets* in West Africa, when tens of thousands of *tirailleurs* (riflemen) returned to West Africa following armistice, the demobilization was contentious and chaotic, and weakened the authority of chiefs.[112] There is much evidence that wartime experiences caused soldiers to question the structures of traditional authority in Northern Rhodesia, rather than the colonial establishment itself.[113] Such veterans rapidly emerged as a self-styled elite whose worldly experience, access to consumer goods, and command of European languages gave them a new status.[114] Elizabeth Schmidt made similar observations regarding former tirailleurs in Guinea.[115] The stress caused by the circumstances of prolonged overseas service, and particularly the social anxieties caused by the men's separation from their wives and families, created tensions in relation to traditional leadership, as soldiers questioned the efficacy of chiefs' management of their family affairs in their absence.

War service had a telling effect on the lives of African servicemen, and in a way intensified the contradictions of imperialism. For the first time in their lives, the men had been to East Africa, the Middle East, Palestine, India, Burma, Madagascar, and Ceylon. Their travels widened their experiences more than during the Great War, when they had fought in neighboring East Africa and met conditions similar to those obtaining at home.[116] The men had fought on equal terms against white-skinned Italians and had no great opinion of them. This resonated especially strongly with servicemen for whom the mystique of white superiority fell victim to the brutality they saw Europeans inflict upon each other.[117] As one European officer from the NRR observed, "as Bwanas [masters], they [Italians] failed to fit into the picture. This was a source of great puzzlement, and frequent questions for their European colleagues. The explanation that there are [different] 'mitundu' [types] of white men too still leaves heads shaking."[118] In Ceylon, men from the NRR fought side by side with British Tommies. Describing one of them, a NRR officer noted that

> this was a white man who rode third class in the trains, was found
> to brawl in the streets, did manual chores and above all did not

> consider himself, still less proclaim himself to be, a superior race. On the contrary, British Tommies are friendly egalitarians and amiable standers of drinks. These are clearly not 'Bwanas' [Masters] – they are never called anything but 'Azungu' [whites].[119]

As pointed out by Killingray, however, all of this does not mean that whites were viewed as superhuman beings by all Africans before the war.[120] To argue otherwise would do a disservice to the astuteness and experience of many Africans, some of whom had for a long time been interacting with whites in towns, mission stations, and other places both within and outside the country.

Serving in the army entailed experiences not dissimilar to those encountered by African migrant workers. Like labor migrants, service in the army brought changes to the servicemen. One such effect was the transformation of race relations. Those African servicemen from Northern Rhodesia who served with the 5th Battalion in the Middle East as laborers mixed with British and other colonized people on equal terms. As they were not combatant troops and therefore, perhaps, not subject to such rigid discipline as existed in the other eight combatant battalions of the NRR, this was easier to undertake. The consequence of this situation was that, on occasion, servicemen mingled with communities surrounding their camps. Military camps have always served as a magnet for prostitutes and African encampments were no exception.[121] Some African servicemen frequented brothels used by European troops and had intercourse with white women. In spite of incessant efforts by military authorities to minimize contact between Africans and local white women in the various theaters of war, African servicemen and white women found each other at every opportunity.[122] A government official in Northern Rhodesia remarked, "Letters from these men to their friends in this country have been intercepted and have shown that the Africans are proud of having slept with white women."[123] Such sexual encounters were common in Italy, India, Burma, and north Africa whenever African servicemen were on leave and went to visit in town. The all-male military institution, long absence from wives and girlfriends, and confinement to encampments all encouraged a climate of sexual hunger and hope.[124] Moreover, the servicemen possessed money, which enticed the foreign women to engage in sexual relations with them. Sexual relations across the color line challenged racial concepts regarding the sanctity of white womanhood and the notions of white superiority upon which colonial rule was based.[125]

This chapter has examined how Northern Rhodesian ex-servicemen experienced home life after the Second World War, the problems they encountered, and the society into which they were reintegrated. For most African ex-servicemen, war service heightened their frustrations by raising expectations that the postwar Northern Rhodesian economy could not satisfy. Many African servicemen felt cheated by the workings of a blatantly racialized demobilization exercise. This made them restless and discontented compared to their European counterparts. Despite this, they remained concerned mainly with personal and domestic matters, such as the welfare of their family or how best to invest the limited funds made available to them in recognition of their services. Thus, the chapter refutes the notion that the altogether limited political role of war veterans in post–Second World War Africa was merely a result of their insignificant numbers. My argument is that what mainly constrained African ex-servicemen politically was their focus on immediate private welfare and survival in the new postwar society. It is, therefore, reasonable to conclude that the war was more vital in the social transformation of African servicemen than it was in the political sphere.

Conclusion

I N EXPLORING THE FULL SOCIOECONOMIC AND POLITICAL IMPACT of the Second World War on colonial Zambia, I have focused on a number of broad themes, all of which bring out the interconnectedness of international and local dynamics and events. I have done this by drawing on the toolkit of "war and society." This is because, from time immemorial, warfare has always had far-reaching social, economic, and political ramifications on society. For example, the need to mobilize material resources to execute a war has economic effects on belligerent citizens and governments. In the same vein, those who remain home also get hurt, not only in strictly economic terms, but also through strains on marriages and family relationships, mental disorders, and juvenile delinquency. Politically, war can lead to the defeat of authoritarian governments, the correction of injustices, and the rise of nationalism. Thanks to the adoption of this approach, I believe I have cast new light on the importance of the Second World War to the Zambian economy and state, even though local African servicemen did not invest their political agency in the rise of nationalism in the country.

The most visible way in which the war is remembered in Zambia today is through the cenotaph erected in the Ridgeway area of Lusaka. At an annual commemorative ceremony there on Remembrance Sunday in November, the state president leads members of the diplomatic corps, serving military personnel, veterans, and senior government officials in laying wreaths in honor of Zambians who died in the two world wars. Similar ceremonies are conducted in the various provincial capitals where other cenotaphs exist. The war is also remembered through naming the country's army barracks after places where the Northern Rhodesia Regiment (NRR) saw active war service.

Thus, the country's nine army barracks have the following names: Arakan, Burma, Chindwin, Kohima, Tug Argan, Taung Up, Gondar, Mawlaik, and Kalewa. These names are mainly from Asia, as well as some from the horn of Africa, where the NRR fought alongside Allied troops.

Colonial racism and pseudoscientific theories have been shown to have had a shaping influence on recruitment for the NRR, the theme of chapter 1. Racial characterizations informed colonial societies during the war, just as they did before, and would do, after it. "Martial race" theory adapted from nineteenth-century India shaped the recruitment of personnel for the army. From the late nineteenth century onward, local groups such as the Ila, Ngoni, and Bemba were considered the best soldierly material in the country. It was from these groups that the majority of servicemen in the NRR were drawn. Unlike the "martial race" par excellence, the Kamba of Kenya, whose skills had little to do with any particular cultural characteristic or precolonial military tradition, the aforementioned Northern Rhodesian peoples did have a long history of militarism.

Enlistment for military service in wartime, however, was also extended to "nonmartial" ethnic groups so as to mobilize the largest possible number of men. Although reliance on martial race theory was relaxed, recruitment parties still focused on the Eastern, Northern, and Southern Provinces, the traditional sources of military labor. Supposedly nonmartial groups such as the Chewa, Nsenga, and Kunda who lived near the martial Ngoni thus also featured prominently among NRR recruits. For such groups, military service was a source of income like any other form of employment. Some of these neighboring groups actually identified themselves as Ngoni, Ila, or Bemba simply to be employed by the army. By negotiating their way into the army in this way, ingenious individuals demonstrated that martial race identity was not wholly a colonial construct. This is reminiscent of what Cynthia Enloe calls the "Gurkha syndrome."[1]

Although the colonial government drew on the influence of chiefs and made use of propaganda material to reach potential recruits, Africans themselves did not play a purely passive role. Many of them were influenced by pull or push factors, such as the desire to seek employment and earn an income, the ambition to learn a trade and to prove their masculinity, or even the prestige of wearing a military uniform. This demonstrates that Africans had a perspective of their own on the conflict that should be acknowledged

Conclusion

and investigated by historians. The evidence which I have presented in this book points to the capacity of the majority of the local population to think for themselves and invent strategies to either counter or oppose the demands of colonial officials and traditional leaders.

Indeed, while some individuals and groups viewed military service as an opportunity, others actively opposed recruitment for the war effort. People refused to join the army for several reasons: religious beliefs, anti-British feelings, fear of dying on the frontline, inadequate remuneration, unfulfilled government promises made during the First World War, and indifference. Local Africans who did not want to be enlisted for war service used various strategies. Some went into temporary hiding in the bush when they learned of the presence of a recruiting party in their vicinity. Others, especially those living in outlying areas, simply crossed into neighboring territories for safety. For some, migrating to seek better employment opportunities in urban areas or neighboring countries was the only solution to avoid military service. This resistance, once again, shows the extent of African agency during the Second World War. More organized and ideologically motivated forms of resistance to the colony's war effort came from both the European and the African members of the Watch Tower movement and from the members of the Afrikaner community, who opposed Northern Rhodesia's participation in the war because they supported the Axis powers, many of them sympathizing with Nazi ideology.

The local economic consequences of the fall of the Allied nations' Southeast Asian colonies were examined in chapter 2. The loss of Southeast Asia ushered in a new period of metropolitan economic control and regulation, and stepped up the imperial extraction of natural resources such as rubber and beeswax from Northern Rhodesia. The colony also revitalized the iron-smelting and rope-making industries in order to fill the gap created by the lack of these commodities on the local market due to war conditions in Southeast Asia. My analysis, however, has also concluded that local rural industries were beset by many challenges, beginning with the low prices offered by the British Ministry of Supply for such produce. The predicament in which Britain found itself forced it to backtrack on earlier commitments: indeed, at the outbreak of the conflict, in an effort to win sympathy from its African subjects, Britain's propaganda campaign against Axis powers had stressed the need for a fair trade relationship between the metropole and the colonies. The attempt to revive local rural industries also exposed the difference in opinion between local colonial officials on the ground and imperial officials in London. Colonial administrators agitated for fairer prices for African produce in order to increase the production of commodities which were urgently required by the Allies. But these efforts did not bear fruit, as the Colonial Office continued to oppose the paying of economic prices, claiming that high costs could fuel the rate of inflation in the colony at a time when there were not many goods on which people could spend their income. The low prices hampered the quantities and quality of the commodities produced. For example, while hoes and axes started being produced in certain areas of the territory, the quantities churned out were so negligible that they could not meet local demand. This meant that the shortage of farming implements persisted.

Likewise, the war had a direct impact on the lives of ordinary people once the shortage of consumer commodities hit the country, as discussed in chapter 3. This shortage was caused by, among other factors, the lack of raw materials in the metropole for manufacturing goods, the unavailability of exports in the industrialized world, and German submarine warfare that sank Africa-bound cargo ships. Unscrupulous traders took advantage of the situation by resorting to hoarding, profiteering, and selling items on the black market. Echoing measures adopted in Britain, the colonial government tried to solve some of these challenges by embarking upon rationing and price controls. These policies were aimed at ensuring a fairer system for distributing goods. But, as I have argued, these austerity measures were difficult to implement for fear of riling the local people. Thus, the equality of sacrifice principle envisaged by the imperial government could not be attained. This was because metropolitan and peripheral conditions were very different insofar as the motivation for participating in the war was concerned. In the colonies, for example, consumption was reduced by consumer-goods price inflation as part of the experience of total war, whereas in the mother country, the government could hold out the promise of increased social consumption after the war in return for acquiescing in direct and immediate sacrifice in wartime.[2] This explains why the Northern Rhodesian government did its best to ensure that maize meal was made available to the local African population at affordable prices. The colonial government also introduced measures aimed at curbing the rate of inflation, such as issuing bonds and

Conclusion

encouraging people to save money. It further tried to regulate the prices of consumer goods by deploying price control mechanisms. This measure, however, yielded little success, as traders used other ingenious methods to evade being caught by state agents. All in all, it is clear that in wartime the colonial government came to play a more direct role in the Northern Rhodesian economy than it did previously.

Chapter 4 focused on a little-known way that the Northern Rhodesian home front was affected by the Second World War: the hosting of Polish refugees on behalf of imperial Britain. Following the prewar grant of a guarantee of protection to Poland, Britain was compelled to offer that country assistance if the Axis attacked it. When this eventually occurred, Britain relied on its vast colonial empire to save Polish souls, and Northern Rhodesia was no exception. However, the Polish refugees were ostracized by the host society mainly on racial lines. The major reason for discouraging the settlement of the Poles was to prevent the emergence of that "poor white" problem which was proving a source of great anxiety in many parts of the British Empire. As in the case of the recruitment of Northern Rhodesia Africans for the army, racial stereotyping based on colonial pseudoscientific theories determined the way that the Poles were treated in colonial Zambia.

Northern Rhodesia's major contribution to the Allied war effort, of course, concerned the provision of base metals—the subject of chapter 5. The colony was the single most important source of copper in the sterling area, a position which led the British Ministry of Supply to closely tie the colony to the British war economy. The British government bought the copper produced in the colony at a uniform price throughout the war period as a result of the closure of the London Metal Exchange at the beginning of hostilities in 1939. In accordance with economic warfare, the metal could not be sold to Axis powers or their agents. The outcome of this scenario was that war acted as a catalyst in changing the financial fortunes of the mining industry, the colony, and the region at large. Production of copper for the Allies, however, was threatened by such obstacles as industrial action six months into the war, high wartime taxation, and shortage of supplies.

The expansion and development of the mining industry affected the agricultural sector too, given the need to feed miners in order not to disrupt production. But Northern Rhodesia's agriculture was threatened by droughts and the shortage of farming implements under wartime restrictions. This situation prompted the imperial government to intervene in the acquisition of food stocks for the colony. Another measure was the resort to coerced African labor on European settler farms so that production could be maintained. This was in line with similar policies adopted elsewhere in the empire. The use of conscripted labor was against the ILO Convention of 1930, to which Britain was a signatory. Therefore, the decline in the moral standing of Britain during wartime was not limited to buying African products at below-market prices, but extended to labor conscription, too. It was another example of desperation on the part of Britain to win the war at whatever cost.

As the war drew to a close, the colonial administration was anxious about how ex-servicemen would be reabsorbed into civilian life. The evidence shows that most ex-servicemen were not going to return to their mainly rural homes unchanged. As with the recruitment process for the military, the structure of demobilization was also based on a system of racial hierarchy. Africans had been recruited into the NRR to help the imperial government based on the principle of togetherness or fraternity, but, at the end of the war, local servicemen were denied the same entitlements as their European counterparts on account of their race. European ex-servicemen received more favorable rewards from the state than their fellow African soldiers. The colonial government rewarded European servicemen for their participation in the war with land grants, higher gratuities, medical care, business and educational loans, and employment opportunities. On the other hand, the gratuities afforded to Africans were as much as three times less than those of Europeans. This situation, it must be added, was widespread throughout the empire, and not peculiar to Northern Rhodesia. Despite (or perhaps because of) this, African ex-servicemen concentrated on personal affairs, such as seeking employment and the general welfare of their families, rather than becoming active in the struggle for political independence. Thus, contrary to older academic arguments, I have contended that military service did not transform African servicemen into politically active citizens and ready-made nationalists. I further noted that the rise of nationalist politics went back to the prewar years. But the war itself did contribute to the growth of a politically versatile African voice, and some ex-servicemen at least contributed to politics at the grassroots level, where they vented their frustration with the demobilization exercise at their traditional leaders who had contributed to their being recruited into the army.

Conclusion

My contention throughout has been that it is only by means of in-depth case studies that a full appreciation of the lived experiences of Africans during the Second World War can be gained. Using previously unexplored archival materials and oral interviews, I have, for the first time, examined the main political, social, and economic dimensions of the Second World War in colonial Zambia. There is a strong relationship between the social, economic, and political processes set in motion by the Second World War and the dynamics which would eventually lead to the development of Zambian nationalism and statehood. A full "war and society" approach reveals the importance of the Second World War to the development of a new Zambian economy and state anchored on increased dollar earnings from copper exports, although local servicemen did not collectively invest their political agency in the country's nationalist politics. This brings into sharp relief the contradictoriness of political processes on the eve of decolonization on the continent: on the one hand, servicemen took part in the Second World War as imperial subjects; on the other, the momentous socioeconomic changes occasioned by the same conflict set Zambia on the path to autonomy and ultimately independence. The nuancing of the idea that the mobilization and demobilization of African servicemen contributed to pro-independence sentiment and organization is indeed one of the book's major historiographical contributions. Should this work persuade more central African specialists of the validity of "war and society" approaches, then my aim will have been accomplished.

Notes

INTRODUCTION

1. Martina Hjertman et al., "The Social Impacts of War: Agency and Everyday Life in the Borderland during the Early Seventeenth Century," *International Journal of History and Archaeology* 22 (2018): 241.

2. Hans Speier, "The Effects of War on the Social Order," *Annals of the American Academy of Political and Social Science* 218 (November 1941): 88.

3. Speier, 89.

4. Speier, 89.

5. Bill Nasson, *Abraham Esau's War: A Black South African War in the Cape, 1899–1902* (Cambridge: Cambridge University Press, 2008). See also Peter Warwick, *Black People and the South African War, 1899–1902* (Cambridge: Cambridge University Press, 1983).

6. V. Upeniece, "War and Society," *International Interdisciplinary Scientific Conference: Society. Health. Welfare* (2014): 1–5; available online at SHS Web of Conferences 30 (2016), doi: 10.1051/shsconf/20163000009.

7. Upeniece, 3.

8. Upeniece, 1.

9. Upeniece, 1.

10. Chama Mutemi Kadansa, interview with the British Broadcasting Corporation (BBC), Ndola, 17 July 1989.

11. Jeremy Black, *World War Two: A Military History* (London: Routledge, 2003), xiv. However, varying casualty figures exist, reflecting, in particular, very different estimates for Soviet and Chinese casualties.

12. An appropriate date for the beginning of the conflict in Europe is 1 September 1939, but in Asia, the parallel struggle arising from Japanese aggression and imperialism began with the invasion of Manchuria in 1931. For details, see Black, *World War Two*, 31–35. Furthermore, it could be argued that for Africans, the war actually started in 1935, when Italy conquered Abyssinia, which fascist forces later used as a base for the conquest of British Somaliland in mid-1940. See, for example, Gerhard L. Weinberg, *A World*

Notes to Pages 3–6

at Arms: A Global History of World War Two (Melbourne: Cambridge University Press, 1994), 503.

13. Ashley Jackson, "The Empire/Commonwealth and the Second World War," *Round Table* 100, no. 412 (February 2011): 67.

14. Jackson, 66. For a more detailed discussion regarding the role of the dominions in the war, see Andrew Stewart, *Empire Lost: Britain, the Dominions and the Second World War* (London: Continuum, 2008), especially chapters 2 and 3.

15. Jackson, "Empire/Commonwealth," 71.

16. Ashley Jackson, *The British Empire and the Second World War* (London: Hambledon Continuum, 2006), 180.

17. Jackson, "Empire/Commonwealth," 68.

18. Jackson, 68.

19. Black, *World War Two*, 56.

20. Kevin Shillington, *History of Africa* (London: Palgrave Macmillan, 2005), 279.

21. John D. Hargreaves, *Decolonization in Africa* (London: Routledge, 1996), 51.

22. John Keegan, *The Second World War* (London: Random House Books, 1989), 212; and Basil H. Liddell Hart, *History of the Second World War* (London: Cassell, 1970), 121–22.

23. Jackson, *British Empire*, 42.

24. See, for example, Ashley Jackson, *Botswana, 1939–1945: An African Country at War* (Oxford: Oxford University Press, 1999).

25. Northern Rhodesia became the independent nation of Zambia on 24 October 1964. Throughout this study, use is made of the colonial name.

26. Cited in Jackson, "Empire/Commonwealth," 66.

27. Judith A. Byfield, "Women, Race, and War: Political and Economic Crisis in Wartime Abeokuta (Nigeria)," in *Africa and World War II*, ed. Judith A. Byfield et al. (New York: Cambridge University Press, 2015), 147–65.

28. Chama Mutemi Kadansa, interview with the BBC, Ndola, 6 June 1989.

29. Lewis H. Gann, *A History of Northern Rhodesia: Early Days to 1953* (London: Chatto and Windus, 1964), 327–28.

30. Kadansa, interview, 6 June 1989.

31. Rabson Chombola, interview with the BBC, Ndola, 10 August 1989.

32. Chama Mutemi Kadansa, interview with the BBC, Ndola, 11 June 1989.

33. John Darwin, *Britain and Decolonisation: The Retreat from Empire in the Post-war World* (London: Palgrave, 1988), 48; and Jackson, *British Empire*, 43–52.

34. D. A. Low and John M. Lonsdale, "Towards the New Order, 1945–63," in *History of East Africa*, vol. 3, ed. D. A. Low and Alison Smith (London: Clarendon, 1976), 300.

35. Hargreaves, *Decolonization*, 52.

36. Nicholas J. Westcott, "The Impact of the Second World War on Tanganyika, 1939–49," in *Africa and the Second World War*, ed. David Killingray and Richard Rathbone (Basingstoke, UK: Palgrave Macmillan, 1986), 144.

37. Rosaleen Smyth, "War Propaganda during the Second World War in Northern Rhodesia," *African Affairs* 83, no. 332 (July 1984): 345.

Notes to Pages 7–9

38. Joseph Chinama Mulenga, interview with the BBC, Lusaka, 6 June 1989.

39. Gann, *History of Northern Rhodesia*, 327.

40. Jackson, *Botswana*, 123.

41. Jackson, *British Empire*, especially chapter 4.

42. Jackson, 43.

43. Jackson, 232.

44. Ashley Jackson, "Motivation and Mobilisation for War: Recruitment for the British Army in Bechuanaland Protectorate, 1941–1942," *African Affairs* 96 (1997): 400.

45. Michael Cowen and Nicholas Westcott, "British Imperial Economic Policy during the War," in Killingray and Rathbone, *Africa and the Second World War*, 20–67; Toyin Falola, "'Salt Is Gold': The Management of Salt Scarcity in Nigeria during World War II," *Canadian Journal of African Studies* 26, no. 2 (1992): 412–36; and Westcott, "Impact of the Second World War."

46. John Lonsdale, "The Depression and the Second World War in the Transformation of Kenya," in Killingray and Rathbone, *Africa and the Second World War*, 97–142.

47. Brian Mokopakgosi, "The Impact of the Second World War: The Case of the Kweneng in the Then Bechuanaland Protectorate, 1939–1950," in Killingray and Rathbone, *Africa and the Second World War*, 160–80; and Hoyini K. Bhila, "The Impact of the Second World War on the Development of Peasant Agriculture in Botswana, 1939–1956," *Botswana Notes and Records* 16 (1984): 63–71.

48. Bhila, "Impact of the Second World War," 63.

49. Timothy Stapleton, *African Police and Soldiers in Colonial Zimbabwe* (Rochester, NY: University of Rochester Press, 2011); David Killingray, "Military and Labour Recruitment in the Gold Coast during the Second World War," *Journal of African History* 23, no. 1 (1982): 83–95; Jackson, "Motivation and Mobilization for War"; Ashley Jackson, "Bad Chiefs and Sub-tribes: Aspects of Recruitment for the British Army in Bechuanaland Protectorate, 1941–42," *Botswana Notes and Records* 28 (1996): 87–96; Albert Grundlingh, "The King's Afrikaners?: Enlistment and Ethnic Identity in the Union of South Africa's Defence Force during the Second World War," *Journal of African History* 40 (1999): 351–65; Louis W. F. Grundlingh, "The Recruitment of South African Blacks for Participation in the Second World War," in Killingray and Rathbone, *Africa and the Second World War*, 181–203; Louis W. F. Grundlingh, "'Non-Europeans Should Be Kept Away from the Temptations of Towns': Controlling Black South Africans during the Second World War," *International Journal of African Historical Studies* 25, no. 3 (1992): 539–60; Hamilton Sipho Simelane, "Labor Mobilization for the War Effort in Swaziland, 1940–1942," *International Journal of African Historical Studies* 26, no. 3 (1993): 541–74; and Mary Nambulelo Ntabeni, "Military Labour Mobilisation in Colonial Lesotho during World War II, 1940–1943," *Scientia Militaria: South African Journal of Military Studies* 36, no. 2 (2008): 36–59.

50. Allister E. Hinds, "Colonial Policy and Processing of Groundnuts: The Case of Georges Calil," *International Journal of African Historical Studies* 19, no. 2 (1986): 261–73; Allister E. Hinds, "Government Policy and the Nigerian Palm Oil Export Industry, 1939–49," *Journal of African History* 38, no. 3 (1997): 459–78; Robin Palmer, "The

Nyasaland Tea Industry in the Era of International Tea Restrictions, 1933–1950," *Journal of African History* 26, no. 2 (1985): 215–39; Toyin Falola, "Cassava Starch for Export in Nigeria during the Second World War," *African Economic History* 18 (1989): 73–98; and Nhamo Samasuwo, "Food Production and War Supplies: Rhodesia's Beef Industry during the Second World War, 1939–1945," *Journal of Southern African Studies* 29, no. 2 (June 2003): 487–502.

51. Raymond Dumett, "Africa's Strategic Minerals during the Second World War," *Journal of African History* 26 (1985): 381–408.

52. P. T. Bauer, "Origins of the Statutory Export Monopolies of British West Africa," *Business History Review* 28, no. 3 (September 1954): 197–213; Rod Alence, "Colonial Government, Social Conflict and State Involvement in Africa's Open Economies: The Origins of the Ghana Cocoa Marketing Board, 1939–46," *Journal of African History* 42, no. 3 (2001): 397–416; David Meredith, "The Colonial Office, British Business Interests and the Reform of Cocoa Marketing in West Africa, 1937–1945," *Journal of African History* 29, no. 2 (1988): 285–300; David Meredith, "State Controlled Marketing and Economic 'Development': The Case of West African Produce during the Second World War," *Economic History Review*, n.s., 39, no. 1 (February 1986): 77–91; Gavin Williams, "Marketing without and with Marketing Boards: The Origins of State Marketing Boards in Nigeria," *Review of African Political Economy* 34 (December 1985): 4–15; Laurens van der Laan, "Marketing West Africa's Export Crops: Modern Boards and Trading Companies," *Journal of Modern African Studies* 25, no. 1 (March 1987): 1–24; Laurens van der Laan, "The Selling Policies of African Export: Marketing Boards," *African Affairs* 85, no. 340 (July 1986): 365–83; and Nicholas J. Westcott, "The East African Sisal Industry, 1929–1949: The Marketing of a Colonial Commodity during Depression and War," *Journal of African History* 25 (1984): 445–61.

53. See, for instance, Frank Furedi, *The New Ideology of Imperialism* (London: Pluto Press, 1994); and Bothwell A. Ogot and W. R. Ochieng', eds., *Decolonization and Independence in Kenya, 1940–93* (Athens: Ohio University Press, 1995).

54. David W. Throup, *Economic and Social Origins of Mau Mau, 1945–53* (Athens: Ohio University Press, 1988); and David Anderson, *Histories of the Hanged: Britain's Dirty War in Kenya and the End of Empire* (New York: W. W. Norton, 2005).

55. Darwin, *Britain and Decolonisation*; Hargreaves, *Decolonization in Africa*; and Peter J. Cain and Antony G. Hopkins, *British Imperialism: Crisis and Deconstruction, 1914–1990* (London: Longman, 1993).

56. Gabriel O. Olusanya, "The Role of Ex-servicemen in Nigerian Politics," *Journal of Modern African Studies* 6, no. 2 (August 1968): 221–32; and Eugene P. A. Schleh, "The Post-war Careers of Ex-servicemen in Ghana and Uganda," *Journal of Modern African Studies* 6, no. 2 (August 1968): 203–20.

57. Michael Crowder, "The 1939–45 War and West Africa," in *History of West Africa*, vol. 2, ed. J. F. A. Ajayi and Michael Crowder (Cambridge: Cambridge University Press, 1974), 665–92.

58. Richard Rathbone, "Businessmen in Politics: Party Struggle in Ghana, 1949–57," *Journal of Development Studies* 9, no. 3 (October 1973): 391–401; and Simon Baynham,

Notes to Pages 11–12

"The Ghanaian Military: A Bibliographic Essay," *West African Journal of Sociology and Political Science* 1, no. 1 (October 1975): 83–107.

59. Rathbone, "Businessmen in Politics," 392; and Baynham, "Ghanaian Military," 84.

60. Adrienne M. Israel, "Ex-servicemen at the Crossroads: Protests and Politics in Post-war Ghana," *Journal of Modern African Studies* 30, no. 2 (1992): 359–68; and Adrienne M. Israel, "Measuring the War Experience: Ghanaian Soldiers in World War II," *Journal of Modern African Studies* 25, no. 1 (1987): 159–68.

61. Rita Headrick, "African Soldiers in World War II," *Armed Forces and Society* 4, no. 3 (1978): 502–26.

62. Jackson, *Botswana*; Ashley Jackson, "African Soldiers and Imperial Authorities: Tensions and Unrest during the Service of High Commission Territories' Soldiers in the British Army, 1941–46," *Journal of Southern African Studies* 25, no. 4 (December 1999): 645–65; Louis W. F. Grundlingh, "Prejudices, Promises and Poverty: The Experiences of Discharged and Demobilised Black South African Soldiers after the Second World War," *South African Historical Journal* 26 (1992): 116–35; Hamilton Sipho Simelane, "Veterans, Politics and Poverty: The Case of Swazi Veterans in the Second World War," *South African Historical Journal* 38 (1998): 144–70; Frank Furedi, "The Demobilized African Soldier and the Blow to White Prestige," in *Guardians of Empire: the Forces of the Colonial Powers c. 1700–1964*, ed. David Killingray and David Omissi (Manchester: Manchester University Press, 1999), 179–97; Joanna Lewis, *Empire State-Building: War and Welfare in Kenya, 1925–52* (Athens: Ohio University Press, 2000); and Stapleton, *African Police and Soldiers.*

63. The dissatisfaction of servicemen at the end of the war was not unique to the African continent either. It affected colonial forces from Asia and the Caribbean as well—especially with regard to perceived broken recruitment promises and delayed demobilization. In fact, the fight for better conditions did not always follow the end of the war, as cases of protest and mutiny sometimes preceded its conclusion. India, Trinidad, and the Cayman Islands all offer relevant examples in this respect. See, for example, Daniel O. Spence, *Colonial Naval Culture and British Imperialism, 1922–67* (Manchester: Manchester University Press, 2015); Daniel O. Spence, "'They Had the Sea in Their Blood': Caymanian Naval Volunteers in the Second World War," in *Transnational Soldiers: Foreign Military Enlistment in the Modern Era*, ed. Nir Arielli and Bruce Collins (New York: Palgrave Macmillan, 2013), 105–23; Dipak Kumar Das, *Revisiting Talwar: A Study in the Royal Indian Navy Uprising of February 1946* (New Delhi: Ajanta, 1993); and Anirudh Deshpande, *British Military Policy in India, 1900–1945: Colonial Constraints and Declining Power* (New Delhi: Manohar, 2005).

64. Gregory Mann, *Native Sons: West African Veterans and France in the Twentieth Century* (Durham, NC: Duke University Press, 2006), 144.

65. Mann, 145.

66. Nancy Lawler, *Soldiers of Misfortune: Ivoirien Tirailleurs of World War II* (Athens: Ohio University Press, 1992).

67. Myron J. Echenberg, *Colonial Conscripts: The Tirailleurs Sénégalais in French West Africa, 1857–1960* (Portsmouth, NH: Heinemann, 1991).

Notes to Pages 12–16

68. Mann, *Native Sons*, 117.

69. Mann, 23.

70. Frederick Cooper, *Decolonization and African Society: The Labor Question in French and British Africa* (Cambridge: Cambridge University Press, 1996), 111.

71. Cooper, *Decolonization and African Society*, 225–60; and Frederick Cooper, *Africa since 1940: The Past of the Present* (Cambridge: Cambridge University Press, 2002).

72. Ian Spencer, "Settler Dominance, Agricultural Production and the Second World War in Kenya," *Journal of African History* 21, no. 4 (1980): 497–514.

73. David Johnson, "Settler Farmers and Coerced African Labour in Southern Rhodesia," *Journal of African History* 33 (1992): 111–28; David Johnson, *World War Two and the Scramble for Labour in Colonial Zimbabwe, 1939–1948* (Harare: University of Zimbabwe Publications, 2000); and Kenneth P. Vickery, "The Second World War Revival of Forced Labor in the Rhodesias," *International Journal of African Historical Studies* 22, no. 3 (1989): 423–37.

74. John Iliffe, *A Modern History of Tanganyika* (Cambridge: Cambridge University Press, 1979).

75. Keith Jeffery, "The Second World War," in *The Oxford History of the British Empire*, vol. 4, *The Twentieth Century*, ed. Judith M. Brown and Wm. Roger Louis (Oxford: Oxford University Press, 1999), 312; William M. Freund, "Labour Migration to the Northern Nigerian Tin Mines, 1903–1945," *Journal of African History* 22, no. 1 (1981): 73–84; and B. W. Hodder, "Tin Mining on the Jos Plateau of Nigeria," *Economic Geography* 35, no. 2 (1959): 109–22.

76. Jackson, *Botswana*.

77. Jackson, 19.

78. David Killingray, *Fighting for Britain: African Soldiers in the Second World War* (Woodbridge: James Currey, 2010); and Jackson, *British Empire*.

79. Killingray, *Fighting for Britain*, 1.

80. Judith A. Byfield, "Preface," in *Africa and World War II*, ed. Judith A. Byfield et al. (New York: Cambridge University Press, 2015), xvii–xxiii.

81. Byfield, xix.

82. Byfield, xix.

83. Byfield, xx.

84. Byfield, xx.

85. Samwiiri Lwanga-Lunyiigo, "Uganda's Long Connection with the Problem of Refugees: From the Polish Refugees of World War II to the Present," in *Uganda and the Problem of Refugees*, ed. A. G. G. Gingyera Pinycwa (Kampala: Makerere University Press, 1998), 1–21.

86. David Kiyaga-Mulindwa, "Uganda: A Safe Haven for Polish Refugees, 1942–1951," *Uganda Journal* 46, no. 1 (2000): 67–72.

87. Baxter Tavuyanago, Tasara Muguti, and James Hlongwana, "Victims of the Rhodesian Immigration Policy: Polish Refugees from the Second World War," *Journal of Southern African Studies* 38, no. 4 (2012): 951–65.

Notes to Pages 16–20

88. Tavuyanago, Muguti, and Hlongwana, 965.

89. Jochen Lingelbach, "Polish Refugees in British Colonial East and Central Africa during and after World War Two" (DPhil thesis, Universität Leipzig, 2017).

90. Lingelbach, 232.

91. L. F. G. Anthony, "The Second World War," in *The Story of the Northern Rhodesia Regiment*, ed. William Vernon Brelsford (Lusaka: Government Printer, 1954), 75–102.

92. William Vernon Brelsford, ed., *The Story of the Northern Rhodesia Regiment* (Lusaka: Government Printer, 1954).

93. Smyth, "War Propaganda," 345–58.

94. Kusum Datta, "Farm Labour, Agrarian Capital and the State in Colonial Zambia: The African Labour Corps, 1942–52," *Journal of Southern African Studies* 14, no. 3 (April 1988): 371–92; and Vickery, "Second World War Revival."

95. Andrew D. Roberts, "Notes towards a Financial History of Copper Mining in Northern Rhodesia," *Canadian Journal of African Studies* 16, no. 2 (1982): 347–59; Andrew D. Roberts, "Northern Rhodesia: The Post-war Background, 1945–1953," in *Living the End of Empire: Politics and Society in Late Colonial Zambia*, ed. Jan-Bart Gewald, Marja Hinfelaar, and Giacomo Macola (Leiden: Brill, 2011), 15–24; and Lewis H. Gann, "The Northern Rhodesian Copper Industry and the World of Copper, 1923–1953," *Rhodes-Livingstone Journal* 18 (1955): 1–18.

96. Lawrence Butler, *Copper Empire: Mining and the Colonial State in Northern Rhodesia, c. 1930–1964* (Houndsmill, UK: Palgrave Macmillan, 2007).

97. Ackson M. Kanduza, *The Political Economy of Underdevelopment in Northern Rhodesia, 1918–1960: A Case Study of Customs Tariff and Railway Freight Policies* (Lanham, MD: University Press of America, 1986).

98. Samuel N. Chipungu, *The State, Technology and Peasant Differentiation in Zambia: A Case Study of the Southern Province, 1930–1986* (Lusaka: Historical Association of Zambia, 1988).

99. Studies which touch on this question are Rosaleen Smyth, "War Propaganda during the Second World War in Northern Rhodesia," *African Affairs* 83, no. 332 (1984): 345–58; Gann, "Northern Rhodesian Copper Industry"; Roberts, "Financial History of Copper Mining," 347–59; and Butler, *Copper Empire*. Perhaps the only exception to this state of affairs is Hugh Macmillan and Frank Shapiro's study on Jewish settlers in colonial Zambia, *Zion in Africa: The Jews of Zambia* (London: I. B. Tauris, 2017). The Jews did not enter Northern Rhodesia as official refugees, but were in fact escaping rising anti-Semitism in the Soviet Union and Germany during the interwar period.

100. Killingray, *Fighting for Britain*, 3.

101. Claude Lévi-Strauss, *Structural Anthropology* (New York: Basic Books, 1963), 16–17.

102. Gayatri Chakravorty Spivak, "Can the Subaltern Speak?," in *Marxism and the Interpretation of Culture*, ed. Cary Nelson and Lawrence Grossberg (Urbana: University of Illinois Press, 1988), 217–313.

103. Killingray, *Fighting for Britain*, 3.

Notes to Pages 23–25

CHAPTER 1: MILITARY LABOR RECRUITMENT AND MOBILIZATION

1. *Mutende*, no. 44, 12 September 1939. Insertions in square brackets indicate wordings found in other printed versions of this speech.

2. Rosaleen Smyth, "War Propaganda during the Second World War in Northern Rhodesia," *African Affairs* 83, no. 332 (1984): 346.

3. *Mutende*, no. 44, 12 September 1939.

4. It is a source of historiographical debate that the Second World War did not start in 1939 but at different times for different people. It could be argued that, for Africans, the war actually started when Italy conquered Abyssinia in 1935 and, for East Asians, when Japan invaded Manchuria in 1937. For a discussion on this aspect, see Jeremy Black, *World War Two: A Military History* (London: Routledge, 2003), 31–35; Christopher Bayly and Tim Harper, *Forgotten Armies: Britain's Asian Empire and the War with Japan* (London: Penguin, 2004); Christopher Bayly and Tim Harper, *Forgotten Wars: The End of Britain's Asian Empire* (London: Penguin, 2007); Thomas Marvin Williamsen, "The Second Sino-Japanese War, 1931–1945," in *World War II in Asia and the Pacific and the War's Aftermath, with General Themes: A Handbook of Literature and Research*, ed. Loyd E. Lee (Westport, CT: Greenwood, 1998), 27–44; Michael A. Barnhart, "International Relations and the Origins of the War in Asia and the Pacific War," in Lee, *World War II in Asia and the Pacific*, 5–24; and David Killingray, *Fighting for Britain: African Soldiers during the Second World War* (Woodbridge, UK: James Currey, 2010), 7, 50–53.

5. *Mutende*, Special Edition, 3 September 1939.

6. *Mutende*, Special Edition, 3 September 1939.

7. National Archives of Zambia (hereafter NAZ) NP1/13/13 Loc 4840, Editor, *Mutende* (Lusaka) to Provincial Commissioner, Northern Province (Kasama), 14 September 1939.

8. See especially, Killingray, *Fighting for Britain*; Mary Nombulelo Ntabeni, "Military Labour Mobilisation in Colonial Lesotho during World War II, 1940–1943," *Scientia Militaria: South African Journal of Military Studies* 36, no. 2 (2008): 36–59; Ashley Jackson, "Bad Chiefs and Sub-tribes: Aspects of Recruitment for the British Army in Bechuanaland Protectorate, 1941–42," *Botswana Notes and Records* 28 (1996): 87–96; Ashley Jackson, *Botswana, 1939–45: An African Country at War* (Oxford: Oxford University Press, 1999); Ashley Jackson, "Motivation and Mobilization for War: Recruitment for the British Army in Bechuanaland Protectorate, 1941–42," *African Affairs* 96, no. 384 (1997): 399–417; David Killingray, "Labour Mobilisation in British Colonial Africa for the War Effort, 1939–46," in *Africa and the Second World War*, ed. David Killingray and Richard Rathbone (Basingstoke, UK: Palgrave Macmillan, 1986), 68–96; David Killingray, "Military and Labour Recruitment in the Gold Coast during the Second World War," *Journal of African History* 23, no. 1 (1982): 83–95; and Hamilton Sipho Simelane, "Labor Mobilization for the War Effort in Swaziland, 1940–1942," *International Journal of African Historical Studies* 26, no. 3 (1993): 541–74.

9. *Mutende*, no. 44, 12 September 1939.

10. See, for example, NAZ NP1/13/13 Loc4840, Chief Mporokoso (Mporokoso) to District Commissioner (Mporokoso), 7 September 1939; NAZ1/13/13 Loc4840, Chief

184

Notes to Pages 25–29

Nsama (Mporokoso) to District Commissioner (Mporokoso), 7 September 1939; NAZ NP1/13/13 Loc4840, Chief Mukupa Katandula (Mporokoso) to District Commissioner (Mporokoso), 7 September 1939; Chief Nsokolo (Abercorn) to District Commissioner (Abercorn), 7 September 1939. See also *Mutende*, no. 45, 26 September 1939, for messages of loyalty from Senior Chiefs Kambombo, Magodi, and Mwase from Lundazi district.

11. See, for example, Jackson, *Botswana*, 34; Jackson, "Motivation and Mobilization," 406–7; Killingray, "Military and Labour Recruitment"; and Simelane, "Labor Mobilization."

12. NAZ SP4/2/9 Loc 5082, Mazabuka District Tour Report no. 7 of 1939.

13. Alicia C. Decker, *In Idi Amin's Shadow: Women, Gender, and Militarism in Uganda* (Athens: Ohio University Press, 2014), 6.

14. Decker, 6.

15. NAZ SEC1/1758 Vol. I, Information Officer (Lusaka) to Chief Secretary (Lusaka), 22 April 1940.

16. NAZ SEC1/1758 Vol. I, Information Officer to Chief Secretary, 22 April 1940; and Smyth, "War Propaganda," 352.

17. NAZ SEC1/76, Chief Secretary (Lusaka) to All District Commissioners, 26 October 1939; NAZ SEC1/1758 Vol. I, Information Officer (Lusaka) to Chief Secretary (Lusaka), 22 April 1940.

18. Smyth, "War Propaganda," 352.

19. NAZ SEC1/1758 Vol. I, Information Officer to Chief Secretary, 22 April 1940.

20. NAZ SEC2/425, Chief Secretary (Lusaka) to Information Officer (Lusaka), 26 June 1940; and NAZ SEC1/1758 Vol. I, Chief Secretary (Lusaka) to Chief Secretary (Zomba, Nyasaland), 7 August 1940.

21. NAZ SEC1/1758 Vol. I, Information Officer to Chief Secretary, 22 April 1940.

22. NAZ SEC1/1758 Vol. I, Information Officer to Chief Secretary, 22 April 1940. For a comparative analysis, see Louis W. F. Grundlingh, "The Military, Race, and Resistance: The Conundrums of Recruiting Black South African Men during the Second World War," in *Africa and World War II*, ed. Judith A. Byfield et al. (New York: Cambridge University Press, 2015), 75.

23. Grundlingh, "Military, Race, and Resistance," 75.

24. Rosaleen Smyth, "Britain's African Colonies and British Propaganda during the Second World War," *Journal of Imperial and Commonwealth History* 14 (1985): 69.

25. NAZ SEC2/1122, Minutes of the Twenty-Seventh Meeting of the African Film Library and Purchasing Committee held at Kitwe on 20 June 1944. See also Grundlingh, "Military, Race, and Resistance," 75.

26. Smyth, "War Propaganda," 349.

27. NAZ SEC2/1122, African Film Library and Purchasing Committee Annual Report for 1941; NAZ SEC2/1280, Report on the Provision of Films at Chitokoloki Mission, 13 July 1942; and Smyth, "War Propaganda," 350.

28. Smyth, "Britain's African Colonies," 74.

29. *Bantu Mirror*, 30 January 1940. Such propaganda was historically ironic because Britain herself was renowned for "stealing" other countries, making her the world's

Notes to Pages 29–33

leading colonial power. What can be deduced from this propaganda campaign is that during war, Britain ignored her own frailties in order to win the sympathy of her colonial subjects.

30. As recently shown by Driss Maghraoui with reference to wartime Morocco, French authorities resorted to similar techniques. See Driss Maghraoui, "The Moroccan 'Effort de Guerre' in World War II," in Byfield et al., *Africa and World War II*, 89–108.

31. NAZ EP4/2/9 Loc 5477 Lundazi Tour Report no. 10 of 1940.

32. *Mutende*, no. 46, October 1939.

33. NAZ SEC1/1758 Vol. II, Report on Public Opinion for Barotse Province for February and March 1942, 1 April 1942.

34. NAZ SEC1/1758 Vol. I, Information Officer (Lusaka) to Chief Secretary (Lusaka), 22 April 1940.

35. Elizabeth Colson Research and Documentation Centre (hereafter ECRDC) FLE-LAB, Chief Secretary (Lusaka) to Director, Rhodes-Livingstone Institute (Livingstone), 8 July 1943.

36. NAZ SEC1/1758 Vol. I, Director of the Rhodes-Livingstone Institute (Livingstone) to Chief Secretary (Lusaka), 8 July 1943.

37. NAZ SEC1/1758 Vol. I, Director of the Rhodes-Livingstone Institute to Chief Secretary, 8 July 1943.

38. NAZ SEC1/1758 Vol. I, Director of the Rhodes-Livingstone Institute to Chief Secretary, 8 July 1943.

39. *Mutende*, 4 October 1940.

40. NRG, *Legislative Council Debates of the 3rd Session of the 7th Council, 20 November–10 December 1943* (Lusaka: Government Printer, 1944), 17.

41. Black, *World War Two*, 56.

42. Black, 45–56; and Basil H. Liddell Hart, *History of the Second World War* (London: Cassell, 1970), 109.

43. Ashley Jackson, *The British Empire and the Second World War* (London: Hambledon Continuum, 2006), 173.

44. Black, *World War Two*, 89.

45. Black, 88.

46. See, for example, Eugene L. Rasor, "The Japanese Attack on Pearl Harbor," in Lee, *World War II in Asia and the Pacific*, 45–55; Ken Kotani, "Pearl Harbor: Japanese Planning and Command Structure," in *The Pacific War Companion: From Pearl Harbor to Hiroshima*, ed. Daniel Marston (Oxford: Osprey, 2005), 29–45; and Gerhard L. Weinberg, *A World at Arms: A Global History of World War II* (Cambridge: Cambridge University Press, 1994).

47. Black, *World War Two*, 100.

48. Liddell Hart, *History*, 121.

49. Lewis H. Gann, *A History of Northern Rhodesia: Early Days to 1953* (London: Chatto and Windus, 1963), 327. In 1939, the African population in the country was estimated at 1,300,000 and that of European origins at 20,000. The exact number of men

Notes to Pages 33–38

who served in African colonial forces is not always easy to calculate. Certain men served for a short term, some reenlisted, and others enlisted in neighboring territories.

50. Gann, *History of Northern Rhodesia*, 328.

51. Simelane, "Labor Mobilization," 550.

52. John D. Hargreaves, *Decolonisation in Africa* (London: Routledge, 1996), 55.

53. Killingray, "Military and Labour Recruitment," 89, 91, and 95; and Grundlingh, "Military, Race, and Resistance," 102.

54. Killingray, "Labour Mobilisation," 77.

55. Jackson, "Motivation and Mobilization," 407.

56. Jackson, *Botswana*, 44.

57. NAZ SEC1/1638 Vol. III, Mendulu Tengetetu Banda (Gatooma, Southern Rhodesia) to Tom Maridikani, (Rambi Village, Chief Zingalume, Fort Jameson), 16 March 1943. Misale and Mazambani were the most popular routes used by labor migrants from the eastern parts of Northern Rhodesia to and from Southern Rhodesia.

58. NAZ SEC1/1638 Vol. III, Provincial Commissioner, Eastern Province (Fort Jameson) to Chief Secretary (Lusaka), 6 April 1943.

59. John Edward Stephenson, *Chirupula's Tale: A Bye-Way in African History* (London: Geoffrey Bless, 1937), 22, 188; and Lewis H. Gann, *The Birth of a Plural Society: The Development of Northern Rhodesia under the British South Africa Company, 1894–1914* (Manchester: Manchester University Press, 1958).

60. LM2/3/4/1/6/1, J. Maclaren, General Manager, Mufulira Mine (Mufulira) to Lt. Col. A. Stephenson, Commander, Sub Area HQ (Lusaka), 28 August 1940; and LM2/3/4/1/6/1, A. Stephenson, Commander, Sub Area HQ (Lusaka) to J. Maclaren, General Manager, Mufulira Copper Mine (Mufulira), 2 August 1940. See also Grundlingh, "Military, Race, and Resistance," 100.

61. LM2/3/4/4/1/1/8/4, Recruiting Posters by Information Office, Lusaka, Northern Rhodesia, 1939–1945.

62. LM2/3/4/4/1/1/8/5, Kampanje Kalila, Shamwale! Lowani Usikari!, n.d., ca. 1943.

63. Killingray, *Fighting for Britain*, 48.

64. LM2/3/4/1/6/1, Information Officer (Lusaka) to Commander, Sub Area Headquarters (Lusaka), 24 September 1949.

65. See, for example, *Mutende*, April 1940; and *Mutende*, no. 63, June 1940.

66. Rita Headrick, "African Soldiers in World War II," *Armed Forces and Society* 4 (1978): 504; and A. G. Dickson, "Studies in War-Time Organisation: The Mobile Propaganda Unit, East Africa Command," *African Affairs* 44, no. 174 (January 1945): 10.

67. Giacomo Macola, *The Gun in Central Africa: A History of Technology and Politics* (Athens: Ohio University Press, 2016), 156.

68. Macola, 157.

69. NAZ SEC1/1773, District Commissioner (Fort Jameson) to Provincial Commissioner, Eastern Province (Fort Jameson), 5 October 1943.

70. NAZ SEC1/1773, District Commissioner to Provincial Commissioner, 5 October 1943; and NAZ SEC1/1771, Intelligence Report for 1 October–15 November 1943 for Western Province and Kaonde-Lunda Province, 18 November 1943.

Notes to Pages 38–42

71. NAZ SEC1/1773, Report by Ackson Mwale on the Mobile Propaganda Unit, ca. September/October 1943.

72. ECRDC FLE-LAB, Barotse Civil Wars.

73. Rightson Kangwa, interview with the British Broadcasting Corporation (BBC), Ndola, 1989.

74. Alfred Tembo, "Rubber Production in Northern Rhodesia during the Second World War, 1942–1946," *African Economic History* 41 (2013): 242.

75. Justin Master Phiri, interview with the BBC, Ndola, 1989.

76. LM2/3/4/4/1/1/10, Information Officer (Lusaka) to Lt. Colonel W. A. Dimoline (Lusaka), 8 March 1940; NAZ EP4/2/9 Loc 5477, Lundazi District Tour Report no. 1 of 1940; and NAZ EP4/2/9 Loc 5477, Lundazi Tour Report no. 7 of 1940.

77. Killingray, *Fighting for Britain*, 95.

78. Gilbert Malama Zulu, interview with the BBC, Lusaka, 1989. See also Macola, *Gun in Central Africa*, 152.

79. LM2/3/4/4/1/1/8, Broadcast Talk to Africans by 2nd Lieutenant K. Thompson, 16 October 1940, from Lusaka. *Askari* is a Swahili term for African soldiers. The term was widely used by colonial and military officials to refer to African servicemen. The singular form is *msikari*.

80. NAZ SEC1/1766 Vol. II, Extract from Minutes of the Second Meeting of the Northern Province Western Areas, Provincial Council held at Kawambwa on 8–9 May 1945.

81. Bernard Nchindila, "Pan-African Issues in Zambian Bemba Literature: The Case of Stephen Mpashi's *Cekesoni aingila ubusoja* (1950) [Jackson joins the Military]," paper presented at the European Conference on African Studies, SOAS, London, 2013, 2–3.

82. Jackson, *British Empire*, 188.

83. NAZ SP4/2/19 Loc 5084, District Commissioner (Namwala) to Provincial Commissioner, Southern Province (Livingstone), 31 October 1942.

84. NAZ SEC1/1775, Provincial Commissioner, Barotse Province (Mongu) to Chief Secretary (Lusaka), 1 April 1943.

85. NAZ SEC1/1758 Vol. I, Provincial Commissioner, Northern Province (Kasama) to Chief Secretary (Lusaka), 11 December 1940; see also NAZ SEC1/1638 Vol. III, District Commissioner (Kasama) to Provincial Commissioner, Northern Province (Kasama), 18 March 1943; NAZ SEC1/1758 Vol. I, Provincial Commissioner, Central Province (Broken Hill) to Chief Secretary (Lusaka), 29 November 1940; and NAZ SEC1/1758 Vol. I, Provincial Commissioner, Central Province (Broken Hill) to Chief Secretary (Lusaka), 5 December 1940.

86. NAZ SEC1/1638 Vol. III, Chief Secretary (Lusaka) to Public Relations Officer, NRR Southern Area HQ (Lusaka), 27 August 1943.

87. NAZ SEC1/1638 Vol. III, Extract from Minute from Secretary for Native Affairs (Lusaka) to Chief Secretary (Lusaka), 10 August 1943.

88. NAZ SEC1/1638 Vol. III, Commander, Southern Sub-Area (Lusaka) to Chief Secretary (Lusaka), 13 September 1943; and Grundlingh, "Military, Race, and Resistance," 99.

188

Notes to Pages 42–47

89. NAZ SEC2/181, District Commissioners' Conference, Northern Province held at Kasama from 22–27 February 1943. See also Grundlingh, "Military, Race, and Resistance," 100.

90. Decker, *In Idi Amin's Shadow*, 8.

91. This was a common motive for many colonial servicemen elsewhere and not just in the Northern Rhodesian or African context. For a comparative case in Trinidad, see Annette Palmer, "The Politics of Race and War: Black Soldiers in the Caribbean Theater during the Second World War," *Military Affairs* 47, no. 2 (April 1983): 59.

92. Samson B. D. Muliango, interview with the BBC, Lusaka, 11 July 1989.

93. LM2/3/4/1/6/1, Information Officer (Lusaka) to Officer Commanding Northern Rhodesia Regiment, Service Corp (Bwana Mkubwa, Ndola), 29 August 1940; and Headrick, "African Soldiers," 505.

94. Lesa Kasansayika, interview with the BBC, Ndola, 24 November 1989.

95. Chama Mutemi Kadansa, interview with the BBC, Ndola, 17 July 1939.

96. Joseph Chinama Mulenga, interview with the BBC, Lusaka, 6 June 1989. See also Killingray, "African Voices," 430.

97. Muliango, interview cited. See also Grundlingh, "Military, Race, and Resistance," 104.

98. Kadansa, interview cited. See also Kapasa Makasa, *Zambia's March to Political Freedom* (Nairobi: Heinemann, 1981), 15.

99. Mulenga, interview cited.

100. Muliango, interview cited.

101. Rabson Chombola, interview with the BBC, Ndola, 24 November 1989.

102. Simelane, "Labor Mobilization," 549; Ntabeni, "Military Labour," 42; and Louis Wilhelm Fredrick Grundlingh, "South African Blacks in the Second World War" (DLitt et Phil thesis, Rand Afrikaans University, 1986), 83–84.

103. Killingray, "Military and Labour Recruitment," 88.

104. SEC1/1638 Vol. III, Major H. Ockerdon, Infantry Training Centre to Chief Secretary, 2 April 1943; and NAZ SEC1/1638 Vol. III, Secretary, Office of the Conference of East African Governors (Nairobi) to Chief Secretary (Lusaka), 22 March 1943.

105. NAZ SEC1/1638 Vol. III, Major H. Ockerdon, Infantry Training Centre (Lusaka) to Chief Secretary (Lusaka), 2 April 1943.

106. SEC1/1638 Vol. III, Major H. Ockerdon, Infantry Training Centre to Chief Secretary, 2 April 1943.

107. NAZ SEC1/1638 Vol. III, Chief Secretary (Lusaka) to Commander, East Africa Command HQ (Nairobi), 9 December 1942.

108. NAZ SEC1/1638 Vol. III, Chief Secretary to Commander, East Africa Command HQ, 9 December 1942. See also Killingray, *Fighting for Britain*, 84.

109. Timothy H. Parsons, "'Wakamba Warriors Are Soldiers of the Queen': The Evolution of the Kamba as a Martial Race, 1890–1970," *Ethnohistory* 46, no. 4 (1999): 672.

110. Parsons, "'Wakamba Warriors,'" 673.

111. Gann, *History of Northern Rhodesia*, 325–26.

Notes to Pages 47–49

112. Gann, 326. See also Northern Rhodesia Government (NRG), *Northern Rhodesia Regiment Annual Report for the Year Ending 1936* (Lusaka: Government Printer, 1937), 5; and NRG, *Northern Rhodesia Regiment Annual Report for the Year Ending 1938* (Lusaka: Government Printer, 1939), 3.

113. John Iliffe, *Honour in African History* (Cambridge: Cambridge University Press, 2005), 227–45.

114. A comprehensive history of the Ngoni people is William Rau, "Mpezeni's Ngoni of Eastern Zambia, 1870–1920" (PhD diss., University of California, Los Angeles, 1974). See also Gann, *Birth of a Plural Society.*

115. Macola, *Gun in Central Africa*, 157. This is quite different from the Kenyan context, where the Kamba people were classified as martial due to a combination of economic and political realities in the 1930s. In the early phase of colonial rule, the Kamba had little interest in joining the army. By the early 1930s, however, the Kamba featured prominently in the King's African Rifles (KAR) due to the economic hardships they faced owing to severe famines and droughts. For details, see Parsons, " 'Wakamba Warriors,' " 674–95.

116. LM2/3/4/1/8/2, Regimental History, Notes, n.d.

117. For a comparative discussion, see Daniel Owen Spence, "Imperial Transition, Indianisation and Race: Developing National Navies in the Subcontinent, 1947–64," *South Asia: Journal of South Asian Studies* 37, no. 2 (June 2014): 326–27.

118. Cynthia H. Enloe, *Ethnic Soldiers: State Security in Divided Societies* (Athens: University of Georgia Press, 1980), 25.

119. Gregory Mann, *Native Sons: West African Veterans and France in the Twentieth Century* (Durham, NC: Duke University Press, 2006), 16.

120. Mann, 16.

121. NAZ SP4/2/9 Loc 5082, Mazabuka Tour Report no. 7 of 1939.

122. Jackson, *British Empire*, 187; and Killingray, *Fighting for Britain*, 45.

123. Killingray, *Fighting for Britain*, 58.

124. NAZ EP4/2/9 Loc 5477, Lundazi District Special Tour Report no. 1 of 1947.

125. NAZ SP4/2/9 Loc 5082, Mazabuka District Tour Report no. 7 of 1939; and NAZ SP4/2/9 Loc 5082, Mazabuka Tour Report no. 9 of 1939.

126. Samuel N. Chipungu, *The State, Technology and Peasant Differentiation in Southern Zambia, 1890–1980* (Lusaka: Historical Association of Zambia, 1988); and Kenneth P. Vickery, *Black and White in Southern Zambia: The Tonga Plateau Economy and British Imperialism, 1890–1939* (New York: Greenwood, 1986).

127. NAZ SP4/2/9 Loc 5082, Mazabuka Tour Report no. 7 of 1939.

128. NAZ SP4/2/9 Loc 5082, Mazabuka Tour Report no. 9 of 1939.

129. NAZ SEC1/1758 Vol. II, Provincial Commissioner, Barotse Province (Mongu) to Chief Secretary (Lusaka), 10 April 1941. See also NAZ SEC1/1758 Vol. I, Provincial Commissioner, Barotse Province (Mongu) to Chief Secretary (Lusaka), Secretary for Native Affairs (Lusaka), Director of Intelligence and Censorship (Lusaka), and Information Officer (Lusaka), 26 September 1940.

130. NAZ SP4/2/19 Loc 5084, Report on Public Opinion in Northern Rhodesia for January 1941; NAZ SEC1/1758 Vol. I, Provincial Commissioner, Barotse Province

Notes to Pages 50–52

(Mongu) to Chief Secretary (Lusaka), 3 December 1940; and NAZ SEC1/1758 Vol. I, Barotse Province Report on Public Opinion for January 1941, n.d., ca. February 1941.

131. R. Philpott, "The Mongu-Mulobezi Labour Route," *Rhodes-Livingstone Journal* 3 (1945): 51; and NAZ SP2/1/1, Annual Report for Southern and Barotse Province for the Year Ending 31 December 1941.

132. Philpott, "Mongu-Mulobezi Labour Route," 54.

133. NAZ EP4/2/5 Loc 5476, Fort Jameson Tour Report no. 10 of 1940.

134. NAZ EP4/2/5 Loc 5476, Fort Jameson Tour Report no. 10 of 1940; and NAZ EP4/2/5 Loc 5476, Fort Jameson Tour Report no. 13 of 1940.

135. NAZ EP4/2/5 Loc 5476, Fort Jameson Tour Report no. 12 of 1940.

136. NAZ EP4/2/5 Loc 5476, Fort Jameson Tour Report no. 12 of 1940. For a continental perspective about this strategy, see Killingray, "Labour Mobilisation," 78.

137. Cross-border resistance to state policies has been discussed by Alfred Tembo, "The Colonial State and African Agriculture in Chipata District of Northern Rhodesia, 1895–1964" (MA diss., University of Zambia, 2010).

138. NAZ SEC1/1758 Vol. II, Report on Public Opinion for Barotse Province for June 1941.

139. Mann, *Native Sons*, 18.

140. NAZ EP4/2/9 Loc 5477, Lundazi District Tour Report no. 8 of 1940. See also NAZ SEC1/1638 Vol. III, Chief Secretary (Lusaka) to Chief Secretary, Southern Rhodesia (Salisbury), 21 January 1943; NAZ SEC1/1758 Vol. I, Eastern Province Report on Public Opinion for the Month of August 1940, n.d., ca. October 1940.

141. NAZ EP4/2/9 Loc 5477, Lundazi District Tour Report no. 7 of 1940. See also NAZ SEC1/1758 Vol. I, Eastern Province Report on Public Opinion for September 1940.

142. Killingray, "Labour Mobilisation," 79.

143. See, for example, Hoyini K. Bhila, "The Impact of the Second World War on the Development of Peasant Agriculture in Botswana, 1939–1956," *Botswana Notes and Records* 16 (1984): 63–71; Wazha G. Morapedi, "Migrant Labour and the Peasantry in the Bechuanaland Protectorate, 1930–1965," *Journal of Southern African Studies* 25, no. 2 (1999): 197–214; and M. Leepile, "The Impact of Migrant Labour on the Economy of Kweneng 1940–1980," *Botswana Notes and Records* 13 (1981): 33–43.

144. The notion that the absence of males from households for long periods of time had only negative effects has been dismissed by some scholars because Africans devised coping strategies. See, for example, Tembo, "The Colonial State"; Yizenge A. Chondoka, "Labour Migration and Rural Transformation in Chama District, North-Eastern Zambia, 1890–1964" (PhD diss., University of Toronto, 1992); and William Watson, *The Social Structure of the Mambwe of Northern Rhodesia* (Manchester: Manchester University Press, 1957).

145. NAZ SEC1/1758 Vol. II, Eastern Province Report on Public Opinion for November 1941, 1 December 1941.

146. NAZ SEC1/1758 Vol. II, Southern Province Report on Public Opinion for November 1941, ca. December 1941.

147. Decker, *In Idi Amin's Shadow*, 10.

Notes to Pages 52–56

148. See, for example, NAZ SEC1/1758 Vol. II, Provincial Commissioner, Central Province (Broken Hill) to Chief Secretary (Lusaka), 5 December 1940; NAZ SEC1/1758 Vol. II, Provincial Commissioner, Central Province (Broken Hill) to Chief Secretary (Lusaka), 29 November 1940; NAZ SEC1/1758 Vol. II, Eastern Province Monthly Report on Public Opinion for September 1940; NAZ SEC1/1758 Vol. I, Provincial Commissioner, Kaonde-Lunda Province (Kasempa) to Chief Secretary (Lusaka), 2 April 1941; NAZ SEC1/1758 Vol. I, Northern Rhodesia Report on Public Opinion for December 1940; and NAZ SEC1/1728 Vol. VII, His Excellency The Governor's Tour to the Copperbelt, 15–22 June 1942.

149. NAZ EP4/2/9 Loc 5477, Lundazi District Tour Report no. 7 of 1940.

150. *Bulawayo Chronicle*, 20 January 1941.

151. Jackson, *British Empire*, 236.

152. NAZ SEC1/1650 Vol. I, Llewelyn V. Phillips (Lusaka) to Sir John Maybin, Governor (Lusaka), 12 June 1940.

153. NAZ SEC1/1650 Vol. I, D. H. Liebenberg (Lusaka) to Governor (Lusaka), 15 June 1940; NAZ SEC1/1650 Vol. I, S. P. Lofford (Nkana) to Governor (Lusaka), 18 June 1940; NAZ SEC1/1650 Vol. I, A. Boshoff (Nkana) to Governor (Lusaka), 18 June 1940; NAZ SEC1/1650 Vol. I, R. Oxenford Stanhope (Luanshya) to Governor (Lusaka), 28 June 1940.

154. NAZ SEC1/1758 Vol. II, Provincial Commissioner, Western Province (Ndola) to Chief Secretary (Lusaka), 2 July 1942.

155. NAZ SEC1/1650 Vol. II, Governor (Lusaka) to Secretary of State for the Colonies (London), 20 April 1949.

156. NAZ SEC1/1758 Vol. II, Report on Public Opinion for Central Province for the Month of March 1942, 8 April 1942.

157. NAZ SEC1/1758 Vol. II, Provincial Commissioner, Central Province (Broken Hill) to Chief Secretary (Lusaka), 13 June 1941.

158. NAZ SEC1/1758 Vol. II, Intelligence Report for Western Province for the Month of February 1942, 6 March 1942.

159. A nuanced discussion of this organization is contained in Christoph Marx, *Oxwagon Sentinel: Radical Afrikaner Nationalism and the History of the Ossewabrandwag* (Berlin: Lit Verlag, 2008).

160. NAZ SEC1/1758 Vol. II, Intelligence Report for Western Province for the Month of February 1942, 6 March 1942; and NAZ SEC1/1758 Vol. II, Provincial Commissioner, Central Province (Broken Hill) to Chief Secretary (Lusaka), 4 October 1944.

161. NAZ SEC1/1758 Vol. II, Provincial Commissioner, Central Province (Broken Hill) to Chief Secretary (Lusaka), 10 March 1942.

CHAPTER 2: SOUTHEAST ASIA, A DESPERATE BRITAIN,
AND THE REVIVAL OF AFRICAN RURAL INDUSTRIES

1. Raymond Dumett, "Africa's Strategic Minerals during the Second World War," *Journal of African History* 26, no. 4 (1985): 381.

2. Judith A. Byfield, "Women, Rice, and War: Political and Economic Crisis in Wartime Abeokuta (Nigeria)," in *Africa and World War II*, ed. Judith A. Byfield et al. (New York: Cambridge University Press, 2015), 156.

Notes to Pages 56–59

3. Judith A. Byfield, Preface to Byfield et al., *Africa and World War II*, xix.

4. Ashley Jackson, "The Empire/Commonwealth and the Second World War," *Round Table* 100, no. 412 (February 2011): 69.

5. Judith A. Byfield, "Producing for the War," in Byfield et al., *Africa and World War II*, 24.

6. Byfield, Preface, xix.

7. Alfred Tembo, "Rubber Production in Northern Rhodesia (Zambia) during the Second World War, 1942–1946," *African Economic History* 41 (2013): 223–55.

8. Cullen Gouldsbury and Hubert Sheane, *The Great Plateau of Northern Rhodesia: Being Some Impressions of the Tanganyika Plateau* (London: Edward Arnold, 1911), 332–37.

9. R. H. Hobson, "Rubber: A Footnote to Northern Rhodesian History," *Occasional Papers of the Rhodes-Livingstone Museum* 13 (1960): 493.

10. Achim von Oppen, *Terms of Trade and Terms of Trust: The History and Contexts of Pre-colonial Market Production around the Upper Zambezi and Kasai* (Munster: Lit Verlag, 1992), 162.

11. See, for example, von Oppen, *Terms of Trade*; Robert Joseph Papstein, "The Upper Zambezi: A History of the Luvale People, 1000–1900" (PhD diss., University of California, Los Angeles, 1978); and Gouldsbury and Sheane, *Great Plateau of Northern Rhodesia*.

12. National Archives of Zambia (hereafter NAZ) SEC2/273, Secret Statement by the Raw Materials Department, Ministry of Supply, November 1943; and Allister E. Hinds, "Government Policy and the Nigerian Palm Oil Export Industry, 1939–49," *Journal of African History* 38, no. 3 (1997): 462.

13. *Bulawayo Chronicle*, 25 June 1942; and Hobson, "Rubber," 493.

14. NAZ SEC2/273, Secret Statement on Raw Materials.

15. *Planter and Tanganyika Advertiser*, June 1942; *Bulawayo Chronicle*, 25 June 1942; and William G. Clarence-Smith, "Africa's 'Battle for Rubber' in the Second World War," in Byfield et al., *Africa and World War II*, 166–82. Ceara is wild rubber obtained from any of certain South American rubber trees of the genus *Manihot*, especially *Manihot carthaginensis glaziovii*. Para rubber is a type of natural rubber obtained from South American rubber trees of the genus *Hevea*, especially *Hevea brasiliensis*.

16. *Bulawayo Chronicle*, 8 May 1942; *Bulawayo Chronicle*, 20 May 1942; and *Bulawayo Chronicle*, 21 May 1942.

17. See, for example, Gouldsbury and Sheane, *Great Plateau of Northern Rhodesia*, 332–37; von Oppen, *Terms of Trade*; and Papstein, "Upper Zambezi."

18. NAZ SEC2/273, Notes by Chief Secretary to Provincial Commissioners' Conference, February 1942; NAZ SEC2/273, Director of Agriculture (Mazabuka) to Chief Secretary (Lusaka), 16 February 1942; NAZ SEC2/273, Director of Agriculture (Mazabuka) to Chief Secretary (Lusaka) and Controller of Customs (Livingstone), 8 January 1937; NAZ SEC2/273, Provincial Commissioner, Barotse Province (Mongu) to Chief Secretary (Lusaka), 3 February 1942; NAZ SEC2/273, Director of Agriculture (Mazabuka) to Chief Secretary (Lusaka), 16 February 1942; NAZ SEC2/273, Chief Secretary (Lusaka) to Director of Agriculture (Mazabuka), 5 January 1937; *Nyasaland News*, no. 30 of 1942.

Notes to Pages 59–61

19. NAZ SEC2/273, Notes by Chief Secretary, February 1942; NAZ SEC2/273, Director of Agriculture to Chief Secretary, 16 February 1942; and NAZ SEC2/273, Provincial Commissioner, Barotse Province to Chief Secretary, 3 February 1942.

20. Tembo, "Rubber Production," 231.

21. NAZ SEC2/273, J. H. Vivian and Company (Johannesburg) to Rhokana Corporation Limited (Nkana), 22 April 1942.

22. NAZ SEC2/273, Director of Agriculture (Mazabuka) to Dunlop South Africa Limited (Durban), 18 April 1942; and J. H. Vivian and Company to Rhokana Corporation Limited, 22 April 1942.

23. NAZ SEC2/273, Chief Buyer, Dunlop South Africa Limited (Durban) to Director of Agriculture (Mazabuka), 4 May 1942; NAZ SEC2/273, General Manager, South Africa Rubber Manufacturing Company Limited (Howick) to Director of Agriculture (Mazabuka), 12 May 1942.

24. NAZ SEC2/273, Chief Buyer, Dunlop South Africa to Director of Agriculture, 4 May 1942; and NAZ SEC2/273, General Manager, South Africa Rubber Manufacturing Company Limited to Director of Agriculture, 12 May 1942.

25. NAZ SEC2/273, Director of Agriculture (Mazabuka) to General Manager, South Africa Rubber Manufacturing Company Limited (Howick), 19 May 1942; NAZ SEC2/273, Provincial Commissioner, Western Province (Ndola) to Chief Secretary (Lusaka), 26 June 1942; and NAZ SEC2/273, Provincial Commissioner (Kasempa) to Chief Secretary (Lusaka), 28 September 1942.

26. NAZ SEC 2/273, Provincial Commissioner (Kasempa) to Governor (Lusaka), 4 July 1943.

27. NAZ SEC2/273, Chief Secretary (Lusaka) to Provincial Commissioner (Mongu), 2 December 1942.

28. NAZ SEC2/273, Provincial Commissioner, Northern Province (Kasama) to Chief Secretary (Lusaka), 27 April 1942; and NAZ SEC2/273, Officer-in-Charge, Kaonde-Lunda Province (Kasempa) to Chief Secretary (Lusaka), 29 May 1942.

29. NAZ SEC2/273, Officer-in-Charge, Kaonde-Lunda Province (Kasempa) to District Commissioner (Mwinilunga), 27 April 1942; and NAZ SEC2/273, Officer-in-Charge, Kaonde-Lunda Province to Chief Secretary, 29 May 1942.

30. NAZ SEC2/273, Officer-in-Charge, Kaonde-Lunda Province to Chief Secretary, 29 May 1942.

31. Tembo, "Rubber Production," 232.

32. Tembo, 233.

33. Tembo, 234–43.

34. NAZ SEC2/273, Statement from the Secretary of State (London), to Chief Secretary (Lusaka), 26 February 1943.

35. NAZ SEC2/273, Statement from Secretary of State to Chief Secretary, 26 February 1943.

36. NAZ SEC2/273, Secretary of State (London) to Governor (Lusaka), 27 October 1943.

Notes to Pages 61–65

37. NAZ SEC2/273, Statement from Secretary of State to Chief Secretary, 26 February 1943.

38. NAZ SEC2/273, Director of Agriculture (Mazabuka) to Chief Secretary (Lusaka), 12 April 1943; and NRG, *Department of Agriculture Annual Report for the Year 1944* (Lusaka: Government Printer, 1945), 4.

39. NAZ SEC2/273, Deputy Controller of Rubber, Ministry of Supply (London) to Governor (Lusaka), 23 February 1945; see also *Department of Agriculture Annual Report for the Year 1944*, 3, where higher production figures are given: 40.7 tons and 117.5 tons for 1943 and 1944, respectively.

40. NAZ SEC2/273, Secretary of State for the Colonies (London) to Governor (Lusaka), 10 December 1945.

41. NAZ SEC2/273, Director of Agriculture (Mazabuka) to Chief Secretary (Lusaka), 20 September 1945.

42. NAZ SEC2/273, Chief Secretary (Lusaka) to All Provincial Commissioners, Director of Agriculture, All District Commissioners, The Accountant-General, The Auditor, 6 October 1945.

43. Tembo, "Rubber Production," 246.

44. Elizabeth Colson, "The Tonga and the Shortage of Implements," *Rhodes-Livingstone Journal* 14 (1954): 37.

45. Colson, 37.

46. Colson, 37.

47. Ashley Jackson, *The British Empire and the Second World War* (London: Hambledon Continuum, 2006), 44; Madhusree Mukerjee, *Churchill's Secret War: The British Empire and the Ravaging of India during World War Two* (New York: Basic Books, 2010); and Bennett S. Siamwiza, "A History of Famine in Zambia c. 1825–1949" (PhD thesis, University of Cambridge, 1998), 279.

48. NAZ SEC2/271, Director of Agriculture (Mazabuka) to Chief Secretary (Lusaka), 11 September 1942.

49. NAZ SEC2/271, G. Emrys, Director, Plows (Pty) Ltd (Cape Town) to African Lakes Company (Ndola), 3 June 1942.

50. NAZ SEC2/271, G. Emrys, Director, Plows (Pty) Ltd, to African Lakes Company, 3 June 1942; and NAZ SEC2/271, District Superintendent, African Lakes Company (Ndola) to Import Controller and Director of Civil Supplies (Lusaka), n.d.

51. NAZ SEC2/271, District Commissioner (Abercorn) to traders, 13 January 1942.

52. NAZ SEC2/271, Chief Secretary's Tour Report of Northern Province, 3 August 1943; see also NAZ SEC2/271, Notes on the Making of Native Hoes by R. H. Howard, Agricultural Supervisor for Northern Province, November 1942.

53. NAZ SEC2/271, British South Africa Company (Lusaka) to Chief Secretary (Lusaka), 16 June 1942; and NAZ SEC2/271, Chief Secretary (Lusaka) to All Provincial Commissioners and District Commissioners, 1 July 1942.

54. NAZ SEC2/271, Chief Secretary to All Provincial Commissioners and District Commissioners, 1 July 1942.

Notes to Pages 65–67

55. NAZ SEC2/271, Chief Secretary to All Provincial Commissioners and District Commissioners, 1 July 1942.

56. Quoted in E. R. Wicker, "Colonial Development and Welfare, 1929–1957: The Evolution of a Policy," *Social and Economic Studies* 7, no. 4 (December 1958): 181.

57. NAZ SEC2/271, Extract from Minutes of the 4th Meeting of the Finance Sub-committee of the Native Development Board held at Lusaka on Monday 20th July 1942.

58. NAZ SEC2/271, Extract from Minutes of the Finance Sub-committee, 20th July 1942.

59. NAZ SEC2/271, Note for Circulation to the Finance Sub-committee of the Native Development Board, July 1942.

60. NAZ SEC2/271, Note for Circulation to the Finance Sub-committee, July 1942.

61. NAZ SEC2/271, Chief Secretary (Lusaka) to Provincial Commissioner, Northern Province (Kasama), 24 July 1942.

62. NAZ SEC2/271, Chief Secretary's Tour Report of Northern Province, 3 August 1943.

63. NAZ SEC2/271, Note for Circulation to the Finance Sub-committee, July 1942; and ibid., Extract from Minutes of the Finance Sub-committee, 20 July 1942.

64. NAZ SEC2/271, Note for Circulation to the Finance Sub-committee, July 1942.

65. NAZ SEC2/271, Extract from Minutes of the Finance Sub-committee, 20 July 1942.

66. NAZ SEC2/271, Provincial Commissioner, Central Province (Broken Hill) to Chief Secretary (Lusaka), 18 August 1942.

67. NAZ SEC2/271, Provincial Commissioner, Kaonde-Lunda Province (Kasempa) to Chief Secretary (Lusaka), 18 September 1942.

68. NAZ SEC2/271, Provincial Commissioner, Kaonde-Lunda Province to Chief Secretary, 18 September 1942.

69. NAZ SEC2/271, District Commissioner (Ndola) to Provincial Commissioner, Western Province (Ndola), 4 August 1942.

70. NAZ SEC2/271, Senior Agricultural Officer (Abercorn) to Director of Agriculture (Mazabuka), 29 September 1942.

71. NAZ SEC2/271, District Commissioner (Kawambwa) to Provincial Commissioner, Northern Province (Kasama), 27 November 1942 (emphasis in the original).

72. NAZ SEC2/271, District Commissioner (Lundazi) to Provincial Commissioner, Eastern Province (Fort Jameson), 1 December 1942.

73. NAZ SEC2/271, Provincial Commissioner, Eastern Province (Fort Jameson) to Chief Secretary (Lusaka), 11 December 1942.

74. NAZ SEC2/271, Note for Executive Council, 21 December 1942.

75. NAZ SEC2/271, Note for Executive Council, 21 December 1942.

76. NAZ SEC2/271, Chief Secretary (Lusaka) to Provincial Commissioners for Eastern Province (Fort Jameson) and Northern Province (Kasama), 15 January 1943.

77. NAZ SEC2/271, Chief Secretary (Lusaka) to Accountant-General (Lusaka), 14 April 1943; and Chief Secretary (Lusaka) to Provincial Commissioner, Northern Province (Kasama), 14 April 1943.

196

Notes to Pages 67–70

78. NAZ SEC2/271, District Commissioner (Abercorn) to Provincial Commissioner, Northern Province (Kasama), 1 February 1943.

79. NAZ SEC2/271, Provincial Commissioner, Northern Province (Kasama) to Chief Secretary (Lusaka), 6 April 1944.

80. NAZ SEC2/271, District Commissioner (Balovale) to Provincial Commissioner, Kaonde-Lunda (Kasempa), 30 April 1943. See also NAZ SEC2/271, Provincial Commissioner, Northern Province (Kasama) to Chief Secretary (Lusaka), 6 April 1945.

81. NAZ SEC2/271, Chief Secretary (Lusaka) to Supplies Representative of the Government of Northern Rhodesia (Johannesburg), 19 October 1942; and NAZ SEC2/271, Controller of Imports (Livingstone) to Supplies Representative of the Government of Northern Rhodesia (Johannesburg), 8 July 1942.

82. NAZ SEC2/271, Chief Secretary (Lusaka) to Provincial Commissioner, Eastern Province (Fort Jameson), 9 April 1943; and NAZ SEC2/271, Acting Chief Secretary (Lusaka) to Provincial Commissioner, Northern Province (Kasama), 15 March 1944.

83. NAZ SEC2/271, Chief Secretary (Lusaka) to Provincial Commissioner, Northern Province (Kasama), 15 September 1943.

84. NAZ SEC2/271, Acting Chief Secretary (Lusaka) to Provincial Commissioner, Northern Province (Kasama), 15 March 1944.

85. NAZ SEC2/271, Provincial Commissioner, Northern Province (Kasama) to Chief Secretary (Lusaka), 23 August 1945.

86. Thaddeus Sunseri, "World War II and the Transformation of the Tanzanian Forests," in Byfield et al., *Africa and World War II*, 238.

87. Von Oppen, *Terms of Trade*, 159.

88. See, for example, Chewe Mebbiens Chabatama, "Peasant Farming, the State, and Food Security in North-Western Province of Zambia, 1902–1964" (PhD diss., University of Toronto, 1999), 183.

89. Von Oppen, *Terms of Trade*, 155.

90. NAZ SEC1/45, Extract from Minutes of Meeting of the Native Development Board held at Lusaka on 24 February 1940; and NAZ SEC1/45, Chief Secretary (Lusaka) to Director of Agriculture (Mazabuka), 6 March 1940.

91. Byfield, "Producing for the War," 24.

92. Byfield, 32.

93. NAZ SEC2/271, Controller of Customs (Livingstone) to Chief Secretary (Lusaka), 23 June 1942; and NAZ SEC2/271, Chief Secretary (Lusaka) to Provincial Commissioner, Kaonde-Lunda Province (Kasempa), 16 November 1942.

94. NAZ SEC2/271, Extract from Letter from Messrs Mann and Bishop Ltd (London) received by Barclays Bank (Lusaka) on 18 June 1942; see also NAZ SEC2/271, Messrs Mann and Bishop Ltd (London) to Barclays Bank (London), 20 August 1942; and NAZ SEC2/271, Chief Secretary (Lusaka) to Director of Agriculture (Mazabuka), 8 October 1942.

95. NAZ SEC2/271, Messrs Mann and Bishop Ltd to Barclays Bank, 18 June 1942.

96. NAZ SEC2/271, Chief Secretary (Lusaka) to Provincial Commissioner, Kaonde-Lunda Province (Kasempa), 16 November 1942.

Notes to Pages 70–74

97. NAZ SEC2/271, Secretary for Native Affairs (Lusaka) to Financial Secretary (Lusaka), 17 October 1942. The concept of "economic warfare" has been explained by Martin Fritz, "Economic Warfare," in *The Oxford Companion to the Second World War*, ed. I. C. B. Dear (Oxford: Oxford University Press, 1995), 318–21; and Jackson, *British Empire*, 48.

98. NAZ SEC1/45, *Gazette of the Union of South Africa*, 14 August 1942.

99. NAZ SEC2/45, Report on Beeswax Development Work in Northern Rhodesia Submitted to the Native Development Board, 5 October 1940.

100. NAZ SEC1/45, Report on Beeswax Development.

101. NAZ SEC1/45, Report on Beeswax Development.

102. NAZ SEC1/45, Report on Beeswax Development.

103. Byfield, "Producing for the War," 32.

104. NAZ SEC1/45, Report on Beeswax Development.

105. NAZ SEC1/45, Report on Beeswax Development.

106. NAZ SEC1/45, Report on Beeswax Development.

107. NAZ SEC1/45, Report on Beeswax Development.

108. NAZ SEC1/45, Report on Beeswax Development.

109. NAZ SEC1/45, Report on Beeswax Development.

110. NAZ SEC1/45, Report on Beeswax Development.

111. NAZ SEC1/45, Report on Beeswax Development.

112. NAZ SEC1/45, Report on Beeswax Development.

113. NAZ SEC1/45, Report on Beeswax Development.

114. Byfield, "Producing for the War," 32.

115. NAZ SEC1/45, Report on Beeswax Development; and NAZ SEC2/45, Chief Secretary (Lusaka) to Director of Agriculture (Mazabuka), 6 March 1940.

116. NAZ SEC2/45, Secretary for Native Affairs (Lusaka) to Financial Secretary (Lusaka), 22 January 1943.

117. NAZ SEC2/45, Director of Agriculture (Mazabuka) to Chief Secretary (Lusaka), 10 October 1942.

118. NAZ SEC2/45, Secretary for Native Affairs (Lusaka) to Financial Secretary (Lusaka), 17 October 1942; and NAZ SEC2/45, Chief Secretary to Director of Agriculture (Mazabuka), 8 October 1942.

119. NAZ SEC2/45, Extract taken from a record of an Interview with Mr B. P. Rudge of Balovale with the Chief Secretary, 27 November 1942; and NAZ SEC2/45, Chief Secretary (Lusaka) to Accountant-General (Lusaka), 15 December 1942.

120. NAZ SEC2/45, Accountant General (Lusaka) to Chief Secretary (Lusaka), 19 December 1942.

121. NAZ SEC2/45, Provincial Commissioner, Kaonde-Lunda (Kasempa) to Chief Secretary (Lusaka), 4 January 1943; and NAZ SEC2/45, Secretary for Native Affairs (Lusaka) to Chief Secretary (Lusaka), 13 January 1943.

122. NAZ SEC3/491, Extract from Mporokoso Tour Report no. 7 of 1933, 18 December 1933.

123. NAZ SEC3/491, Chief Secretary (Lusaka) to Provincial Commissioner, Barotse Province (Mongu), 30 October 1935.

Notes to Pages 74–77

124. NAZ SEC3/491, Secretary for Native Affairs (Lusaka) to Chief Secretary (Lusaka), 24 January 1934; NAZ SEC3/491, District Commissioner (Senanga) to Provincial Commissioner, Barotse Province (Mongu), 9 October 1935; and NAZ SEC3/491, Chief Secretary (Lusaka) to Provincial Commissioner, Barotse Province (Mongu), 30 October 1935.

125. NAZ SEC3/491, Director of Agriculture (Mazabuka) to Chief Secretary (Lusaka), 16 February 1942.

126. NAZ SEC3/491, Director of Agriculture to Chief Secretary, 16 February 1942.

127. NAZ SEC3/491, Circular from Colonial Office (London) to Chief Secretary (Lusaka), 30 January 1942; and NAZ SEC3/491, Note for Provincial Commissioners' Conference, 10 March 1942.

128. NAZ SEC3/491, Chief Secretary (Lusaka) to All Provincial Commissioners, 23 April 1942.

129. NAZ SEC3/491, Note for Provincial Commissioners' Conference, 10 March 1942.

130. Quoted in Wicker, "Colonial Development and Welfare," 182.

131. NAZ SEC3/491, North Western Rhodesia Cooperative Society (Ndola) to Acting Chief Secretary (Lusaka), 19 June 1942.

132. NAZ SEC3/491, E. W. Tarry (Lusaka) to Officer-in-Charge, Central Province (Broken Hill), 19 June 1942.

133. NAZ SEC3/491, District Commissioner (Abercorn) to Provincial Commissioner, Northern Province (Kasama), 22 May 1942.

134. NAZ SEC3/491, Chief Secretary (Lusaka) to Post Master-General (Livingstone), and Government Printer (Lusaka), 17 June 1942.

135. NAZ SEC3/491, Officer-in-Charge, Central Province (Broken Hill) to Chief Secretary (Lusaka), 18 June 1942; and NAZ SEC3/491, Chief Secretary (Lusaka) to Officer-in-Charge, Central Province (Broken Hill), 22 June 1942.

136. NAZ SEC3/491, Note for Provincial Commissioners' Conference, 10 March 1942.

137. NAZ SEC3/491, Note for Provincial Commissioners' Conference, 10 March 1942.

138. NAZ SEC3/491, Note for Provincial Commissioners' Conference, 10 March 1942.

139. NAZ SEC3/491, Note for Provincial Commissioners' Conference, 10 March 1942.

140. NAZ SEC3/491, Director of African Education (Mazabuka) to Chief Secretary (Lusaka), 13 March 1942.

141. NAZ SEC3/491, Commissioner of Police (Livingstone) to Chief Secretary (Lusaka), 26 March 1942.

142. NAZ SEC3/491, Extract of the Meeting of the Finance Sub-committee of the Native Development Board held at Lusaka on Monday 20 July 1942; and NAZ SEC3/491, Chief Secretary (Lusaka) to All Provincial Commissioners, 24 July 1942.

143. NAZ SEC3/491, Director of Agriculture (Mazabuka) to Provincial Commissioner, Barotse Province (Mongu), 24 August 1942; NAZ SEC3/491, District Commissioner (Sesheke) to Chief Secretary (Lusaka), 8 September 1942.

144. NAZ SEC3/491, Provincial Commissioner, Central Province (Broken Hill) to Chief Secretary (Lusaka), 31 October 1942.

145. NAZ SEC3/491, Chief Secretary (Lusaka) to Provincial Commissioner, Central Province (Broken Hill), 7 November 1942.

Notes to Pages 77–82

146. NAZ SEC3/491, Provincial Commissioner, Central Province (Broken Hill) to Chief Secretary (Lusaka), 13 January 1943.

147. NAZ SEC3/491, Provincial Commissioner, Central Province to Chief Secretary, 13 January 1943.

148. NAZ SEC3/491, Provincial Commissioner, Northern Province (Kasama) to Post Master-General (Livingstone), 5 August 1942.

CHAPTER 3: WAR AND THE ECONOMICS OF THE HOME FRONT

1. F. Crawford, Chief Secretary, *Legislative Council Debates*, 8 December 1947.

2. Carolyn A. Brown, "African Labor in the Making of World War II," in *Africa and World War II*, ed. Judith A. Byfield et al. (New York: Cambridge University Press, 2015), 45.

3. Ashley Jackson, *The British Empire and the Second World War* (London: Hambledon Continuum, 2006), 235.

4. National Archives of Zambia (hereafter NAZ) SEC1/1362, Note for Executive Council by the Chief Secretary, ca. 1944.

5. M. R. D. Foot and P. Stansky, "United Kingdom," in *The Oxford Companion to the Second World War*, ed. I. C. B. Dear (Oxford: Oxford University Press, 1995), 1134.

6. David Killingray and Richard Rathbone, "Introduction," in *Africa and the Second World War*, ed. David Killingray and Richard Rathbone (Basingstoke, UK: Palgrave Macmillan, 1986), 8.

7. P. T. Bauer, "Origins of the Statutory Export Monopolies of British West Africa," *Business History Review* 28, no. 3 (1954): 205. For a detailed discussion of the Japanese strategic conquest of Southeast Asian Allied colonies, see Basil H. Liddell Hart, *History of the Second World War* (London: Cassell, 1970), 212–38.

8. Thaddeus Sunseri, "World War II and the Transformation of the Tanzanian Forests," in Byfield et al., *Africa and World War II*, 238.

9. NAZ SEC1/1362, Note for Executive Council, ca. 1944. See also Richard Overy, "World Trade and World Economy," in Dear, *Oxford Companion to the Second World War*, 1284–85.

10. Cited in Jackson, *British Empire*, 48.

11. Jackson, *British Empire*, 48.

12. Michael Cowen and Nicholas Westcott, "British Imperial Economic Policy during the Second World War," in Killingray and Rathbone, *Africa and the Second World War*, 40.

13. John D. Hargreaves, *Decolonization in Africa* (London: Routledge, 1996), 55. See also Jackson, *British Empire*, 44.

14. NAZ SEC1/1362, Note for Executive Council, ca. 1944. See also Foot and Stansky, "United Kingdom," 1154–56.

15. Cowen and Westcott, "British Imperial Economic Policy," 41.

16. Cowen and Westcott, 41.

17. Quoted in M. F. Hill, *Permanent Way: The Story of the Kenya and Uganda Railway*, 2d ed. (Nairobi: East African Railways and Harbours, 1961), 258.

Notes to Pages 82–87

18. See especially Catherine R. Schenk, *The Decline of Sterling: Measuring the Retreat of an International Currency, 1945–1992* (Cambridge: Cambridge University Press, 2010), 37–80; and Gerold Krozewski, "Sterling, the 'Minor' Territories, and the End of Formal Empire, 1939–1958," *Economic History Review* 46, no. 2 (1993): 239–65.

19. NAZ SEC1/1362, Note for Executive Council, ca. 1944.

20. *The Times*, 14 April 1943.

21. Rosaleen Smyth, "War Propaganda during the Second World War in Northern Rhodesia," *African Affairs* 83, no. 332 (July 1984): 348.

22. NRG, Report of the Northern Rhodesia Supply Mission to the United Kingdom (Lusaka: Government Printer, 1944), 4; and Northern News, 24 October 1946.

23. NRG, *Report of the Northern Rhodesia Supply Mission*, 4.

24. NRG, 5.

25. NRG, 5.

26. NRG, 5.

27. NRG, 5.

28. NRG, 3.

29. See, for example, Samuel N. Chipungu, *The State, Technology and Peasant Differentiation in Southern Zambia: A Case Study of the Southern Province, 1890–1980* (Lusaka: Historical Association of Zambia, 1988).

30. Killingray and Rathbone, "Introduction," 8.

31. Killingray and Rathbone, 8.

32. NAZ SEC3/42, Note for Executive Council, ca. 1947; NAZ SEC3/88, Extract of Minute no. 522/43 from Postmaster-General (Livingstone) to Chief Secretary (Lusaka), 7 September 1943; and NAZ SEC3/88, Governor (Lusaka) to Secretary of State for the Colonies (London), 14 February 1947.

33. NAZ SEC3/87, Posts and Telegraphs: Proposed Savings Bank Scheme for African Ranks in H. M. Forces, 9 June 1941.

34. NAZ SEC1/704, Auditor General (Lusaka) to Chairman, Legislative Council Committee on Taxation (Lusaka), 29 September 1945.

35. NAZ SEC3/42, Note for Executive Council, ca. 1947.

36. NAZ SEC3/42, Note for Executive Council, ca. 1947.

37. For a comparative discussion on these issues elsewhere, see Ashley Jackson, *Botswana, 1939–1945: An African Country at War* (Oxford: Oxford University Press, 1999), 142.

38. NAZ SP4/2/6 Loc 5081, Mazabuka Tour Report no. 1 of 1947.

39. NAZ SP4/2/6 Loc 5081, Mazabuka Tour Report no. 1 of 1947.

40. NAZ SEC3/45, S. K. Patel and C. C. Patel v. The Crown, in the High Court of Northern Rhodesia. See also Lewis H. Gann, *A History of Northern Rhodesia: Early Days to 1953* (London: Chatto and Windus, 1964), 349.

41. NAZ SEC3/44 Vol. I, Price Controller (Lusaka) to Chief Secretary (Lusaka), 28 April 1947.

42. Jackson, *Botswana*, 140.

43. NAZ SEC3/485, Confidential Correspondence from Provincial Commissioner, Western Province (Ndola) to Chief Secretary (Lusaka), 5 May 1943.

Notes to Pages 87–90

44. NAZ SEC3/44 Vol. II, Extract from the Sixth Meeting of the African Provincial Council for the Western Province held at Luanshya on 9–10 July 1947.

45. NAZ SEC3/75, Commissioner of Police (Lusaka) to Chief Secretary (Lusaka), 18 September 1947; and NRG, *Legislative Council Debates*, 24 September 1947. See also NAZ SEC3/44 Vol. I, Commissioner of Police (Lusaka) to Financial Secretary (Lusaka), 10 July 1947.

46. NAZ SEC3/45, Record of Meeting in the Office of the Labour Commissioner at 9:30 on Friday 16 November 1947.

47. NAZ SEC1/1758 Vol. II, Report on Public Opinion for the Western Province for the Month of June 1941, 2 July 1941. Prosecution of some traders for profiteering by selling items above the control prices was equally adopted in Nigeria—with a varying degree of success; see Judith A. Byfield, "Women, Rice, and War: Political and Economic Crisis in Wartime Abeokuta (Nigeria)," in Byfield et al., *Africa and World War II*, 157.

48. Cowen and Westcott, "British Imperial Economic Policy," 20–67. For a detailed discussion of rationing schemes in Britain during the war, see Foot and Stansky, "United Kingdom," 1135.

49. NAZ SEC1/1620, Report of the Chairman of the Mufulira Copper Production Committee 12th Meeting held on Tuesday 15 June 1943 at 4PM in the Office of the District Commissioner.

50. NAZ SEC3/485, Emergency Powers (Rationing) Regulations, 1944.

51. NAZ SEC3/485, Emergency Powers (Rationing) Regulations, 1944.

52. NAZ SEC3/485, Emergency Powers (Rationing) Regulations, 1944.

53. NAZ SEC3/485, Emergency Powers (Rationing) Regulations, 1944.

54. NRG, *Legislative Council Debates*, 16 September 1947.

55. NRG, *Legislative Council Debates*, 16 September 1947.

56. *Mutende*, November 1946.

57. Judith A. Byfield, Preface to Byfield et al., *Africa and World War II*, xx.

58. NAZ SEC3/42, Emergency Powers (Control of Prices and Hoarding) Regulations, July 1942.

59. NAZ SEC3/42, Director of Civil Supplies to Financial Secretary, 1 March 1944; and *Bulawayo Chronicle*, 24 September 1943.

60. NAZ SEC3/42, Director of Civil Supplies to Financial Secretary.

61. Black market is used here to mean buying and selling at prices above those officially fixed, or in quantities or for purposes not permitted by the rationing regulations. It normally appears wherever there are artificial restrictions on the ordinary operations of a market.

62. See, for example, Jackson, *British Empire*, 48.

63. A nuanced discussion on these aspects is contained in Schenk, *Decline of Sterling*, 60–79; and Overy, "World Trade and World Economy," 1283.

64. NAZ SEC3/44 Vol. I, Chief Secretary (Lusaka) to E. Leishman (Kitwe), 13 August 1947. See also Nicholas J. Westcott, "The Impact of the Second World War on Tanganyika, 1939–49," in Killingray and Rathbone, *Africa and the Second World War*, 144–45.

65. NAZ SEC1/1362, Colonial Office Circular no. 18889/23/42.

Notes to Pages 90–92

66. NRG, *Legislative Council Debates*, 9 June 1947.

67. NAZ SEC3/44 Vol. I, Price Controller (Lusaka) to Financial Controller (Lusaka), 23 July 1947.

68. NRG, *Legislative Council Debates*, Hansard no. 57, 9 June 1947, columns 144 and 237, pp. 317, 394; and NAZ SEC3/44 Vol. I, Price Controller (Lusaka) to Financial Secretary (Lusaka), 31 March 1947.

69. NRG, *Legislative Council Debates*, 10 May 1943; *Bulawayo Chronicle*, 24 September 1943; NAZ SEC3/485, Confidential Correspondence from Provincial Commissioner, Western Province (Ndola) to Chief Secretary (Lusaka), 5 May 1943; *Livingstone Mail*, 26 September 1947; *Bulawayo Chronicle*, 1 September 1947; *Bulawayo Chronicle*, 3 September 1947; *Bulawayo Chronicle*, 14 August 1947; *Bulawayo Chronicle*, 27 August 1947; *Northern News*, 28 August 1947; *Bulawayo Chronicle*, 30 August 1947; *Northern News*, 28 August 1947; and *Northern News*, 14 September 1947.

70. NAZ SEC1/1770, Report on Public Opinion for Central Province for July 1942, 3 August 1942.

71. NAZ SEC1/1770, Report on Public Opinion for Central Province for July 1942, 3 August 1942.

72. NRG, *Interim Report of the Commission of Inquiry into the Cost of Living* (Lusaka: Government Printer, 1946), 7.

73. NAZ SEC1/1362, Colonial Office Circular No. 18889/23/42; and NAZ SEC3/45, Memorandum on Price Control ca. 1947. See also *Northern News*, 7 August 1947; and NAZ SEC3/44 Vol. I, Price Controller (Lusaka) to Financial Secretary (Lusaka), 31 March 1947.

74. NRG, *Maize Meal (Wholesale Prices) Order of 1942* (Lusaka: Government Printer, 1942).

75. NRG, *Maize Meal (Wholesale Prices) Order of 1942*.

76. Cowen and Westcott, "British Imperial Economic Policy," 20–67.

77. NRG, *Interim Report of the Commission of Inquiry into the Cost of Living*, 6.

78. NRG, 6.

79. NRG, *Legislative Council Debates*, 3 December 1947.

80. NRG, *Legislative Council Debates*, 3 December 1947.

81. NRG, *Legislative Council Debates*, 3 December 1947; and Mining Industry Archive [hereafter MIA] 14.3.3F, Statement by the Secretary of State for the Colonies on the State of British Territories in East and Central Africa, 1945–1950, 137.

82. Killingray and Rathbone, "Introduction," 8. For a comparative perspective elsewhere, see Daniel Owen Spence, "Beyond *Talwar*: A Cultural Reappraisal of the 1946 Royal Indian Navy Mutiny," *Journal of Imperial and Commonwealth History* 46, no. 3 (2015): 489–508.

83. NAZ SEC1/1362, Provincial Commissioner, Western Province (Ndola) to Chief Secretary (Lusaka), 20 August 1941.

84. NAZ SEC1/1362, Labour Officer (Mufulira) to Labour Commissioner (Lusaka), 22 July 1943. See also *Bulawayo Chronicle*, 11 June 1947; *Northern News*, 24 October 1946; *Sunday Times*, 13 October 1946; and *Bulawayo Chronicle*, 10 May 1946; NAZ SEC1/1362,

Notes to Pages 93–94

Labour Commissioner (Lusaka) to Chief Secretary (Lusaka), 3 September 1943; NRG, *Legislative Council Debates*, 16 December 1941, 353–54; NAZ SEC1/1728 Vol. VII, Record of His Excellency the Governor's Meeting with Representatives of the Broken Hill African Community held at the Town Location on Wednesday 24 June 1942 at 11:30; NAZ SEC1/1758 Vol. II, Intelligence Report for Western Province for the Month of February 1942, 6 March 1942; NAZ SEC1/1758 Vol. II, Report on Public Opinion for Central Province, 8 March 1942; and Gann, *History of Northern Rhodesia*, 349.

85. Ackson Kanduza, *The Political Economy of Underdevelopment in Northern Rhodesia, 1918–1960: A Case Study of Customs Tariff and Railway Freight Policies* (Lanham, MD: University of America Press, 1986), 186. For customs purposes, Northern Rhodesia was divided into two areas: the Zambezi Basin Area, south of a line drawn from the southeast corner of the Katanga pedicle to Fife on the Tanganyika border, which contained all the important industries and accounted for the vast bulk of the trade of the Territory; and the area north of this line, which was included in the conventional Congo Basin Area, but which was of negligible importance from the commercial point of view. In the area within the Congo Basin, no preference could be granted, and customs duty was charged at the empire rate on all goods, whatever their country of origin.

86. NAZ SEC1/1620, Chairman's Report of the 18th Meeting of the Mufulira Copper Production Committee held on Tuesday 16 November 1943 at 4PM in the Office of the District Commissioner.

87. Richard N. Gardner, *Sterling-Dollar Diplomacy in Current Perspective: The Origins and the Prospects of Our International Economic Order* (New York: Columbia University Press, 1980), 308.

88. A. R. Conan, *The Problem of Sterling* (London: Macmillan, 1966), 38.

89. The most vocal being the Northern Rhodesia Civil Servants' Association and the Associated Chambers of Commerce.

90. NRG, *Interim Report of the Commission of Inquiry into the Cost of Living*, 6. For the price index in other countries, see Judith A. Byfield, "Producing for the War," in Byfield et al., *Africa and World War II*, 39.

91. Lawrence Butler, *Copper Empire: Mining and the Colonial State in Northern Rhodesia, c. 1930–1964* (Houndsmill, UK: Palgrave Macmillan, 2007), 69.

92. NAZ SEC1/1363, A Report of Some Aspects of African Living Conditions on the Copperbelt of Northern Rhodesia by A. L. Saffery, 3 January 1943.

93. See Cowen and Westcott, "British Imperial Economic Policy," 59.

94. NAZ SEC3/48 Vol. III, Interim Report of the Cost of Living Advisory Committee presented by the Minister of Labour and National Service to Parliament by Command of His Majesty, London, March 1947.

95. NAZ SEC1/1362, Note for Executive Council on Cost of Living Allowances for Africans, ca. 1946.

96. NAZ SEC1/1362, Chief Secretary (Lusaka) to Heads of Department and Provincial Commissioners, 23 July 1946.

97. NAZ SEC1/1362, Chief Secretary (Lusaka) to North Eastern Rhodesia Agricultural and Commercial Association (Lusaka), 11 April 1946.

Notes to Pages 94–100

98. NAZ SEC1/1362, Note for Executive Council, ca. 1946.

99. NAZ SEC1/1362, Extract from Despatch from Governor (Lusaka) to Sec of State (London), 25 February 1943.

100. NAZ SEC2/200, Western Province Newsletter for the Fourth Quarter of 1946; and NAZ SEC2/241, Tours by Members Nominated to Represent Native Interests, Report on the Copperbelt Tour, 21 February 1947.

101. NAZ SEC2/200, Western Province Newsletter for the Fourth Quarter of 1946; and NAZ SEC2/241, Report on the Copperbelt Tour, 21 February 1947.

102. NAZ SEC2/74, Annual Report on African Affairs for the Year 1947: Central Province.

CHAPTER 4: STRANGERS IN OUR MIDST

1. My sources do not permit an examination of African perceptions of the Poles in detail. Since the refugees were kept more or less confined, they are unlikely to have made a great impression on Africans.

2. Nicoli Nattrass and Jeremy Seekings, "The Economy and Poverty in the Twentieth Century in South Africa," in *The Cambridge History of South Africa*, vol. 2, *1885–1994*, ed. Robert Ross, Anne Kelk Mager, and Bill Nasson (Cambridge: Cambridge University Press, 2012), 533.

3. Lewis H. Gann, *A History of Northern Rhodesia: Early Days to 1953* (London: Chatto and Windus, 1964), 331.

4. Hugh Macmillan with Frank Shapiro, *Zion in Africa: The Jews of Zambia* (London: I. B. Tauris, 2017), 113.

5. National Archives of Zambia (hereafter NAZ) SEC3/49 Vol. II, Chief Immigration Officer's Notes on Statistics concerning Non-native Employees Supplied by Mines and Other Employers, n.d. but 1948. See also NAZ SEC3/49 Vol. I, Northern Rhodesia Immigration Statistics Summary for 1947.

6. NAZ SEC3/55, Provincial Commissioner, Western Province (Ndola) to Chief Secretary (Lusaka), 28 June 1938. See also NAZ SEC3/55, Provincial Commissioner, Western Province to Chief Secretary, 22 March 1938.

7. *Bulawayo Chronicle*, 1 August 1938.

8. *Bulawayo Chronicle*, 1 August 1938; and *Livingstone Mail*, 3 August 1938.

9. *Bulawayo Chronicle*, 2 August 1938.

10. NAZ SEC3/55, Chief Immigration Officer (Livingstone) to Chief Secretary (Lusaka), 1 November 1938.

11. Martin R. Rupiah, "The History of the Establishment of Internment Camps and Refugee Settlements in Southern Rhodesia, 1938–1952," *Zambezia* 22, no. 2 (1995): 145.

12. Jochen Lingelbach, "Polish Refugees in British Colonial East and Central Africa during and after World War Two" (DPhil thesis, Universität Leipzig, 2017), 28. Several hundred thousand Polish residents of the annexed territory became targets of the mass expulsions carried out in the eastern parts of Poland by Soviet troops. Many were deported to Siberia and Soviet Central Asia. The deportations targeted both Polish elites and Poles of all social categories from peasants to the intelligentsia. These

205

Notes to Pages 100–103

removals were aimed at crushing Polish political and social life in order to safeguard Soviet domination.

13. NAZ SEC1/1703 Vol. I, British High Commissioner (Jerusalem) to Governor (Lusaka), 21 July 1941.

14. NAZ SEC1/1703 Vol. I, Chief Secretary to the East Africa Conference of Governors (Nairobi) to Governor (Lusaka), 18 June 1941.

15. NAZ SEC1/1703 Vol. I, Officer in Charge of War Evacuees (on special train in Mafikeng) to Governor (Lusaka), 5 August 1941. See also Macmillan with Shapiro, *Zion in Africa.*

16. Lingelbach, "Polish Refugees," 27.

17. Robert I. Rotberg, *Black Heart: Gore-Browne and the Politics of Multiracial Zambia* (Berkeley: University of California Press, 1977), 237. The gender disparity in the refugee population could be ascribed to the fact that while whole families were arrested by the authorities in Poland, the male household heads were usually separated from the rest of the family.

18. NAZ SEC1/1703 Vol. I, Director of War Evacuees and Camps (Lusaka) to Chief Secretary (Lusaka), 22 July 1943. See also Mary-Ann Sandifort, "The Forgotten Story of Polish Refugees in Zambia," *Bulletin and Record*, June 2015, 20–21.

19. NAZ SEC1/1703 Vol. I, Director of War Evacuees and Camps (Lusaka) to Chief Secretary (Lusaka), 22 July 1943. See also Sandifort, "Forgotten Story of Polish Refugees," 20–21.

20. NAZ SEC1/1703 Vol. I, Emergency Immigration.

21. NAZ SP4/2/19, District Commissioner (Livingstone) to Provincial Commissioner, Southern Province (Livingstone), 12 June 1942.

22. NAZ SEC1/1700, Chief Secretary to the Conference of East African Governors (Nairobi) to Chief Secretary (Lusaka), 18 June 1941.

23. Rotberg, *Black Heart*, 236.

24. Rotberg, 237.

25. Rotberg, 236.

26. NAZ SEC1/1703 Vol. II, Director of War Evacuees and Camps (Lusaka) to Acting Chief Secretary (Lusaka), 16 March 1944.

27. NAZ SP4/2/19, District Commissioner (Livingstone) to Provincial Commissioner, Southern Province (Livingstone), 12 June 1942.

28. Rupiah, "History of the Establishment of Internment Camps," 151.

29. NAZ SEC1/1701 Vol. I, Director of War Evacuees and Camps (Lusaka) to Chief Secretary (Lusaka), 9 September 1943.

30. Baxter Tavuyanago, Tasara Muguti, and James Hlongwana, "Victims of the Rhodesian Immigration Policy: Polish Refugees from the Second World War," *Journal of Southern African Studies* 38, no. 4 (2012): 959.

31. NAZ SEC1/1701 Vol. I, Director of Medical Services (Lusaka) to Director of War Evacuees and Camps (Lusaka), 13 March 1942.

32. Rupiah, "History of the Establishment of Internment Camps," 149.

Notes to Pages 103–106

33. NAZ SEC1/1701 Vol. II, Director of War Evacuees and Camps (Lusaka) to Chief Secretary (Lusaka), 11 October 1945.

34. NAZ SEC1/1703 Vol. II, Regulations under Ordinance no. 5 of 1947.

35. Tavuyanago, Muguti, and Hlongwana, "Victims of the Rhodesian Immigration Policy," 956.

36. NAZ SEC1/1700 Vol. II, Commissioner of Police (Lusaka) to Chief Secretary (Lusaka), 27 February 1946.

37. NAZ SEC1/1703 Vol. II, Director of War Evacuees and Camps (Lusaka) to Chief Secretary (Lusaka), 5 February 1944.

38. NAZ SEC1/1701 Vol. II, Camp Commandant (Fort Jameson) to Director of War Evacuees and Camps (Lusaka), 9 August 1944; and NAZ SEC1/1701 Vol. II, Provincial Commissioner, Eastern Province (Fort Jameson) to Camp Commandant (Fort Jameson), 27 June 1944.

39. NAZ SEC1/1703 Vol. II, Director of War Evacuees and Camps to Chief Secretary, 5 February 1944.

40. NAZ SEC1/1703 Vol. II, Director of War Evacuees and Camps to Chief Secretary, 5 February 1944.

41. NAZ SEC1/1701 Vol. I, Memorandum by Director of War Evacuees and Camps on Expenditure by Polish Evacuees in Lusaka Town, 17 April 1943.

42. NAZ SEC1/1701 Vol. I, Memorandum by Director of War Evacuees and Camps.

43. NAZ SEC1/1701 Vol. I, Acting Director of War Evacuees and Camps (Lusaka) to Chief Secretary (Lusaka), 21 August 1944.

44. NAZ SEC1/1703 Vol. II, Director of War Evacuees and Camps (Lusaka) to Chief Secretary (Lusaka), 2 February 1944.

45. Mary-Ann Sandifort, "World War Two: The Deportation of Polish Refugees to Abercorn Camp in Northern Rhodesia" (MA diss., University of Leiden, 2015), 48.

46. Kaonga W. Mazala, "For Pleasure and Profit: Sex Work in Zambia, c. 1880–1964" (MA diss., University of Zambia, 2013), 35.

47. NAZ SEC1/1703 Vol. II, C. L. Burton, East African Refugee Administration (Nairobi) to Chief Secretary, Conference of Governors, East Africa (Nairobi), 21 September 1944.

48. NAZ SEC1/1701 Vol. II, Conference of Directors and Commissioners of Refugees in East Africa held in Nairobi, 9 January 1942.

49. NAZ SEC1/1701 Vol. I, Minutes of a Meeting between the Polish Consul-General and Director of War Evacuees and Camps held in Livingstone on 26 May 1942.

50. NAZ SEC1/1701 Vol. I, Officer in Charge of War Evacuees (Lusaka) to Chief Secretary (Lusaka), 29 September 1941; and NAZ SP4/2/19, District Commissioner (Livingstone) to Provincial Commissioner, Southern Province (Livingstone), 12 June 1942.

51. Rotberg, *Black Heart*, 237. Mrs Locke-King was the wife of a Methodist minister in Lusaka.

52. Rotberg, *Black Heart*, 237. For a detailed discussion on "miscegenation" in colonial Zambia, see J. B. Milner-Thornton, *The Long Shadow of the British Empire: The*

Notes to Pages 107–110

Ongoing Legacies of Race and Class in Zambia (New York: Palgrave Macmillan, 2012). For a broader perspective, see Ann L. Stoler, "Making Empire Respectable: The Politics of Race and Sexual Morality in 20th-Century Colonial Cultures," *American Ethnologist* 16, no. 4 (1989): 634–60.

53. NAZ SEC1/1701 Vol. II, R. G. Soulsby, Chairman of the Emergency Joint Committee Meeting (Lusaka) to Chief Secretary (Lusaka), 4 November 1943.

54. NAZ SEC1/1701 Vol. II, Soulsby to Chief Secretary, 4 November 1943.

55. Mazala, "For Pleasure and Profit," 45.

56. NAZ SEC1/1701 Vol. II, Extract from Resolutions on Social Welfare adopted by the Synod of the Methodist Church in Northern Rhodesia, November 1943. See also Samwiiri Lwanga-Lunyiigo, "Uganda's Long Connection with the Problem of Refugees: From the Polish Refugees of World War II to the Present," in *Uganda and the Problem of Refugees*, ed. A. G. G. Gingyera Pinycwa (Kampala: Makerere University Press, 1998), 10–12.

57. NAZ SEC1/1701 Vol. II, Chief Secretary (Lusaka) to Mrs R. G. Soulsby (Lusaka), 6 November 1943.

58. NAZ SEC1/1701 Vol. II, Honorary Secretary, Lusaka and District Welfare and Nursing Association (Lusaka) to Chief Secretary (Lusaka), 17 December 1943.

59. NAZ SEC1/1701 Vol. II, R. Welensky (Lusaka) to Chief Secretary (Lusaka), 27 July 1944.

60. NAZ SEC1/1701 Vol. II, Attorney-General (Salisbury) to Minister of Justice (Salisbury), 17 June 1944. See also, in the same file, Director of War Evacuees and Camps (Lusaka) to Provincial Commissioners, Eastern, Western, Central and Southern, 1 June 1944.

61. NAZ SEC1/1701 Vol. I, Manager, Lusaka Hotel (Lusaka) to Officer in Charge of Polish Refugees (Lusaka), 19 September 1941.

62. NAZ SEC1/1701 Vol. II, Polish Group of 22 (Lusaka) to Consul General of Poland (Lusaka), 30 September 1941.

63. NAZ SEC1/1701 Vol. II, Emergency Powers (Control of Movement of War Evacuees) Regulations, 1942.

64. NAZ SEC1/1701 Vol. II, Officer in Charge of War Evacuees (Lusaka) to Chief Secretary (Lusaka), 25 April 1942.

65. NAZ SEC1/1701 Vol. II, Officer in Charge of War Evacuees to Chief Secretary, 25 April 1942.

66. NAZ SEC1/1701 Vol. II, Officer in Charge of War Evacuees to Chief Secretary, 25 April 1942.

67. Rotberg, *Black Heart*, 237; and NAZ SEC1/1771, Intelligence Report for the Month of August 1943, 6 September 1943.

68. NAZ SEC1/1701 Vol. II, Director of War Evacuees and Camps (Lusaka) to Chief Secretary (Lusaka), 9 September 1943.

69. NAZ SEC1/1701 Vol. II, Director of War Evacuees and Camps to Chief Secretary, 9 September 1943.

70. NAZ SEC1/1701 Vol. II, Director of War Evacuees and Camps to Chief Secretary, 9 September 1943.

Notes to Pages 110–116

71. Rotberg, *Black Heart*, 237; NAZ SEC1/1701 Vol. II, Chief Secretary (Lusaka) to Chief Secretary, East Africa Conference of Governors (Nairobi), 8 October 1943; and NAZ SEC1/1701 Vol. II, Director of War Evacuees and Camps (Lusaka) to Chief Secretary (Lusaka), 12 October 1943.

72. See, for example, Gann, *History of Northern Rhodesia*; and James Ferguson, *Expectations of Modernity: Myths and Meanings of Urban Life on the Zambian Copperbelt* (Berkeley: University of California Press, 1999).

73. *Bulawayo Chronicle*, 31 October 1941.

74. NAZ SEC1/1703 Vol. I, Director of War Evacuees and Camps (Lusaka) to Chief Secretary (Lusaka), 15 July 1943; and NAZ SEC1/1703 Vol. I, Chief Secretary (Lusaka) to Chief Secretary, Conference of Governors (Nairobi), 24 July 1943.

75. NAZ SEC1/1703, Vol. I, Chief Secretary to Chief Secretary, Conference of Governors, 24 July 1943.

76. NAZ SEC1/1702, Note for Executive Council, 7 August 1947.

77. NAZ SEC1/1702, Note for Executive Council, 7 August 1947.

78. NAZ SEC1/1702, Note for Executive Council, 7 August 1947.

79. NAZ SEC1/1702, Note for Executive Council, 7 August 1947.

80. NAZ SEC1/1702, Note for Executive Council, 7 August 1947.

81. NAZ SEC1/1702, Note for Executive Council, 7 August 1947.

82. NAZ SEC1/1702, Note for Executive Council, 7 August 1947.

83. Quoted in Anuradha Bhattacharjee, "Polish Refugees in India: During and after the Second World War," *Sarmatian Review* 34, no. 2 (2013): 1752.

84. NAZ SEC1/1702, Note for Executive Council, 7 August 1947.

85. NAZ SEC1/1699, Note for Executive Council, 1 November 1946.

86. NRG, *Legislative Council Debates, 15 November 1948* (Lusaka: Government Printer, 1949); and NAZ SEC1/1702, Minutes of the Committee to Consider Applications for Permanent Residence in Northern Rhodesia held on 16 July 1948. On the other hand, Sandifort puts the figure at 245 ("World War Two," 54).

87. NAZ SEC1/1702, Minutes of the Committee, 16 July 1948.

88. NRG, *Legislative Council Debates, 15 November 1948*.

CHAPTER 5: THE COPPER MINING INDUSTRY
AND THE ALLIED WAR EFFORT

1. Lawrence Butler, *Copper Empire: Mining and the Colonial State in Northern Rhodesia, c. 1930–1964* (Houndsmill, UK: Palgrave Macmillan, 2007), 60.

2. Andrew D. Roberts, "Notes towards a Financial History of Copper Mining in Northern Rhodesia," *Canadian Journal of African Studies* 16, no. 2 (1982): 350.

3. Raymond Dumett, "Africa's Strategic Minerals during the Second World War," *Journal of African History* 26, no. 4 (1985): 393; and Lewis H. Gann, "The Northern Rhodesian Copper Industry and the World of Copper, 1923–52," *Rhodes-Livingstone Journal* 18 (1955): 10.

4. Dumett, "Africa's Strategic Minerals," 381.

209

Notes to Pages 116–120

5. Dumett, 392.

6. Butler, *Copper Empire*, 61; and Elena L. Berger, *Labour, Race and Colonial Rule: The Copperbelt from 1924 to Independence* (Oxford: Oxford University Press, 1974), 54.

7. Dumett, "Africa's Strategic Minerals," 393–94.

8. Dumett, 393.

9. Dumett, 396.

10. Mining Industry Archives (hereafter MIA) 18.4.2A, Governor John Maybin, Address to the nation made at Broken Hill, 26 January 1940.

11. Judith A. Byfield, "Producing for the War," in *Africa and World War II*, ed. Judith A. Byfield et al. (New York: Cambridge University Press, 2015), 40.

12. Butler, *Copper Empire*, 62; and John G. Phillips, "Roan Antelope: Big Business in Central Africa" (PhD thesis, University of Cambridge, 2000), 249.

13. Butler, *Copper Empire*, 63; and Francis L. Coleman, *The Northern Rhodesia Copperbelt, 1899–1962* (Manchester: Manchester University Press, 1971), 144. Lewis H. Gann, *A History of Northern Rhodesia: Early Days to 1953* (London: Chatto and Windus, 1964), 329, puts the figure at £66 per ton.

14. Butler, *Copper Empire*, 63.

15. MIA 18.4.2A, Governor John Maybin, Address to the nation broadcast from Nkana at 6:30PM, 2 February 1940.

16. See, for example, Northern Rhodesia Government (hereafter NRG), *Legislative Council Debates*, June 1940; NRG, *Legislative Council Debates*, 26 May 1943; and NRG, *Address to the Legislative Council by Governor John Maybin, September 1940* (Lusaka, 1941).

17. National Archives of Zambia (hereafter NAZ) SEC1/276, Secret Telegram no. 33 on Instructions to Customs Officers with regard to "Contraband," 2 September 1939.

18. NAZ SEC1/276, Secret Telegram no. 33, 2 September 1939.

19. The official handbook of the British Ministry of Economic Warfare described its aim as being to disorganize the enemy's economy so as to prevent it from carrying on with the war. The ministry was not simply involved in naval blockade but also used such diverse actions as diplomatic negotiations with neutral countries and the bombing of industrial targets. For a detailed examination of Allied economic warfare against the Axis, see Martin Fritz, "Economic Warfare," in *The Oxford Companion to the Second World War*, ed. I. C. B. Dear (Oxford: Oxford University Press, 1995), 318–21.

20. P. T. Bauer, "Origins of the Statutory Export Monopolies of British West Africa," *Business History Review* 28, no. 3 (1954): 202.

21. United Kingdom Department of Overseas Trade, *Report on Economic and Commercial Conditions in Southern Rhodesia, Northern Rhodesia and Nyasaland* (London, May 1939), 29.

22. Ashley Jackson, *The British Empire and the Second World War* (London: Hambledon Continuum, 2006), 48.

23. NAZ SEC1/275, Comptroller of Customs (Lusaka) to Chief Secretary (Lusaka), 2 April 1940. See also NAZ SEC1/276, Export Prohibition Orders: Instructions to Customs Officers with Regard to "Contra Band"; Licences for Exportation of Certain

Notes to Pages 120–122

Commodities; and NAZ SEC1/275, Chief Secretary (Lusaka) to Controller of Customs (Livingstone), 23 October 1939.

24. See Ian Henderson, "The Origins of Nationalism in East and Central Africa: The Zambian Case," *Journal of African History* 11, no. 4 (1970): 591–603; Ian Henderson, "Wage Earners and Political Protest in Colonial Africa: The Case of the Copperbelt," *African Affairs* 72, no. 288 (July 1973): 288–99; Ian Henderson, "Early African Leadership: The Copperbelt Disturbances of 1935 and 1940," *Journal of Southern African Studies* 2, no. 1 (1975): 83–97; M. R. Mwendapole, *A History of the Trade Union Movement in Zambia up to 1968*, ed. Robin H. Palmer and Ian Phimister (Lusaka: University of Zambia, 1977); and Henry S. Meebelo, *African Proletarians and Colonial Capitalism: The Origins, Growth and Struggles of the Zambian Labour Movement to 1964* (Lusaka: Kenneth Kaunda Foundation, 1986).

25. Coleman, *Northern Rhodesia Copperbelt*, 144.

26. NAZ ZP12/1, Evidence, Forster Commission of Inquiry, 574.

27. MIA 18.4.2A, Notes of the Proceedings at a Meeting between Managers and Representatives of the Northern Rhodesia Mine Workers' Union held at Nkana on Friday, 26 January 1940 at 3:15PM.

28. MIA 18.4.2A, Notes of the Proceedings at a Meeting, 26 January 1940.

29. MIA 18.4.2A, C. Wilson, Rhodesian Anglo American of South Africa Ltd (Johannesburg) to Managing Director, Rhokana Corporation Ltd (London), 27 December 1939.

30. Butler, *Copper Empire*, 70; Gann, "Northern Rhodesian Copper Industry," 11; Ronald Prain, *Reflections on an Era: An Autobiography* (Surrey: Metal Bulletin Books, 1981), 79; and Coleman, *Northern Rhodesia Copperbelt*, 146.

31. NAZ SEC1/1728 Vol. X, Report of a Meeting between His Excellency the Governor, the Mine Managements (Nkana, Roan-Antelope, Mufulira and Nchanga) and Deputations of Employees from each of the Mines, held at Nkana on Thursday 7 September 1939 on the Subject of Recruiting for Active Service; NAZ SEC1/1728 Vol. X, Speech Broadcast by His Excellency the Governor from Nkana Station on Friday 2 February 1940 at 6:30 PM; Gann, *History of Northern Rhodesia*, 336; and Berger, *Labour, Race and Colonial Rule*, 99.

32. Butler, *Copper Empire*, 70; and Gann, *History of Northern Rhodesia*, 336.

33. Butler, *Copper Empire*, 70.

34. NRG, *Report of the Commission of Inquiry into Disturbances on the Copperbelt* (hereafter, *Forster Commission*) (Lusaka, 1940), 25.

35. Phillips, "Roan Antelope," 258.

36. See Henry S. Meebelo, *Reaction to Colonialism: A Prelude to the Politics of Independence in Northern Zambia, 1893–1939* (Manchester: Manchester University Press, 1971).

37. Gann, "Northern Rhodesian Copper Industry," 11.

38. *Forster Commission*, 25.

39. *Forster Commission*, 26.

40. Cited in Meebelo, *African Proletarians*, 107.

Notes to Pages 122–126

41. Meebelo, *African Proletarians*, 107.

42. *Forster Commission*, 30–37.

43. Butler, *Copper Empire*, 72; and *Forster Commission*, 32.

44. Timothy Oberst, "Transport Workers, Strikes and the 'Imperial Response': Africa and the Post World War II Conjuncture," *African Studies Review* 31, no. 1 (1988): 119.

45. Carolyn A. Brown, "African Labor in the Making of World War II," in Byfield et al., *Africa and World II*, 56.

46. Byfield, "Producing for the War," 39.

47. Oberst, "Transport Workers," 119.

48. Oberst, 70.

49. NAZ ZP12/1, Evidence, Forster Commission, 559; and Roberts, *History of Zambia*, 203.

50. Colonial Office, *Report of the Commission Appointed to Enquire into the Financial and Economic Position of Northern Rhodesia* (London: H.M.S.O., 1938), 51–54.

51. NAZ ZP12/1, Frank Bedford, Evidence, Forster Commission, 499–500.

52. Butler, *Copper Empire*, 71–72. Although the color bar was officially implemented in 1941, racist tendencies on the mines were as old as the mines themselves.

53. *Forster Commission*, 30, 51–52; and Meebelo, *African Proletarians*, 133. Primarily due to this strike, the first African miners' trade union was registered in 1947.

54. MIA 18.4.2A, Rhokana Corporation (Kitwe) to Rhokana Corporation (London), 20 November 1942. In the same file, see Memorandum of a Meeting which took place at the Ministry of Supply, Bush House, London on Tuesday 15 December 1942; MIA18.4.2A, Memorandum of a Meeting which took place at the Offices of Rhokana Corporation Limited on Tuesday 24 November 1942 at 11:15AM; and MIA 18.4.2A, Rhodesian Anglo American Corporation (Johannesburg) to Rhokana (London), 4 February 1943.

55. Cited in Theodore Gregory, *Ernest Oppenheimer and the Economic Development of Southern Africa* (London: Literary Licencing, 1962), 453.

56. MIA 18.4.2A, Record of Decisions reached at a Meeting held at Kitwe on Tuesday 29 September 1942 at 9:30AM to discuss Matters of Supplies; and MIA18.4.2A, Notes of a Meeting which was held at 11:30AM on Friday 11 June 1943 at the Colonial Office, Dover House, Whitehall, London. See also MIA 18.4.2A, A.D. Storke, Chamber of Mines (Kitwe) to R. L. Prain (London), 29 September 1942; and MIA 18.4.2A, A. D. Storke, Chamber of Mines (Kitwe) to Financial Secretary (Lusaka), 29 September 1942.

57. MIA 18.4.2A, Rhokana Corporation (London) to Rhokana Anglo American (Kitwe), 20 July 1943; and MIA 18.4.2A, Notes of a Meeting which was held at 11:30AM on Friday 11 June 1943 at the Colonial Office, Dover House, Whitehall, London.

58. MIA 18.4.2A, Notes of a Meeting, Friday 11 June 1943.

59. MIA 18.4.2A, Notes of a Meeting, Friday 11 June 1943.

60. MIA 18.4.2A, Rhokana Corporation Limited (London) to Rhodesian Anglo American (Johannesburg), 26 October 1942; and MIA18.4.2A, Rhodesian Anglo American (Johannesburg) to Rhokana Corporation Limited (London), 21 December 1942.

61. MIA 18.4.2A, A. M. Baer, Non-Ferrous Metals Control, Ministry of Supply (London) to R. L. Prain, Roan Antelope Copper Mines Limited (London), 9 March 1943.

Notes to Pages 126–128

62. Gann, *History of Northern Rhodesia*, 329.

63. Butler, *Copper Empire*, 86.

64. Gann, "Northern Rhodesian Copper Industry," 12; Gann, *History of Northern Rhodesia*, 360; and Prain, *Reflections on an Era*, 82–83.

65. Berger, *Labour, Race and Colonial Rule*, 110; Coleman, *Northern Rhodesia Copperbelt*, 146; and Gann, *History of Northern Rhodesia*, 360.

66. Gann, "Northern Rhodesian Copper Industry," 12; and Coleman, *Northern Rhodesia Copperbelt*, 146.

67. Richard N. Gardner, *Sterling-Dollar Diplomacy in Current Perspective: The Origins and the Prospects of Our International Economic Order* (New York: Columbia University Press, 1980), 308.

68. Catherine R. Schenk, *The Decline of Sterling: Measuring the Retreat of an International Currency, 1945–1992* (Cambridge: Cambridge University Press, 2010), 68.

69. Andrew D. Roberts, "Northern Rhodesia: The Post-war Background, 1945–1953," in *Living the End of Empire: Politics and Society in Late Colonial Zambia*, ed. Jan-Bart Gewald, Marja Hinfelaar, and Giacomo Macola (Leiden: Brill, 2011), 16; Roberts, "Notes towards a Financial History," 355; and Prain, *Reflections on an Era*, 88. See also Peter J. Cain and Antony G. Hopkins, *British Imperialism: Crisis and Deconstruction, 1914–1990* (Harlow, UK: Longman, 1993), 269–74; and Peter J. Cain and Antony G. Hopkins, *British Imperialism: Innovation and Expansion, 1688–2000*, 2d ed. (Harlow, UK: Longman, 2001), 625–31. Schenk, *Decline of Sterling*, 69, puts the rate of devaluation at 17 percent.

70. Gann, "Northern Rhodesian Copper Industry," 13. Following devaluation, the value of the pound in relation to the US dollar became $2.80, instead of $4.02.

71. Roberts, "Notes towards a Financial History," 355.

72. *The Economist*, 2 August 1947; and Butler, *Copper Empire*, 115.

73. Phillips, "Roan Antelope," 309.

74. David Killingray and Richard Rathbone, "Introduction," in *Africa and the Second World War*, ed. David Killingray and Richard Rathbone (Basingstoke, UK: Palgrave Macmillan, 1986), 11.

75. Cain and Hopkins, *British Imperialism: Crisis and Deconstruction*, 279; and Cain and Hopkins, *British Imperialism: Innovation and Expansion*, 630.

76. NAZ SEC1/1362, Minutes of the African Governors Conference held in London, 12 November 1947.

77. NAZ SEC1/1362, Minutes of the African Governors Conference.

78. MIA 14.3.3F, Statement by the Secretary of State for the Colonies on the state of British Territories in East and Central Africa, 1945–1950, June 1950, 43.

79. MIA 14.3.3F, Statement by the Secretary of State for the Colonies, 43.

80. Gann, "Northern Rhodesian Copper Industry," 14.

81. *The Economist*, 2 August 1947.

82. Berger, *Labour, Race and Colonial Rule*, 110.

83. Berger, 110.

84. Copper Development Association, *Fifteenth Annual Report* (November 1949), 11–12.

Notes to Pages 128–130

85. Butler, *Copper Empire*, 107; Berger, *Labour, Race and Colonial Rule*, 110; *The Economist*, 2 August 1947; and Gann, "Northern Rhodesian Copper Industry," 1–18.

86. Phillips, "Roan Antelope," 288–89.

87. Phillips, 288–89.

88. Butler, *Copper Empire*, 194.

89. Coleman, *Northern Rhodesia Copperbelt*, 146.

90. Butler, *Copper Empire*, 131.

91. Butler, 3, 4, 271.

92. Butler, 300. For a comparative perspective elsewhere in Africa, see Sarah Stockwell, *The Business of Decolonisation: British Business Strategies in the Gold Coast* (Oxford: Oxford University Press, 2000), 213–14, 220.

93. Andrew D. Roberts, *A History of Zambia* (London: Heinemann, 1976), 212; and Butler, *Copper Empire*, 107.

94. Butler, *Copper Empire*, 131.

95. Butler, 217.

96. Berger, *Labour, Race and Colonial Rule*, 6.

97. See, for example, Daniel O. Spence, *Colonial Naval Culture and British Imperialism, 1922–67* (Manchester: Manchester University Press, 2015), 114–15, 137–41, 249–50; Michael Collins, "Decolonisation and the 'Federal Moment,'" *Diplomacy and Statecraft* 24, no. 1 (2013): 21–40; Nicholas J. Westcott, "Closer Union and the Future of East Africa, 1939–1948: A Case Study in the 'Official Mind of Imperialism,'" *Journal of Imperial and Commonwealth History* 10, no. 1 (1981): 67–88; and Jason Parker, "Remapping the Cold War in the Tropics: Race, Communism, and National Security in the West Indies," *International History Review* 24, no. 2 (2002): 318–47.

98. Gann, "Northern Rhodesia Copper Industry," 14.

99. See, for example, Gann, *History of Northern Rhodesia*, 397–39; Prain, *Reflections on an Era*, 95–133; Gregory, *Ernest Oppenheimer*, 462–63; and especially chapters 5 and 6 in Butler, *Copper Empire*. For more specialized discussion, see Harry Franklin, *Unholy Wedlock: The Failure of the Central African Federation* (London: Faber and Faber, 1963).

100. MIA 14.3.3F, Assistant Manager, Nchanga Consolidated Copper Mining (Chingola) to The Secretary, Rhodesian Anglo American Corporation (London), 26 January 1951.

101. MIA 16.2.3E, Memo on Copper Production, 12 September 1941; MIA 16.2.2D, RACM Minutes of Meeting held on 5 May 1942; MIA 16.2.2E RACM Executive Minutes of Meeting held on 21 April 1942; and MIA 18.4.2A, Assistant Manager, Rhodesian Anglo American Corporation (Johannesburg) to The Secretary (Rhokana Anglo American Corporation (Kitwe), 22 April 1951.

102. MIA 18.4.2A, Notes of a Meeting with the Acting Director of Trade, Transport and Industry and the Controller of Customs held at Kitwe on 18 February 1952 at 7:30PM.

103. MIA 18.4.2A, American Metal Company Limited (New York) to Rhokana Corporation (Kitwe), 10 January 1951.

Notes to Pages 130–133

104. MIA 18.4.2A, American Metal Company Limited (New York) to Rhodesian Anglo American (Kitwe), 27 June 1951.

105. Butler, *Copper Empire*, 148.

106. *The Star*, 25 June 1952.

107. NAZ SEC1/704, Commissioner of Income Tax (Ndola) to Chief Secretary (Lusaka), 25 January 1941. See also *Financial Times*, 21 November 1941.

108. *East Africa and Rhodesia*, 24 May 1945.

109. *South African Mining Journal*, 13 January 1940, 611; and Phillips, "Roan Antelope," 252.

110. Prain, *Reflections on an Era*, 100. See also Butler, *Copper Empire*, 149–50.

111. Butler, *Copper Empire*, 148; and Dumett, "Africa's Strategic Minerals," 395.

112. Roberts, "Notes towards a Financial History," 354.

113. *Financial Times*, 5 December 1940.

114. *Financial Times*, 5 December 1940.

115. *The Times*, 1 November 1940.

116. *The Times*, 1 November 1940.

117. NAZ SEC1/704, Commissioner of Income Tax (Ndola) to Financial Secretary (Lusaka), 16 February 1948.

118. *The Star*, 25 June 1952.

119. Butler, *Copper Empire*, 202. See also the relevant sections in Prain, *Reflections on an Era*; and Gregory, *Ernest Oppenheimer*.

120. Berger, *Labour, Race and Colonial Rule*, 8.

121. *The Scotsman*, 28 October 1940; *The Economist*, 2 November 1940; *City Press*, 2 November 1940; and MIA 16.2.2D, Roan Antelope Copper Mine, Minutes of Meeting held on 4 July 1941.

122. Berger, *Labour, Race and Colonial Rule*, 8.

123. Butler, *Copper Empire*, 66; Berger, *Labour, Race and Colonial Rule*, 54; and Gann, "Northern Rhodesian Copper Industry," 10.

124. Phillips, "Roan Antelope," 255.

125. Jackson, *British Empire*, 236; Dumett, "Africa's Strategic Minerals," 394; and Butler, *Copper Empire*, 69. The exaggerated figure of 200,000 miners is given by Samuel N. Chipungu, *The State, Technology and Peasant Differentiation in Southern Zambia, 1890–1980* (Lusaka: Historical Association of Zambia, 1988), 62. For urban growth in other parts of British West and East Africa, see Byfield, "Producing for the War," 36.

126. W. J. Busschau, *Report on the Development of Secondary Industries in Northern Rhodesia* (Lusaka: Government Printer, 1945), 22. See also Berger, *Labour, Race and Colonial Rule*.

127. Gann, *History of Northern Rhodesia*, 331. For a fuller discussion, see especially chapter 7 of Bennett S. Siamwiza, "A History of Famine in Zambia, c. 1825–1949" (PhD thesis, University of Cambridge, 1998).

128. Robert E. Baldwin, *Economic Development and Export Growth: A Study of Northern Rhodesia, 1920–1960* (Berkeley: University of California Press, 1966), 155.

Notes to Pages 133–137

129. NRG, *Department of Agriculture Annual Report for the Year 1941* (Lusaka: Government Printer, 1942), 1.

130. NRG, *Department of Agriculture Annual Report for the Year 1941*, 1. For a discussion on increased consumption levels of fish on the Copperbelt during the war, see, for example, J. Chilonge, "Poverty in the Midst of Abundance: The Case of Fishermen of Samfya District, 1935–1970" (MA diss., University of Zambia, 2011), especially chapter 2.

131. NRG, *Legislative Council Debates*, 28 November 1940.

132. Jackson, *British Empire*, 235.

133. Jackson, 235.

134. Jackson, 235.

135. Ackson M. Kanduza, *The Political Economy of Underdevelopment in Northern Rhodesia, 1918–1960: A Case of Customs Tariffs and Railway Freight Policies* (Lanham, MD: University Press of America, 1986), 169.

136. Kanduza, 169.

137. Chipungu, *State, Technology and Peasant Differentiation*, 62. See also Chewe Mebbiens Chabatama, "Peasant Farming, the State, and Food Security in the North-Western Province of Zambia, 1902–1964" (PhD diss., University of Toronto, 1999).

138. NRG, *Department of Agriculture Annual Report for the Year 1944* (Lusaka: Government Printer, 1945), 2; and Chipungu, *State, Technology and Peasant Differentiation*, 62. See also Chabatama, "Peasant Farming, the State and Food Security."

139. David Killingray, "Labour Mobilisation in British Colonial Africa for the War Effort, 1939–46," in Killingray and Rathbone, *Africa and the Second World War*, 82–83.

140. Killingray, 84–86.

141. Keith Jeffery, "The Second World War," in *The Oxford History of the British Empire*, vol. 4, *The Twentieth Century*, ed. Judith Brown and Wm. Roger-Louis (Oxford: Oxford University Press, 1999), 312.

142. Charles van Onselen, *Chibaro: African Mine Labour in Southern Rhodesia, 1900–1933* (London: Pluto, 1976), 99.

143. See W. M. Freund, "Labour Migration to the Northern Nigerian Tin Mines, 1903–1945," *Journal of African History* 22, no. 1 (1981): 73–84; and B. W. Hodder, "Tin Mining on the Jos Plateau of Nigeria," *Economic Geography* 35, no. 2 (1959): 109–22.

144. Killingray, "Labour Mobilisation," 70.

145. International Labour Organisation (ILO), *Report and Questionnaire on Forced Labour* (Geneva: ILO, 1929), 1–2; and ILO, *Conventions and Recommendations, 1919–1937* (Geneva: ILO, 1939), 179–93.

146. David Killingray, *Fighting for Britain: African Soldiers in the Second World War* (Woodbridge, UK: James Currey, 2010), 44.

147. Brown, "African Labor in the Making of World War II," 62.

148. For a detailed discussion, see Madhusree Mukerjee, *Churchill's Secret War: The British Empire and the Ravaging of India during World War Two* (New York: Basic Books, 2010). See also Brown, "African Labor in the Making of World War II," 44.

149. Killingray, "Labour Mobilisation," 88.

216

Notes to Pages 137–143

150. NAZ SEC1/59, Director of Agriculture (Mazabuka) to Chief Secretary (Lusaka), 2 November 1939. The discussion that follows in this chapter was first published as "Coerced African Labour for Food Production in Northern Rhodesia (Zambia) during the Second World War, 1942–1945," *South African Historical Journal* 68, no. 1 (2016): 50–68.

151. NAZ SEC1/59, Director of Agriculture (Mazabuka) to Chief Secretary (Lusaka), 2 November 1939.

152. NAZ SEC1/59, Director of Agriculture to Chief Secretary, 2 November 1939.

153. *Bulawayo Chronicle*, 3 November 1939.

154. Kenneth P. Vickery, "Saving Settlers: Maize Control in Northern Rhodesia," *Journal of Southern African Studies* 11, no. 2 (1985): 212–34.

155. NRG, *Emergency Powers (Recruitment of Farm Labour) Regulation 1942* (Lusaka: Government Printer, 1942).

156. NRG, *Emergency Powers (Recruitment of Farm Labour) Regulation 1942*.

157. NRG, *Emergency Powers (Recruitment of Farm Labour) Regulation 1942*.

158. Killingray, "Labour Mobilisation," 75.

159. NAZ SEC1/1346, Chairman's Report of the Second ALAB Meeting, 3 February 1942.

160. Kenneth P. Vickery, "The Second World War Revival of Forced Labor in the Rhodesias," *International Journal of African Historical Studies* 22, no. 3 (1989): 434. For a discussion on the implementation of forced labor in French West Africa, see Catherine Bogosian Ash, "Free to Coerce: Forced Labor during and after the Vichy Years in French West Africa," in Byfield et al., *Africa and World War II*, 109–26.

161. Kusum Datta, "Farm Labour, Agrarian Capital and the State in Colonial Zambia: The African Labour Corps, 1942–52," *Journal of Southern African Studies* 14, no. 3 (April 1988): 379.

162. Datta, 379–80.

163. Datta, 378.

164. NAZ SEC1/1346, Governor (Lusaka) to Colonial Secretary (London), 26 November 1942.

165. Quoted in Vickery, "Second World War," 434.

166. Vickery, "Second World War," 434.

167. See Kenneth P. Vickery, *Black and White in Southern Zambia: The Tonga Plateau Economy and British Imperialism, 1890–1939* (New York: Greenwood, 1986), 195–210; and Vickery, "Saving Settlers."

168. Cain and Hopkins, *British Imperialism: Innovation and Expansion*, 63.

CHAPTER 6: DEMOBILIZATION AND THE GREAT DISAPPOINTMENT OF WAR SERVICE

1. Rabson Chombola, interview with the British Broadcasting Corporation (hereafter BBC), Ndola, 10 August 1989.

2. *Mutende*, no. 212, 28 February 1946.

Notes to Pages 143–146

3. Timothy Parsons, "No Country Fit for Heroes: The Plight of Disabled Kenyan Veterans," in *Africa and World War II*, ed. Judith A. Byfield et al. (New York: Cambridge University Press, 2015), 127.

4. See especially Michael Crowder, "The 1939–45 War and West Africa," in *History of West Africa*, vol. 2, ed. J. F. A. Ajayi and Michael Crowder (London: Columbia University Press, 1974), 665–92; Crowder, "The Second World War: Prelude to Decolonization," in *The Cambridge History of Africa*, vol. 8, *c. 1940–c. 1975*, ed. Michael Crowder (Cambridge: Cambridge University Press, 1984), 8–51; Gabriel O. Olusanya, "The Role of Ex-servicemen in Nigerian Politics," *Journal of Modern African Studies* 6, no. 2 (1968): 221–32; and Eugene P. A. Schleh, "The Post-war Careers of Ex-servicemen in Ghana and Uganda," *Journal of Modern African Studies* 6, no. 2 (1968): 203–20. An earlier version of this chapter appeared as "Frustrated Expectations: Experiences of Northern Rhodesian (Zambian) Ex-servicemen in the Post–Second World War Era," *War in History* 24, no. 2 (2017): 195–216.

5. David Killingray, *Fighting for Britain: African Soldiers in the Second World War* (Woodbridge, UK: James Currey, 2010), 179.

6. Ashley Jackson, *The British Empire and the Second World War* (London: Hambledon Continuum, 2006), 174.

7. See, for example, Jeremy Black, *World War Two: A Military History* (London: Routledge, 2003), 129–58. By 1943 the availability of massive resources following the introduction of Lend-Lease in March 1941 enabled the Allies to attack on a number of fronts at once. The Allies also benefited from the extent to which the Germans had used up important military assets during their ultimately ill-fated offensives in Russia and North Africa in 1942, while the Japanese had done the same at Midway.

8. National Archives of Zambia (hereafter NAZ), SEC1/1766 Vol. I, Circular from the Secretary of State (London) to All Governors, 12 July 1943.

9. NAZ SEC1/1766 Vol. I, Circular from Secretary of State to All Governors.

10. NAZ SEC1/1766 Vol. I, Circular from Secretary of State to All Governors.

11. Killingray, *Fighting for Britain*, 180; and David Killingray, "African Voices from Two World Wars," *Historical Research* 74, no. 186 (2001): 440.

12. Gregory Mann, *Native Sons: West African Veterans and France in the Twentieth Century* (Durham, NC: Duke University Press, 2006), 116.

13. Anirudh Deshpande, *British Military Policy in India, 1900–1945: Colonial Constraints and Declining Power* (New Delhi: Manohar, 2005).

14. NAZ SEC1/1766 Vol. I, Minutes of a Meeting of the Employment of African Soldiers Sub-committee held in the Secretariat on 3 February 1943 at 2:15 pm; and NAZ SEC1/1766 Vol. I, Minutes of the Meeting of the Employment of African Soldiers Sub-committee held in the Central Offices on Tuesday 17 August 1943 at 9 am.

15. NAZ SEC1/1766 Vol. I, Minutes of a Meeting of the Post-war Problems (African) Committee held on 8 September 1945.

16. NAZ SEC1/1766 Vol. II, Northern Rhodesia Chamber of Mines (Kitwe) to Chief Secretary (Lusaka), 20 August 1945; NAZ SEC1/1768, Minutes of the Serenje District After-Care Committee held on 15 January 1946; NAZ SEC1/1766 Vol. I, Minutes

Notes to Pages 146–149

of the First Meeting of the Balovale District After-Care Committee held on 2 October 1945; and NAZ SEC1/1766 Vol. I, Minutes of Chinsali After-Care Committee Meeting held at 9am on Saturday 19 January 1946.

17. NAZ SEC1/1766 Vol. I, Interim Report no. 7 of the Nyasaland Protectorate Post-war Development Committee, n.d., ca.1945.

18. NAZ SEC1/1766 Vol. I, Minutes of the Meeting of the Post-war Problems (African) Committee held on 17 January 1946.

19. Livingstone Museum 2/3/4/1/6/3, *The Green 'Un': The Magazine of the 94 Independent Garrison Company: The King's African Rifles* (June–November 1946).

20. Killingray, *Fighting for Britain*, 184.

21. Killingray, 185.

22. Killingray, 187.

23. Chama Mutemi Kadansa, interview with the BBC, Ndola, 17 July 1989.

24. NAZ SEC1/1768, Minutes of the Third Meeting of Namwala After-Care Committee held on 29 October 1945; and NAZ SEC1/1768, Minutes of the Third Meeting of the Mwinilunga After-Care Committee held on 20 November 1945.

25. NAZ SEC1/1768, Minutes of the Third Meeting of the Namwala After-Care Committee held on 29 October 1945.

26. Sergeant-Major Joseph Chinama Mulenga, interview with the BBC, Lusaka, 6 June 1989.

27. NAZ SEC2/1135, Report on Tour to Madagascar from 4 January to 4 February 1943, dated 22 February 1943.

28. The impact of labor migration on colonial Zambia has been discussed by, among others, Yizenge A. Chondoka, "Labour Migration in Chama District, North-Eastern Zambia" (PhD diss., University of Toronto, 1992); Audrey L. Richards, *Land, Labour and Diet in Northern Rhodesia: An Economic Study of the Bemba Tribe* (Hamburg: James Currey, 1995); William Watson, *The Social Structure of the Mambwe of Northern Rhodesia* (Manchester: Manchester University Press, 1957).

29. NAZ SEC1/1766 Vol. I, District Commissioner (Broken Hill) to Provincial Commissioner (Central Province), 15 September 1943.

30. See Luise White, "Prostitution, Identity, and Class Consciousness in Nairobi during World War II," *Signs: Journal of Women and Culture in Society* 11 (1986): 255–73; and Timothy H. Parsons, "'All Askaris Are Family Men': Sex, Domesticity and Discipline in the King's African Rifles, 1902–1964," in *Guardians of Empire: The Armed Forces of the Colonial Powers, c. 1700–1964*, ed. David Killingray and David Omissi (Manchester: Manchester University Press, 1999), 179–97.

31. Killingray, *Fighting for Britain*, 190.

32. NAZ SEC1/1766 Vol. I, Minutes of the Post-war Problems (African) Committee held on 16 January 1946.

33. For specific speeches delivered to the 1st NRR Battalion, see *Mutende*, no. 210, January 1946; and *Mutende*, no. 212, February 1946. More generally, see Kapasa Makasa, *Zambia's March to Political Freedom* (Nairobi: Heinemann, 1981), 15.

Notes to Pages 149–153

34. NRG, *Notes on Demobilisation: Benefits, Rehabilitation, Procedure, etc., for Persons of Northern Rhodesian Origin Serving in the Armed Forces* (Lusaka: Government Printer, 1945), 1.

35. NRG, 2.

36. NRG, 2.

37. Kadansa, interview cited.

38. Carol Summers, "Ugandan Politics and World War II (1939–1949)," in Byfield et al., *Africa and World War II*, 480–98; Killingray, *Fighting for Britain*, 191; Ashley Jackson, "African Soldiers and Imperial Authorities: Tensions and Unrest during the Service of High Commission Territories' Soldiers in the British Army, 1941–46," *Journal of Southern African Studies* 25, no. 4 (December 1999): 645–65; Ashley Jackson, *Botswana, 1939–1945: An African Country at War* (Oxford: Oxford University Press. 1999); Hamilton Sipho Simelane, "Veterans, Politics and Poverty: The Case of Swazi Veterans in the Second World War," *South African Historical Journal* 38 (1998): 144–70; Adrienne M. Israel, "Ex-servicemen at the Crossroads: Protests and Politics in Post-war Ghana," *Journal of Modern African Studies* 30, no. 2 (1992): 359–68; David Killingray, "Soldiers, Ex-servicemen, and Politics in the Gold Coast, 1939–50," *Journal of Modern African Studies* 21, no. 3 (September 1983): 523–34; Olusanya, "Role of Ex-servicemen in Nigerian Politics," 221–32; and Schleh, "Post-war Careers of Ex-servicemen," 203–20.

39. NAZ SEC1/1768, Minutes of the Inaugural Meeting of the Mkushi After-Care Committee held on 17 April 1945.

40. NAZ SEC1/1766, Chief Secretary (Lusaka) to Secretary for Native Affairs (Lusaka), 30 May 1945. See also Killingray, *Fighting for Britain*, 198.

41. Killingray, *Fighting for Britain*, 198.

42. Killingray, 191.

43. NAZ SEC1/1766 Vol. I, District Commissioner (Chinsali) to Provincial Commissioner, Northern Province (Kasama), 5 November 1943; NAZ SEC1/1766 Vol. I, District Commissioner (Lundazi) to Provincial Commissioner, Eastern Province (Fort Jameson), 4 October 1943; and NAZ SEC1/1766 Vol. I, District Commissioner (Kasama) to Provincial Commissioner, Northern Province (Kasama), 19 November 1943.

44. S. J. Simwinga, interview with MUVI TV, Lusaka, ca. 2011.

45. Killingray, "African Voices," 441; and Martin Meredith, *The State of Africa: A History of the Continent since Independence* (London: Simon and Schuster, 2011), 10.

46. NRG, *Legislative Council Debates*, 16 December 1941, 353–54.

47. *Northern News*, 24 October 1946; and *Bulawayo Chronicle*, 10 May 1946.

48. *Mutende*, no. 198, August 1945.

49. *Mutende*, August 1945.

50. NAZ SEC1/1766 Vol. I, Minutes of a Meeting of the Post-war Problems (African) Committee held in Central Offices, Lusaka on Friday 20 July 1945.

51. NAZ SEC1/1768, Mkushi After-Care Committee Progress Report, 28 February 1946; and NAZ SEC1/1768, Minutes of the Third Meeting of the Mwinilunga After-Care Committee held on Tuesday 20 November 1945.

Notes to Pages 153–158

52. NAZ SEC1/1766 Vol. I, Meeting of the Post-war Problems (African) Committee held in Lusaka on 16 February 1946.

53. NRG, *Notes on Demobilisation*, 2. Class A referred to servicemen released after 18 June 1945; Class B meant those released between 16 October 1944 and 7 May 1945. Class C designated men released between 8 May and 18 June 1945.

54. NAZ SEC1/1766 Vol. I, District Commissioner (Chingola) to Provincial Commissioner, Western Province (Ndola), 17 September 1943; see also NAZ SEC1/1766 Vol. I, District Commissioner (Kawambwa) to Provincial Commissioner, Northern Province (Kasama), 2 October 1943; NAZ SEC1/1766 Vol. I, District Commissioner (Chinsali) to Provincial Commissioner, Northern Province (Kasama), 5 November 1943; and NAZ SEC1/1766, Chief Secretary (Lusaka) to Secretary for Native Affairs (Lusaka), 30 May 1945.

55. NAZ SEC1/1766 Vol. II, Private Alfred Hezekiah (HQ South East Asia Command) to The Manager, Government Farm (Mazabuka), 28 July 1945. See also NAZ SEC1/1766 Vol. II, Private Alfred Hezekiah (HQ South East Asia Command) to Chief Secretary (Lusaka), 20 October 1945.

56. NAZ SEC1/1766 Vol. I, Chief Secretary (Lusaka) to Private NRA 1163 Alfred Hezekiah (HQ South East Asia Command), 30 August 1945.

57. NAZ SEC1/1766 Vol. I, Circular from Secretary of State (London) to All Governors, 12 July 1943.

58. C. J. Duder, "Men of the Officer Class': The Participants in the 1919 Soldier Settlement Scheme in Kenya," *African Affairs* 92, no. 366 (1993): 69–87.

59. NRG, *Notes on Demobilisation*, 3; and NRG, *Final Report of the Select Committee Appointed to Examine and Report on the Question of Land Settlement in Northern Rhodesia for Ex-servicemen and Others* (Lusaka: Government Printer, 1945), 7–8.

60. NRG, *Final Report of the Select Committee*, 8.

61. NRG, 9.

62. NRG, 9.

63. Chipo Munzabwa Simunchembu, "Commercial Farming and Social Change in Mkushi District, 1945–1975" (MA diss., University of Zambia, 1989), 26.

64. Simunchembu, 29.

65. NRG, *Department of Agriculture Annual Report for the Year 1951* (Lusaka: Government Printer, 1952), 6.

66. Parsons, "No Country Fit for Heroes," 127.

67. Parsons, 140.

68. Rabson Chombola, interview with the BBC, Ndola, 24 November 1989.

69. NAZ SEC1/1768, Minutes of a Meeting of the Broken Hill After-Care Committee held on 4 February 1947 at 2:15 pm.

70. Parsons, "No Country Fit for Heroes," 130.

71. Parsons, 129.

72. NAZ SEC1/1764, Post-war Problems Notes Circulated to Members of the Post-war Problems (African) Committee, 1943; and NAZ SEC1/1766 Vol. I, Extract from Minutes of the Post-war Problems (African) Committee held in the Chief Secretary's

Notes to Pages 158–161

Office on 20 September 1942; NAZ SEC1/1766 Vol. I, Extract from Minutes of the Post-war Problems (African) Committee Meeting held on 20 October 1943.

73. NAZ SEC1/1764, Post-war Problems Notes.

74. NAZ SEC1/1764, Post-war Problems Notes.

75. NAZ SEC1/1764, Post-war Problems Notes.

76. As we know, unlike in Southern Rhodesia and South Africa, the war did not stimulate much industrial growth in Northern Rhodesia leading to job creation.

77. Killingray, *Fighting for Britain*, 182.

78. NAZ SEC1/1766 Vol. I, Chief Secretary (Lusaka) to Secretary for Native Affairs (Lusaka), 30 May 1945.

79. Mann, *Native Sons*, 79.

80. Myron J. Echenberg, *Colonial Conscripts: The* Tirailleurs Sénégalais *in French West Africa, 1857–1960* (Portsmouth, NH: Heinemann, 1991), 82.

81. Israel, "Ex-servicemen at the Crossroads," 361–62.

82. NAZ SEC1/1766 Vol. I, Minutes of a Meeting of the Employment of African Soldiers Sub-committee held in the Secretary for Native Affairs' Office, Lusaka on Thursday 26 October 1943 at 2PM; and NAZ SEC1/1766 Vol. I, Confidential Analysis of Army Tradesmen (African) Recruited from Northern Rhodesia up to 30 September 1943.

83. NAZ SEC1/1766 Vol. I, Post-war Training and Employment for African Ex-servicemen in Nyasaland, n.d., but ca. 1945.

84. Killingray, *Fighting for Britain*, 195.

85. Killingray, 195. This term referred to a liking for white-collar jobs by African servicemen who had served overseas during this war.

86. Timothy Stapleton, *African Police and Soldiers in Colonial Zimbabwe, 1923–80* (Rochester, NY: University of Rochester Press, 2011), 217.

87. NAZ SEC1/1766 Vol. II, Extract from the Barotse Provincial Newsletter for the First Quarter of 1946, 26 April 1946. See also NAZ SEC1/1766 Vol. II, Labour Commissioner (Lusaka) to Commissioner of Police (Livingstone), 24 September 1946; and NAZ SEC1/1766 Vol. II, Labour Officer (Fort Jameson) to Labour Commissioner (Lusaka), 4 September 1946.

88. Stapleton, *African Police*, 218–19.

89. The color-bar policy arose out of Clause 42 of an agreement on wages and conditions of service for European miners negotiated by the Chamber of Mines and the European Mine Workers' Union in 1946. The effect of this policy was to bar Africans in any category of job where Europeans were employed at the date of the signing of the agreement (see, for example, Duncan Money, "'No Matter How Much or How Little They've Got, They Can't Settle Down': A Social History of Europeans on the Zambian Copperbelt, 1926–1974" (PhD diss., University of Oxford, 2016), 123–62.

90. NAZ SEC1/1766 Vol. I, Minutes of a Meeting of the Post-war Problems (African) Committee held on 16 February 1946.

91. Simelane, "Veterans, Politics and Poverty," 155–56.

92. NAZ SEC1/1766 Vol. I, Post Master-General (Livingstone) to Chief Secretary (Lusaka), 30 May 1945. See also Summers, "Ugandan Politics and World War II," 492.

Notes to Pages 161–165

93. NAZ SEC1/1766 Vol. I, Post Master-General (Livingstone) to Chief Secretary (Lusaka), 30 May 1945.

94. NAZ SEC1/1766 Vol. I, Director of Medical Services (Lusaka) to Secretary for Native Affairs, 23 October 1945; and NAZ SEC1/1766 Vol. II, Extract from Minutes of a Meeting of the Post-War Problems (African) Committee held on 8 September 1945.

95. Quoted in Killingray, *Fighting for Britain*, 198.

96. Notable among these are Olusanya, "Role of Ex-servicemen in Nigerian Politics"; Schleh, "Post-war Careers of Ex-servicemen"; and Crowder, "1939 War and West Africa."

97. Killingray, *Fighting for Britain*; Jackson, *Botswana*; John D. Hargreaves, *Decolonisation in Africa* (London: Routledge, 1996); Louis Willem Fredrick Grundlingh, "South African Blacks in the Second World War" (DLitt et Phil thesis, Rand Afrikaans University, 1986), retrieved from http://www.ujdispace.uj.ac.za (accessed 27 July 2014); and Simelane, "Veterans, Politics and Poverty."

98. NAZ SEC1/1766 Vol. III, Captain F. Johnstone (HQ 21 East Africa Command, Nairobi) to Sir Stewart Gore-Browne (Lusaka), 21 September 1943.

99. Killingray, "Soldiers, Ex-servicemen and Politics," 524–25. See also Hargreaves, *Decolonisation*, 70–71.

100. David Johnson, *World War Two and the Scramble for Labour in Colonial Zimbabwe, 1939–1948* (Harare: University of Zimbabwe Publications, 2000), 27; and Stapleton, *African Police*, 221.

101. See, for example, Jackson, *Botswana*; Simelane, "Veterans, Politics and Poverty"; and Mary Nombulelo Ntabeni, "Military Labour Mobilisation in Colonial Lesotho during World War II, 1940–1943," *Scientia Militaria: South African Journal of Military Studies* 36, no. 2 (2008): 36–59.

102. Joanna Lewis, *Empire State-Building: War and Welfare in Kenya, 1925–52* (Athens: Ohio University Press, 2000), 203, 240.

103. Jackson, *Botswana*, 241.

104. Andrew D. Roberts, *A History of Zambia* (London: Heinemann, 1976), 196–205. For Uganda, see Summers, "Ugandan Politics and World War II," 495–97.

105. Roberts, *History of Zambia*, 197. Livingstonia Mission was founded by the Free Church of Scotland in 1875 near the southern end of Lake Malawi in memory of the Scottish missionary-cum-medical doctor, David Livingstone, who did pioneer missionary work in Malawi in the nineteenth century. This mission station would later become the foremost center for African advancement in Malawi and much of the region in the twentieth century, as many mission stations established in the area originated from there. Many early African nationalists in the region either attended this mission station or were indirectly influenced by its teachings. See, for example, Henry S. Meebelo, *Reaction to Colonialism: A Prelude to the Politics of Independence in Northern Rhodesia, 1893–1939* (Manchester: Manchester University Press, 1971).

106. Kapasa Makasa, *Zambia's March to Political Freedom* (Nairobi: Heinemann, 1981), 41.

107. See, for example, Meebelo, *Reaction to Colonialism*.

108. Mulenga, interview cited.

Notes to Pages 165–172

109. Makasa, *Zambia's March to Political Freedom*, 41.

110. Jackson, *Botswana*, 250.

111. University of Zambia Library Special Collections, Gov.Zam/02/1944, Minutes of the Eastern Province Regional Council held at Fort Jameson on 24 and 25 July 1944; NAZ SEC2/1135, Report on Tour to Madagascar by Information Officer, 22 February 1943; NAZ SEC1/1775, Report on Public Opinion for Barotse Province for April–July 1943; and NAZ SEC1/1775, Report on Public Opinion for Barotse Province for January–June 1944.

112. Mann, *Native Sons*, 73.

113. See, for example, NAZ SEC1/1766 Vol. I, District Commissioner (Mpika) to Provincial Commissioner, Northern Province (Kasama), 29 September 1943; NAZ SEC1/1766 Vol. I, District Commissioner (Kasama) to Northern Province (Kasama), 19 November 1943; NAZ SEC1/1766 Vol. I, District Commissioner (Balovale) to Provincial Commissioner, Western Province (Ndola), 4 November 1943; NAZ SEC1/1766 Vol. I, District Commissioner (Mwinilunga) to Provincial Commissioner, Kaonde Lunda Province (Kasempa), 3 September 1943; NAZ SEC1/1766 Vol. I, District Commissioner (Kawambwa) to Provincial Commissioner, Northern Province (Kasama), 2 October 1943; NAZ SEC1/1766 Vol. I, District Commissioner (Chinsali) to Provincial Commissioner, Northern Province (Kasama), 5 November 1943; and Jackson, *British Empire and the Second World*, 188.

114. Elizabeth Schmidt, "Popular Resistance and Anticolonial Mobilization: The War Effort in French Guinea," in Byfield et al., *Africa and World War II*, 456.

115. Schmidt, 441–61.

116. Lewis H. Gann, *A History of Northern Rhodesia: Early Days to 1953* (London: Chatto and Windus, 1964), 328.

117. Judith A. Byfield, "Preface," in Byfield et al., *Africa and World War II*, 127.

118. NAZ SEC1/1766 Vol. III, Notes by Col. H. McDowell, Lusaka, 11 November 1942. *Mitundu* referred to many ethnic groups or races. Singular form = *mutundu*.

119. NAZ SEC1/1766 Vol. III, Notes by Col. H. McDowell.

120. Killingray, *Fighting for Britain*, 204.

121. Killingray, 108.

122. Killingray, "African Voices," 439.

123. NAZ SEC1/1766 Vol. III, Notes on Northern Rhodesia Asikari, n.d., but ca. November 1944.

124. Killingray, *Fighting for Britain*, 108.

125. Killingray, 110.

CONCLUSION

1. Cynthia H. Enloe, *Ethnic Soldiers: State Security in Divided Societies* (Athens: University of Georgia Press, 1980), 25.

2. Michael Cowen and Nicholas Westcott, "British Imperial Economic Policy during the War," in *Africa and the Second World War*, ed. David Killingray and Richard Rathbone (Basingstoke, UK: Palgrave Macmillan, 1986), 24.

Bibliography

A. PRIMARY SOURCES

1. National Archives of Zambia (NAZ)

I. SECRETARIAT SERIES (SEC1–3)

SEC1/45 Development of Beeswax Industry: Import and Export of Beeswax, 1938.

SEC1/59 Statement on Agricultural Policy during the War: Plans for Agricultural Development: Extract from Bulawayo Chronicle, Friday November 3 1939, War Effort of Northern Rhodesia.

SEC1/76 Production of Vegetable Oils in Northern Rhodesia; Soap Making for the Native Market, Castor Oil and Conversion.

SEC1/95 Regulations Regarding African Application for Rationing Supplies of Staffs; Tour Reports, and Increment of Bonus, 1947–48.

SEC1/275 Exports and Import Licences Issued: Export of Metals; Blister Copper to France; Electrolytic Ingot Bar to Calcutta.

SEC1/276 Export Prohibition Orders: Instructions to Customs Officers with Regard to "Contra Band"; Licences for Exportation of Certain Commodities.

SEC1/703 Post-war Proposals; Expenditure by the Government of Northern Rhodesia between Europeans and Africans; Increment of Allowances; Review of Taxation, 1944–45.

SEC1/704 Notes and Recommendation of Northern Rhodesia Income Tax; Memorandum on Additional Customs and Excise Duties Imposed during the War, 1945–46.

SEC1/1346 Combined Native Farm Labour; Labour Committee, 1940–44.

SEC1/1362 Cost of Living Allowances.

SEC1/1363 Report by Mr A. L. Saffery on the Cost of Living.

SEC1/1620 Copper Production Committee, Copperbelt, 1942–48.

SEC1/1638 Vol. III. Recruitment of African Soldiers and Non-combatant Personnel: Cooks and Waiters.

SEC1/1642 Estimate of Defence Force: Organisation of European Defence Force.

SEC1/1650 Vols. I–II. Compulsory Military Service Exemptions.

SEC1/1675 Extra-territorial Releases: Nursing and Sisters.

SEC1/1693 Compulsory Military Service, 1940–45.

Bibliography

SEC1/1694 Compulsory Regulation of Military, 1940–41.

SEC1/1699 Polish Evacuees General.

SEC1/1700 Refugees from Cyprus, Polish Evacuees General.

SEC1/1701 Vols. I–II. Polish Evacuees Control and Administration of Evacuees Camp Lusaka, Bwana Mkubwa and Abercorn.

SEC1/1702 Committee to Consider Application from Refugees for Permanent Residence in Northern Rhodesia.

SEC1/1703 Refugee Camps General.

SEC1/1728 Vol. VII. His Excellency's Tours to the Copperbelt, 1940–42.

SEC1/1728 Vol. X. His Excellency's Tours to the Copperbelt, September 1939.

SEC1/1728 Vol. XII. His Excellency's Tours: Arrangements and Matters Discussed.

SEC1/1758 Reports on Public Opinion Vols. I–II, 1939–1942.

SEC1/1764 Employment in Industry and Statistical Sub-committee, 1941–43.

SEC1/1766 Vols. I–III. Post-war Problems: African Soldiers Sub-committee; Views of African Soldiers on Post-war Employment; and Reports on Resettlement by District Commissioners; Views of Service Officers of Northern Rhodesian Units on Demobilisation and Resettlement of Northern Rhodesian Askari.

SEC1/1768 Minutes of the Meetings of District After-care Committees.

SEC1/1770 Reports on Public Opinion, 1942–45, Central Province.

SEC1/1771 Reports on Public Opinion, 1942–45, Western Province.

SEC1/1772 Reports on Public Opinion, 1942–43, Northern Province.

SEC1/1773 Reports on Public Opinion, 1942–43, Eastern Province.

SEC1/1774 Reports on Public Opinion, 1942–44, Kaonde-Lunda Province.

SEC1/1775 Reports on Public Opinion, 1942–44, Barotse Province.

SEC2/164 Effect of Italian and Abyssinian War on Natives.

SEC2/181 District Commissioners' Conferences, Northern Province.

SEC2/271 Native Industries: Iron Working.

SEC2/273 Vols. I–V. Native Rubber Industries.

SEC2/278 Rubber Importation of Made Goods to Stimulate Production.

SEC2/425 Broadcasting for Natives including Schools Broadcasting.

SEC2/470 Proposed War Memorial Northern Rhodesia Regiment.

SEC2/1122 Films for Africans: African Film Library and Purchasing Committee.

SEC2/1135 Reports from Information Officers on Visits to Troops.

SEC3/42 Miscellaneous Cost of Living Enquiry by Central Supplies Advisory Board.

SEC3/44 Vols. I–II. Price Control Policy, 1946–49.

SEC3/45 Price Control Advisory Committee, 1947–49.

SEC3/47 Emergency Powers Control of Prices and Board Amendment Regulation.

SEC3/48 Miscellaneous Cost of Living Inquiry.

SEC3/49 Immigration Committee.

SEC3/55 Northern Rhodesia Report of the Local Committee on Refugee Settlement.

SEC3/75 Price Control: General Policy.

SEC3/76 Cost of Living.

SEC3/79 Price Control—General on Oils and Fats.

Bibliography

SEC3/87 Post and Telegraphs Proposed Saving Bank Scheme for African Ranks in HM Forces.
SEC3/88 Post Office Savings Bank Regulations.
SEC3/453 Post-war Development Planning Report by Joint Development Advisor.
SEC3/485 Rationing of Food Stuffs.
SEC3/486 Supplies Control Ordinance.
SEC3/487 Control of Rationed Goods.
SEC3/491 Jute Supplies.
SEC3/492 Soap Rationing for Africans.
SEC3/494 Import Control: General.

II. PROVINCIAL SERIES

EP4/2/5 Loc 5476 Tour Reports Fort Jameson.
EP4/2/9 Loc 5477 Tour Reports Lundazi District, 1939–1946.
EP4/2/10 Loc 5477 Fort Jameson Tour Reports, 1940–48.
NP1/13/13 Loc 4840 1939 War: Loyalty Messages from Chiefs.
SP2/1/1 Loc 3109 Annual Report for Southern Province, 1947.
SP4/2/5 Loc 5081 District Travelling and Tour Reports: Kalomo.
SP4/2/6 Loc 5081 District Travelling: Mazabuka Tour Reports.
SP4/2/9 Loc 5082 District Travelling Tour Reports, 1939: Mazabuka.
SP4/2/19 Loc 5084 Information Reports, Public Opinion and Information on Northern Rhodesia.
SP4/12/35 Loc 5187 Cost of Living for Africans.

2. Mining Industry Archives (MIA)

14.3.3F British Territories in East and Central Africa, 1945–1950.
16.2.2D RACM Directors' Meetings, 1927–1954.
16.2.3E RACM Directors' Meeting Minutes 1954–1962.
18.4.2A, Mine Supplies, April 1942–November 1945, August 1950–December 1955.

3. Livingstone Museum (LM)

LM 2/3/4/1/5/2 Northern Rhodesia Regiment Parades, Programmes, 1935–1956.
LM 2/3/4/1/6/1 NRR Propaganda, Information Newsletters, 1940–1941.
LM 2/3/4/1/6/3 The Crested Crane.
LM 2/3/4/1/8/2 Northern Rhodesia Regimental History.
LM 2/3/4/4/1/1/8/4 Recruiting Posters, Information Office, Lusaka, Northern Rhodesia, 1943.
LM 2/3/4/4/1/1/8 Northern Rhodesia Newsletter, War News, 13 January 1942.
LM 2/3/4/4/1/1/8/5 Kampanje Kalila Shamwale! Lowani Usikari, ca. 1943.

4. Elizabeth Colson Documentation Centre, Institute for Economic and Social Research (INESOR) at the University of Zambia

FLE-LAB 1940 Propaganda in Barotseland.

Bibliography

5. Published Government Reports

I. NORTHERN RHODESIA GOVERNMENT (NRG)

(All NRG published reports listed were printed by the government printer in Lusaka.)

Annual Reports for the Department of Agriculture, 1940–1958. Lusaka.

Emergency Powers (Recruitment of Farm Labour) Regulations, 1942. Lusaka, 1942.

Final Report of the Select Committee Appointed to Examine and Report on the Question of Land Settlement in Northern Rhodesia for Ex-servicemen and Others. Lusaka, 1945.

First Report of the Advisory Committee on Industrial Development. Lusaka, 1946.

Interim Report of the Commission of Inquiry into the Cost of Living. Lusaka, 1946.

Legislative Council Debates, 1940–1950. Lusaka.

Maize Meal (Wholesale Prices) Order of 1942. Lusaka, 1942.

Memorandum on Post-war Development Planning in Northern Rhodesia. Lusaka, 1945.

Northern Rhodesia Regiment Annual Report for the Year Ending 1936. Lusaka, 1937.

Northern Rhodesia Regiment Annual Report for the Year Ending 1938. Lusaka, 1939.

Notes on Demobilisation: Benefits, Rehabilitation, Procedure, etc., for Persons of Northern Rhodesian Origin Serving in the Armed Forces. Lusaka, 1945.

Report of the Commission of Inquiry into Disturbances on the Copperbelt. Lusaka, 1940.

Report of the Northern Rhodesia Supply Mission to the United Kingdom 1944. Lusaka, 1944.

Report of the Commission of Enquiry into the Cost of Living. Lusaka, 1947.

Report on the Development of Secondary Industries in Northern Rhodesia. Lusaka, 1945.

Second Report of the Advisory Committee on Industrial Development. Lusaka, 1947.

Ten Year Development Plan. Lusaka, 1947.

Third Report of the Advisory Committee on Industrial Development. Lusaka, 1948.

II. BRITAIN

Report of the Commission Appointed to Enquire into the Financial and Economic Position of Northern Rhodesia. London, 1938.

Report on Economic and Commercial Conditions in Southern Rhodesia, Northern Rhodesia and Nyasaland. London, May 1939.

Statement of Policy on Colonial Development and Welfare. London, February 1940.

6. Oral Interviews

The interviews with Northern Rhodesia Regiment veterans conducted by the British Broadcasting Corporation (BBC) on the occasion of the fiftieth anniversary of the outbreak of the Second World War are available at the Imperial War Museum in London, while those done by MUVI TV can be accessed at the firm's library in Lusaka.

Chombola, Rabson, interviews with the BBC, Ndola, 10 August 1989 and 24 November 1989.

Kadansa, Chama Mutemi, interviews with the BBC, Ndola, 6 June 1989, 11 June 1989, 4 July 1989, and 17 July 1989.

Kangwa, Rightson, interview with the BBC, Ndola, 1989.

Kantu, Sekwela, interview with the BBC, Ndola, 1989.

Bibliography

Kasansayika, Lesa, interview with the BBC, Ndola, 24 November 1989.
Kazembe, Jim Mibenge, interview with the BBC, Ndola, 1989.
Mulenga, Joseph Chinama, interview with the BBC, Lusaka, 6 June 1989.
Muliango, Samson B. D., interview with the BBC, Lusaka, 11 July 1989.
Phiri, Justin Master, interview with the BBC, Ndola, 1989.
Sakala, Juston Eneya, interview with MUVI TV, Lusaka, 2011.
Simwinga, S. J., interview with MUVI TV, Lusaka, ca. 2011.
Zulu, Gilbert Malama, interview with the BBC, Chisamba, 1989.

7. Newspapers
Bulawayo Chronicle
City Press
Crown Colonist
East Africa and Rhodesia
The Economist
Mutende
Northern News
The Scotsman
South African Mining Journal
The Star
The Times

8. Miscellaneous
Copper Development Association. *Annual Reports, 1939–1953*. London.
International Labour Organisation. *Report and Questionnaire on Forced Labour*. Geneva: ILO, 1929.
———. *Conventions and Recommendations, 1919–1937*. Geneva: ILO, 1939.
Nchindila, Bernard. "Pan-African Issues in Zambian Bemba Literature: The Case of Stephen Mpashi's *Cekesoni aingila ubusoja* (1950) [Jackson joins the military]." Paper presented at the 5th European Conference on African Studies, SOAS, London, 2013.

B. SECONDARY SOURCES

1. Books
Anderson, David. *Histories of the Hanged: Britain's Dirty War in Kenya and the End of Empire*. New York: W. W. Norton, 2005.
Baldwin, Robert E. *Economic Development and Export Growth: A Study of Northern Rhodesia, 1920–1960*. Berkeley: University of California Press, 1966.
Barker, Brian Johnson, Paul Bell, Allan Duggan, Vivien Horler, Vincent le Roux, Portia Maurice, Cecile Reynierse, and Peter Schafer. *Reader's Digest Illustrated History of South Africa: The Real Story*. Cape Town: Oxford, 1988.
Bayly, Christopher, and Tim Harper. *Forgotten Armies: Britain's Asian Empire and the War with Japan*. London: Penguin, 2004.

Bibliography

————. *Forgotten Wars: The End of Britain's Asian Empire*. London: Penguin, 2007.

Berger, Elena L. *Labour, Race and Colonial Rule: The Copperbelt from 1924 to Independence*. Oxford: Oxford University Press, 1974.

Black, Jeremy. *World War Two: A Military History*. London: Routledge, 2003.

Brelsford, William Vernon, ed. *The Story of the Northern Rhodesia Regiment*. Lusaka: Government Printer, 1954.

Butler, Lawrence. *Copper Empire: Mining and the Colonial State in Northern Rhodesia, c. 1930–1964*. Houndsmill, UK: Palgrave Macmillan, 2007.

Byfield, Judith A., Carolyn A. Brown, Timothy Parsons, and Ahmad Alawad Sikainga, eds. *Africa and World War II*. New York: Cambridge University Press, 2015.

Cain, Peter J., and Antony G. Hopkins. *British Imperialism: Innovation and Expansion, 1688–2000*. 2d ed. Harlow, UK: Longman, 2001.

————. *British Imperialism: Crisis and Deconstruction, 1914–1990*. Harlow, UK: Longman, 1993.

Chipungu, Samuel N. *The State, Technology and Peasant Differentiation in Southern Zambia: A Case Study of the Southern Province, 1890–1980*. Lusaka: Historical Association of Zambia, 1988.

Coleman, Francis L. *The Northern Rhodesia Copperbelt, 1899–1962*. Manchester: Manchester University Press, 1971.

Conan, A. R. *The Problem of Sterling*. London: Macmillan, 1966.

Cooper, Frederick. *Africa since 1940: The Past of the Present*. Cambridge: Cambridge University Press, 2002.

————. *Decolonization and African Society: The Labor Question in French and British Africa*. Cambridge: Cambridge University Press, 1996.

Darwin, John. *Britain and Decolonisation: The Retreat from Empire in the Post-war World*. London: Palgrave, 1988.

Das, Dipak Kumar. *Revisiting Talwar: A Study in the Royal Indian Navy Uprising of February 1946*. New Delhi: Ajanta , 1993.

Dear, I. C. B., ed. *The Oxford Companion to the Second World War*. Oxford: Oxford University Press, 1995.

Decker, Alicia C. *In Idi Amin's Shadow: Women, Gender, and Militarism in Uganda*. Athens: Ohio University Press, 2014.

Deshpande, Anirudh. *British Military Policy in India, 1900–1945: Colonial Constraints and Declining Power*. New Delhi: Manohar, 2005.

Echenberg, Myron J. *Colonial Conscripts: The* Tirailleurs Sénégalais *in French West Africa, 1857–1960*. Portsmouth, NH: Heinemann, 1991.

Enloe, Cynthia H. *Ethnic Soldiers: State Security in Divided Societies*. Athens: University of Georgia Press, 1980.

Ferguson, James. *Expectations of Modernity: Myths and Meanings of Urban Life on the Zambian Copperbelt*. Berkeley: University of California Press, 1999.

Franklin, Harry. *Unholy Wedlock: The Failure of the Central African Federation*. London: Faber and Faber, 1963.

Furedi, Frank. *The New Ideology of Imperialism*. London: Pluto Press, 1994.

Bibliography

Gann, Lewis H. *The Birth of a Plural Society: The Development of Northern Rhodesia under the British South Africa Company, 1894–1914.* Manchester: Manchester University Press, 1958.

———. *A History of Northern Rhodesia: Early Days to 1953.* London: Chatto and Windus, 1964.

Gardner, Richard N. *Sterling-Dollar Diplomacy in Current Perspective: The Origins and the Prospects of Our International Economic Order.* New York: Columbia University Press, 1980.

Gouldsbury, Cullen, and Hubert Sheane. *The Great Plateau of Northern Rhodesia: Being Some Impressions of the Tanganyika Plateau.* London: Edward Arnold, 1911.

Gregory, Theodore. *Ernest Oppenheimer and the Economic Development of Southern Africa.* London: Literary Licencing, 1962.

Hargreaves, John D. *Decolonization in Africa.* London: Routledge, 1996.

Hellen, John A. *Rural Economic Development in Zambia, 1890–1964.* Munich: Weltforum Verlag for Inst. F. Wirtschaftsforschung, 1968.

Hill, M. F. *Permanent Way: The Story of the Kenya and Uganda Railway.* 2d ed. Nairobi: East African Railways and Harbours, 1961.

Hochschild, Adam. *King Leopold's Ghost: A Story of Greed, Terror, and Heroism in Colonial Africa.* Boston: Mariner Books, 1998.

Hyam, Ronald, and Peter Henshaw. *The Lion and the Springbok: Britain and South Africa since the Boer War.* Cambridge: Cambridge University Press, 2003.

Iliffe, John. *Honour in African History.* Cambridge: Cambridge University Press, 2005.

———. *A Modern History of Tanganyika.* Cambridge: Cambridge University Press, 1979.

Jackson, Ashley. *Botswana, 1939–1945: An African Country at War.* Oxford: Oxford University Press, 1999.

———. *The British Empire and the Second World War.* London: Hambledon Continuum, 2006.

Johnson, David. *World War Two and the Scramble for Labour in Colonial Zimbabwe, 1939–1948.* Harare: University of Zimbabwe Publications, 2000.

Kanduza, Ackson M. *The Political Economy of Underdevelopment in Northern Rhodesia, 1918–1960: A Case Study of Customs Tariff and Railway Freight Policies.* Lanham, MD: University Press of America, 1986.

Keegan, John. *The Second World War.* London: Random House Books, 1989.

Killingray, David. *Fighting for Britain: African Soldiers in the Second World War.* Woodbridge, UK: James Currey, 2010.

Killingray, David, and David Omissi, eds. *Guardians of Empire: The Armed Forces of the Colonial Powers c. 1700–1964.* Manchester: Manchester University Press, 1999.

Killingray, David, and Richard Rathbone, eds. *Africa and the Second World War.* Basingstoke, UK: Palgrave Macmillan, 1986.

Lawler, Nancy Ellen. *Soldiers of Misfortune: Ivoirien Tirailleurs of World War II.* Athens: Ohio University Press, 1992.

Lee, Loyd E., ed. *World War II in Asia and the Pacific and the War's Aftermath, with General Themes: A Handbook of Literature and Research.* Westport, CT: Greenwood, 1998.

Bibliography

Lévi-Strauss, Claude. *Structural Anthropology*. New York: Basic Books, 1963.

Lewis, Joanna. *Empire State-Building: War and Welfare in Kenya, 1925–52*. Athens: Ohio University Press, 2000.

Liddell Hart, Basil H. *History of the Second World War*. London: Cassell, 1970.

Macmillan, Hugh, with Frank Shapiro. *Zion in Africa: The Jews of Zambia*. London: I. B. Tauris, 2017.

Macola, Giacomo. *The Gun in Central Africa: A History of Technology and Politics*. Athens: Ohio University Press, 2016.

———. *Liberal Nationalism in Central Africa: A Biography of Harry Mwaanga Nkumbula*. New York: Palgrave Macmillan, 2009.

Makasa, Kapasa. *Zambia's March to Political Freedom*. Nairobi: Heinemann, 1981.

Mann, Gregory. *Native Sons: West African Veterans and France in the Twentieth Century*. Durham, NC: Duke University Press, 2006.

Martin, H. J., and Neil Orpen. *South Africa at War: Preparations and Operations on the Home Front, 1939–45*. Vol. 7 of *South African Forces in World War II*. Cape Town: Purnell, 1979.

Martin, Thomas. *Fight or Flight: Britain, France and their Roads from Empire*. Oxford: Oxford University Press, 2014.

Marx, Christoph. *Oxwagon Sentinel: Radical Afrikaner Nationalism and the History of the Ossewabrandwag*. Berlin: Lit Verlag, 2008.

Meebelo, Henry S. *African Proletarians and Colonial Capitalism: The Origins, Growth and Struggles of the Zambian Labour Movement to 1964*. Lusaka: Kenneth Kaunda Foundation, 1986.

———. *Reaction to Colonialism: A Prelude to the Politics of Independence in Northern Zambia, 1893–1939*. Manchester: Manchester University Press, 1971.

Melland, Frank. *In Witch-Bound Africa: An Account of the Primitive Kaonde Tribe and Their Beliefs*. London: Seeley, 1923.

Meredith, Martin. *The State of Africa: A History of the Continent since Independence*. London: Simon and Schuster, 2011.

Milner-Thornton, J. B. *The Long Shadow of the British Empire: The Ongoing Legacies of Race and Class in Zambia*. New York: Palgrave Macmillan, 2012.

Moore, Henrietta L., and Megan Vaughan. *Cutting Down Trees: Gender, Nutrition, and Agricultural Change in the Northern Province of Zambia, 1890–1900*. Portsmouth, NH: Heinemann, 1994.

Mukerjee, Madhusree. *Churchill's Secret War: The British Empire and the Ravaging of India during World War Two*. New York: Basic Books, 2010.

Mwangilwa, Godwin. *Harry Mwaanga Nkumbula: Biography of the 'Old Lion' of Zambia*. Lusaka: Multi Media Publications, 1984.

Mwendapole, M. R. *A History of the Trade Union Movement in Zambia up to 1968*. Edited and with an introduction by Robin H. Palmer and Ian Phimister. Lusaka: University of Zambia, 1977.

Nasson, Bill. *Abraham Esau's War: A Black South African War in the Cape, 1899–1902*. Cambridge: Cambridge University Press, 2008.

Bibliography

Ogot, Bothwell A., and W. R. Ochieng', eds. *Decolonization and Independence in Kenya, 1940–93.* Athens: Ohio University Press, 1995.

Overy, Richard. *The Bombing War: Europe, 1939–1945.* London: Allen Lane, 2014.

Perrings, Charles. *Black Mineworkers in Central Africa: Industrial Strategies and the Evolution of an African Proletariat in the Copperbelt, 1911–1941.* New York: Africana, 1979.

Phimister, Ian. *An Economic and Social History of Zimbabwe, 1890–1948: Capital Accumulation and Class Struggle.* London: Longman, 1988.

———. *Wangi Kolia: Coal, Capital and Labour in Colonial Zimbabwe, 1894–1954.* Johannesburg: Witwatersrand University Press, 1994.

Prain, Ronald L. *Reflections on an Era: An Autobiography.* Surrey: Metal Bulletin Books, 1981.

Richards, Audrey L. *Land, Labour and Diet in Northern Rhodesia: An Economic Study of the Bemba Tribe.* Hamburg: James Currey, 1995.

Roberts, Andrew D. *A History of Zambia.* London: Heinemann, 1976.

Rotberg, Robert I. *Black Heart: Gore-Browne and the Politics of Multiracial Zambia.* Berkeley: University of California Press, 1977.

———. *The Rise of Nationalism in Central Africa: The Making of Malawi and Zambia, 1873–1964.* Cambridge, MA: Harvard University Press, 1965.

Schenk, Catherine R. *The Decline of Sterling: Measuring the Retreat of an International Currency, 1945–1992.* Cambridge: Cambridge University Press, 2010.

Shillington, Kevin. *History of Africa.* London: Palgrave Macmillan, 2005.

Spence, Daniel Owen. *Colonial Naval Culture and British Imperialism, 1922–67.* Manchester: Manchester University Press, 2015.

Stapleton, Timothy. *African Police and Soldiers in Colonial Zimbabwe, 1923–80.* Rochester, NY: University of Rochester Press, 2011.

Stephenson, John Edward. *Chirupula's Tale: A Bye-Way in African History.* London: Geoffrey Bless, 1937.

Stewart, Andrew. *Empire Lost: Britain, the Dominions and the Second World War.* London: Continuum, 2008.

Stockwell, Sarah. *The Business of Decolonisation: British Business Strategies in the Gold Coast.* Oxford: Oxford University Press, 2000.

Throup, David W. *Economic and Social Origins of Mau Mau, 1945–53.* Athens: Ohio University Press, 1988.

van Onselen, Charles. Chibaro: African Mine Labour in Southern Rhodesia, 1900–1933. London: Pluto, 1976.

Vickery, Kenneth P. *Black and White in Southern Zambia: The Tonga Plateau Economy and British Imperialism, 1890–1939.* New York: Greenwood, 1986.

von Oppen, Achim. *Terms of Trade and Terms of Trust: The History and Contexts of Precolonial Market Production around the Upper Zambezi and Kasai.* Munster: Lit Verlag, 1992.

Warwick, Peter. *Black People and the South African War, 1899–1902.* Cambridge: Cambridge University Press, 1983.

Bibliography

Watson, William. *The Social Structure of the Mambwe of Northern Rhodesia*. Manchester: Manchester University Press, 1957.
Weinberg, Gerhard L. *A World at Arms: A Global History of World War II*. Cambridge: Cambridge University Press, 1994.

2. Articles and Chapters

Alence, Rod. "Colonial Government, Social Conflict and State Involvement in Africa's Open Economies: The Origins of the Ghana Cocoa Marketing Board, 1939–46." *Journal of African History* 42, no. 3 (2001): 397–416.
Anthony, L. F. G. "The Second World War." In *The Story of the Northern Rhodesia Regiment*, edited by William Vernon Brelsford, 75–102. Lusaka: Government Printer, 1954.
Baker, Colin. "Depression and Development in Nyasaland, 1929–1939." *Society of Malawi Journal* 27, no. 1 (1974): 7–26.
Barnhart, Michael A. "International Relations and the Origins of the War in Asia and the Pacific War." In Lee, *World War II in Asia and the Pacific*, 5–24.
Bauer, P. T. "Origins of the Statutory Export Monopolies of British West Africa." *Business History Review* 28, no. 3 (1954): 197–213.
Baynham, Simon. "The Ghanaian Military: A Bibliographic Essay." *West African Journal of Sociology and Political Science* 1, no. 1 (October 1975): 83–96.
Bhattacharjee, Anuradha. "Polish Refugees in India during and after the Second World War." *Sarmatian Review* 34, no. 2 (April 2013): 1743–57.
Bhila, Hoyini K. "The Impact of the Second World War on the Development of Peasant Agriculture in Botswana, 1939–1956." *Botswana Notes and Records* 16 (1984): 63–71.
Byfield, Judith A. Preface to Byfield et al., *Africa and World War II*, xvii–xxiii.
———. "Producing for the War." In Byfield et al., *Africa and World War II*, 24–42.
———. "Women, Rice, and War: Political and Economic Crisis in Wartime Abeokuta (Nigeria)." In Byfield et al., *Africa and World War II*, 147–65.
Chipungu, Samuel N. "African Leadership under Indirect Rule in Colonial Zambia." In *Guardians in Their Time: Experiences of Zambians under Colonial Rule, 1980–1964*, edited by Samuel N. Chipungu, 50–73. London: Macmillan, 1992.
Clarence-Smith, William G. "Africa's 'Battle for Rubber' in the Second World War." In Byfield et al., *Africa and World War II*, 166–82.
Collins, Michael. "Decolonisation and the 'Federal Moment.'" *Diplomacy and Statecraft* 24, no. 1 (2013): 21–40.
Colson, Elizabeth. "The Tonga and the Shortage of Implements." *Rhodes-Livingstone Journal* 14 (1954): 37–38.
Cowen, Michael, and Nicholas Westcott. "British Imperial Economic Policy during the Second World War." In Killingray and Rathbone, *Africa and the Second World War*, 20–67.
Crowder, Michael. "Introduction." In *The Cambridge History of Africa*, vol. 8, *c. 1940–c. 1975*, edited by Michael Crowder, 1–7. Cambridge: Cambridge University Press, 1984.

Bibliography

———. "The 1939–45 War and West Africa." In *History of West Africa*, vol. 2, edited by J. F. A. Ajayi and Michael Crowder, 665–92. London: Columbia University Press, 1974.

———. "The Second World War: Prelude to Decolonization." In *The Cambridge History of Africa*, vol. 8, *c. 1940–c. 1975*, edited by Michael Crowder, 8–51. Cambridge: Cambridge University Press, 1984.

Datta, Kusum. "Farm Labour, Agrarian Capital and the State in Colonial Zambia: The African Labour Corps, 1942–52." *Journal of Southern African Studies* 14, no. 3 (April 1988): 371–92.

Dickson, A. G. "Studies in War-Time Organisation: The Mobile Propaganda Unit, East Africa Command." *African Affairs* 44, no. 174 (January 1945): 9–18.

Duder, C. J. "'Men of the Officer Class': The Participants in the 1919 Soldier Settlement Scheme in Kenya." *African Affairs* 92, no. 366 (1993): 69–87.

Dumett, Raymond. "Africa's Strategic Minerals during the Second World War." *Journal of African History* 26, no. 4 (1985): 381–408.

Falola, Toyin. "Cassava Starch for Export in Nigeria during the Second World War." *African Economic History* 18 (1989): 73–98.

———. "'Salt Is Gold': The Management of Salt Scarcity in Nigeria during World War II." *Canadian Journal of African Studies* 26, no. 2 (1992): 412–36.

Foot, M. R. D., and P. Stansky. "United Kingdom." In Dear, *Oxford Companion to the Second World War*, 1130–229.

Fritz, Martin. "Economic Warfare." In Dear, *Oxford Companion to the Second World War*, 318–21.

Furedi, Frank. "The Demobilized African Soldier and the Blow to White Prestige." In Killingray and Omissi, *Guardians of Empire*, 179–97.

Gann, Lewis H. "The Northern Rhodesian Copper Industry and the World of Copper, 1923–52." *Rhodes-Livingstone Journal* 18 (1955): 1–18.

Grundlingh, Albert. "The King's Afrikaners? Enlistment and Ethnic Identity in the Union of South Africa's Defence Force during the Second World War, 1939–45." *Journal of African History* 40 (1999): 351–65.

Grundlingh, Louis W. F. "The Military, Race, and Resistance: The Conundrums of Recruiting Black South African Men during the Second World War." In Byfield et al., *Africa and World War II*, 71–88.

———. "'Non-Europeans Should Be Kept Away from the Temptations of Towns': Controlling Black South Africans during the Second World War." *International Journal of African Historical Studies* 25, no. 3 (1992): 539–60.

———. "Prejudices, Promises and Poverty: The Experiences of Discharged and Demobilised Black South African Soldiers after the Second World War." *South African Historical Journal* 26 (1992): 116–35.

———. "The Recruitment of South African Blacks for Participation in the Second World War." In Killingray and Rathbone, *Africa and the Second World War*, 181–203.

Headrick, Rita. "African Soldiers in World War II." *Armed Forces and Society* 4 (1978): 502–26.

Bibliography

Hjertman, Martina, Sari Nauman, Maria Vretemark, Gwilym Williams, and Anders Kjellin. "The Social Impacts of War: Agency and Everyday Life in the Borderland during the Early Seventeenth Century." *International Journal of Historical Archaeology* 22 (2018): 226–44.

Henderson, Ian. "Early African Leadership: The Copperbelt Disturbances of 1935 and 1940." *Journal of Southern African Studies* 2, no. 1 (1975): 83–97.

———. "The Origins of Nationalism in East and Central Africa: The Zambian Case." *Journal of African History* 11, no. 4 (1970): 591–603.

———. "Wage Earners and Political Protest in Colonial Africa: The Case of the Copperbelt." *African Affairs* 72, no. 288 (July 1973): 288–99.

Hinds, Allister E. "Colonial Policy and Processing of Groundnuts: The Case of Georges Calil." *International Journal of African Historical Studies* 19, no. 2 (1986): 261–73.

———. "Government Policy and the Nigerian Palm Oil Export Industry, 1939–49." *Journal of African History* 38, no. 3 (1997): 459–78.

Hobson, R. H. "Rubber: A Footnote to Northern Rhodesian History." *Occasional Papers of the Rhodes-Livingstone Museum* 13 (1960).

Holbrook, Wendy P. "British Propaganda and the Mobilization of the Gold Coast War Effort, 1939–1945." *Journal of African History* 26, no. 4 (1985): 347–61.

Ibhawoh, Bonny. "Second World War Propaganda, Imperial Idealism and Anti-colonial Nationalism in British West Africa." *Nordic Journal of African Studies* 16, no. 2 (2007): 221–43.

Israel, Adrienne M. "Ex-servicemen at the Crossroads: Protest and Politics in Post-war Ghana." *Journal of Modern African Studies* 30, no. 2 (1992): 359–68.

———. "Measuring the War Experience: Ghanaian Soldiers in World War II." *Journal of Modern African Studies* 25, no. 1 (1987): 159–68.

Jackson, Ashley. "African Soldiers and Imperial Authorities: Tensions and Unrest during the Service of High Commission Territories' Soldiers in the British Army, 1941–46." *Journal of Southern African Studies* 25, no. 4 (December 1999): 645–65.

———. "Bad Chiefs and Sub-tribes: Aspects of Recruitment for the British Army in Bechuanaland Protectorate, 1941–42." *Botswana Notes and Records* 28 (1996): 87–96.

———. "The Empire/Commonwealth and the Second World War." *Round Table* 100, no. 412 (February 2011): 65–78.

———. "Motivation and Mobilization for War: Recruitment for the British Army in Bechuanaland Protectorate." *African Affairs* 96, no. 384 (1997): 399–417.

Jeffery, Keith. "The Second World War." In *The Oxford History of the British Empire*, vol. 4, *The Twentieth Century*, edited by Judith M. Brown and Wm. Roger Louis, 306–28. Oxford: Oxford University Press, 1999.

Johnson, David. "Settler Farmers and Coerced African Labour in Southern Rhodesia." *Journal of African History* 33 (1992): 111–28.

Killingray, David. "African Voices from Two World Wars." *Historical Research* 74, no. 186 (November 2001): 425–43.

Bibliography

———. "Labour Exploitation for Military Campaigns in British Colonial Africa, 1870–1945." *Journal of Contemporary History* 24, no. 3 (1989): 483–501.

———. "Labour Mobilisation in British Colonial Africa for the War Effort, 1939–46." In Killingray and Rathbone, *Africa and the Second World War*, 68–96.

———. "Military and Labour Recruitment in the Gold Coast during the Second World War." *Journal of African History* 23, no. 1 (1982): 83–95.

———. "Soldiers, Ex-servicemen, and Politics in the Gold Coast, 1939–50." *Journal of Modern African Studies* 21, no. 3 (September 1983): 523–34.

Killingray, David, and Richard Rathbone. "Introduction." In Killingray and Rathbone, *Africa and the Second World War*, 1–19.

Kotani, Ken. "Pearl Harbor: Japanese Planning and Command Structure." In *The Pacific War Companion: From Pearl Harbor to Hiroshima*, edited by Daniel Marston, 29–45. Oxford: Osprey, 2005.

Krozewski, Gerold. "Sterling, the 'Minor' Territories, and the End of Formal Empire, 1939–1958." *Economic History Review* 46, no. 2 (1993): 239–65.

Leepile, M. "The Impact of Migrant Labour on the Economy of Kweneng 1940–1980." *Botswana Notes and Records* 13 (1981): 33–43.

Lonsdale, John. "The Depression and the Second World War in the Transformation of Kenya." In Killingray and Rathbone, *Africa and the Second World War*, 97–142.

Low, D. A., and John M. Lonsdale. "Towards the New Order, 1945–63." In *History of East Africa*, vol. 3, edited by D. A. Low and Alison Smith, 297–328. Oxford: Clarendon, 1976.

Lwanga-Lunyiigo, Samwiiri. "Uganda's Long Connection with the Problem of Refugees: From the Polish Refugees of World War II to the Present." In *Uganda and the Problem of Refugees*, edited by A. G. G. Gingyera Pinycwa, 1–21. Kampala: Makerere University Press, 1998.

Marjomaa, Risto. "The Martial Spirit: Yao Soldiers in the British Service in Nyasaland." *Journal of African History* 44, no. 3 (2003): 413–32.

Mbewe, Mary. "Northern Poles." *The Lowdown*, 1 July 2013, 1.

Meredith, David. "The Colonial Office, British Business Interests and the Reform of Cocoa Marketing in West Africa, 1937–1945." *Journal of African History* 29, no. 2 (1988): 285–300.

———. "State Controlled Marketing and Economic 'Development': The Case of West African Produce during the Second World War." *Economic History Review*, n.s., 39, no. 1 (February 1986): 77–91.

Mokopakgosi, Brian. "The Impact of the Second World War: The Case of the Kweneng in the Then Bechuanaland Protectorate, 1939–1950." In Killingray and Rathbone, *Africa and the Second World War*, 160–80.

Moore, R. J. B. "Native Wages and Standard of Living in Northern Rhodesia." *African Studies* 1, no. 2 (1942): 142–48.

Morapedi, Wazha G. "Migrant Labour and the Peasantry in the Bechuanaland Protectorate, 1930–1965." *Journal of Southern African Studies* 25, no. 2 (1999): 197–214.

Bibliography

Musambachime, Mwelwa C. "Dauti Yamba's Contribution to the Rise and Growth of Nationalism in Zambia, 1941–1964." *African Affairs* 90, no. 359 (1991): 259–81.

Ntabeni, Mary Nombulelo. "Military Labour Mobilisation in Colonial Lesotho during World War II, 1940–1943." *Scientia Militaria: South African Journal of Military Studies* 36, no. 2 (2008): 36–59.

Oberst, "Transport Workers, Strikes and the 'Imperial Response': Africa and the Post World War II Conjuncture." *African Studies Review* 31, no. 1 (1988): 117–33.

Olusanya, Gabriel O. "The Role of Ex-servicemen in Nigerian Politics." *Journal of Modern African Studies* 6, no. 2 (1968): 221–32.

Overy, Richard. "World Trade and World Economy." In Dear, *Oxford Companion to the Second World War*, 1282–88.

Palmer, Annette. "The Politics of Race and War: Black Soldiers in the Caribbean Theater during the Second World War." *Military Affairs* 47, no. 2 (April 1983): 59–62.

Palmer, Robin. "The Nyasaland Tea Industry in the Era of International Tea Restrictions, 1933–1950." *Journal of African History* 26, no. 2 (1985): 215–39.

Parker, Jason. "Remapping the Cold War in the Tropics: Race, Communism, and National Security in the West Indies." *International History Review* 24, no. 2 (2002): 318–47.

Parsons, Timothy H. "'All Askaris Are Family Men': Sex, Domesticity and Discipline in the King's African Rifles, 1902–1964." In Killingray and Omissi, *Guardians of Empire*, 179–97.

———. "No Country Fit for Heroes: The Plight of Disabled Kenyan Veterans." In Byfield et al., *Africa and World War II*, 127–44.

———. "'Wakamba Warriors Are Soldiers of the Queen': The Evolution of the Kamba as a Martial Race, 1890–1970." *Ethnohistory* 46, no. 4 (1999): 671–701.

Perrings, Charles. "Conflict and Proletarianisation: An Assessment of the 1935 Mineworkers' Strike on the Northern Rhodesian Copperbelt." *Journal of Southern African Studies* 4, no. 1 (1977): 31–51.

Philpott, R. "The Mongu-Mulobezi Labour Route." *Rhodes-Livingstone Journal* 3 (1945): 50–54.

Rasor, Eugene L. "The Japanese Attack on Pearl Harbor." In Lee, *World War II in Asia and the Pacific*, 45–55.

Rathbone, Richard. "Businessmen in Politics: Party Struggle in Ghana, 1949–57." *Journal of Development Studies* 9, no. 3 (1973): 391–401.

Roberts, Andrew D. "Northern Rhodesia: The Post-war Background, 1945–1953." In *Living the End of Empire: Politics and Society in Late Colonial Zambia*, edited by Jan-Bart Gewald, Marja Hinfelaar, and Giacomo Macola, 15–24. Leiden: Brill, 2011.

———. "Notes towards a Financial History of Copper Mining in Northern Rhodesia." *Canadian Journal of African Studies* 16, no. 2 (1982): 347–59.

Rupiah, Martin R. "The History of the Establishment of Internment Camps and Refugee Settlements in Southern Rhodesia, 1938–1952." *Zambezia* 22, no. 2 (1995): 137–52.

Samasuwo, Nhamo. "Food Production and War Supplies: Rhodesia's Beef Industry during the Second World War, 1939–1945." *Journal of Southern African Studies* 29, no. 2 (June 2003): 487–502.

Bibliography

Sandifort, Mary-Ann. "The Forgotten Story of Polish Refugees in Zambia." *Bulletin and Record*, June 2015, 20–21.

Schleh, Eugene P. A. "The Post-war Careers of Ex-servicemen in Ghana and Uganda." *Journal of Modern African Studies* 6, no. 2 (1968): 203–20.

Schumaker, Lynette. "A Tent with a View: Colonial Officers, Anthropologists, and the Making of the Field in Northern Rhodesia, 1937–1960." *Osiris*, 2d ser., 11 (1996): 237–58.

Seirlis, J. K. "Undoing the United Front? Coloured Soldiers in Rhodesia, 1939–1980." *African Studies* 63, no. 1 (2004): 73–94.

Simelane, Hamilton Sipho. "Labor Mobilization for the War Effort in Swaziland, 1940–1942." *International Journal of African Historical Studies* 26, no. 3 (1993): 541–74.

———. "Veterans, Politics and Poverty: The Case of Swazi Veterans in the Second World War." *South African Historical Journal* 38 (1998): 144–70.

Smyth, Rosaleen. "Britain's African Colonies and British Propaganda during the Second World War." *Journal of Imperial and Commonwealth History* 14 (1985): 65–82.

———. "War Propaganda during the Second World War in Northern Rhodesia." *African Affairs* 83, no. 332 (July 1984): 345–58.

Speier, Hans. "The Effects of War on the Social Order." *Annals of the American Academy of Political and Social Science* 218 (November 1941): 87–96.

Spence, Daniel Owen. "Beyond *Talwar*: A Cultural Reappraisal of the 1946 Royal Indian Navy Mutiny." *Journal of Imperial and Commonwealth History* 46, no. 3 (2015): 489–508.

———. "Imperial Transition, Indianisation and Race: Developing National Navies in the Subcontinent, 1947–64." *South Asia: Journal of South Asian Studies* 37, no. 2 (June 2014): 323–38.

———. " 'They Had the Sea in Their Blood': Caymanian Naval Volunteers in the Second World War." In *Transnational Soldiers: Foreign Military Enlistment in the Modern Era*, edited by Nir Arielli and Bruce Collins, 105–23. New York: Palgrave Macmillan, 2013.

Spencer, Ian. "Settler Dominance, Agricultural Production and the Second World War in Kenya." *Journal of African History* 21, no. 4 (1980): 497–514.

Spivak, Gayatri Chakravorty. "Can the Subaltern Speak?" In *Marxism and the Interpretation of Culture*, edited by Cary Nelson and Lawrence Grossberg, 217–313. Urbana: University of Illinois Press, 1988.

Stoler, Ann L. "Making Empire Respectable: The Politics of Race and Sexual Morality in 20th-Century Colonial Cultures." *American Ethnologist* 16, no. 4 (1989): 634–60.

Summers, Carol. "Ugandan Politics and World War II (1939–1949)." In Byfield et al., *Africa and World War II*, 480–98.

Sunseri, Thaddeus. "World War II and the Transformation of the Tanzanian Forests" In Byfield et al., *Africa and World War II*, 238–56.

Tavuyanago, Baxter, Tasara Muguti, and James Hlongwana. "Victims of the Rhodesian Immigration Policy: Polish Refugees from the Second World War." *Journal of Southern African Studies* 38, no. 4 (2012): 951–65.

Bibliography

Taylor, Robert H. "Colonial Forces in British Burma: A National Army Postponed." In *Colonial Armies in Southeast Asia*, edited by Tobias Rettig and Karl Hack, 185–201. London: Routledge, 2006.

Tembo, Alfred. "Rubber Production in Northern Rhodesia during the Second World War, 1942–1946." *African Economic History* 41 (2013): 223–55.

Upeniece, V. "War and Society." *International Interdisciplinary Scientific Conference: Society. Health. Welfare* (2016): 1–5. Online at SHS Web of Conferences 30 (2016), doi: 10.1051/shsconf/20163000009.

van der Laan, Laurens. "Marketing West Africa's Export Crops: Modern Boards and Trading Companies." *Journal of Modern African Studies* 25, no. 1 (March 1987): 1–24.

———. "The Selling Policies of African Export: Marketing Boards." *African Affairs* 85, no. 340 (July 1986): 365–83.

Vickery, Kenneth P. "The Second World War Revival of Forced Labor in the Rhodesias." *International Journal of African Historical Studies* 22, no. 3 (1989): 423–37.

Westcott, Nicholas J. "Closer Union and the Future of East Africa, 1939–1948: A Case Study in the 'Official Mind of Imperialism.'" *Journal of Imperial and Commonwealth History* 10, no. 1 (1981): 67–88.

———. "The East African Sisal Industry, 1929–1949: The Marketing of a Colonial Commodity during Depression and War." *Journal of African History* 25 (1984): 445–61.

———. "The Impact of the Second World War on Tanganyika, 1939–49." In Killingray and Rathbone, *Africa and the Second World War*, 143–59.

White, Luise. "Prostitution, Identity, and Class Consciousness in Nairobi during World War II." *Signs: Journal of Women and Culture in Society* 11 (1986): 255–73.

Wicker, E. R. "Colonial Development and Welfare, 1929–1957: The Evolution of a Policy." *Social and Economic Studies* 7, no. 4 (December 1958): 170–92.

Williams, Gavin. "Marketing without and with Marketing Boards: The Origins of State Marketing Boards in Nigeria." *Review of African Political Economy* 34 (December 1985): 4–15.

Williamsen, Thomas Marvin. "The Second Sino-Japanese War, 1931–1945." In Lee, *World War II in Asia and the Pacific*, 27–44.

Wright, Marcia. "An Old Nationalist in New Nationalist Times: Donald Siwale and the State in Zambia, 1948–1963." *Journal of Southern African Studies* 23, no. 2 (1997): 339–51.

Zeleza, Tiyambe. "The Political Economy of British Colonial Development and Welfare in Africa." *Transafrican Journal of History* 15 (1985): 139–61.

3. Theses and Dissertations

Chabatama, Chewe Mebbiens. "Peasant Farming, the State, and Food Security in the North-Western Province of Zambia, 1902–1964." PhD diss., University of Toronto, 1999.

Chondoka, Yizenge A. "Labour Migration in Chama District, North-Eastern Zambia." PhD diss., University of Toronto, 1992.

Grundlingh, Louis Willem Fredrick. "South African Blacks in the Second World War." DLitt et Phil thesis, Rand Afrikaans University, 1986.

Bibliography

Lingelbach, Jochen. "Polish Refugees in British Colonial East and Central Africa during and after World War Two." DPhil thesis, Universität Leipzig, 2017.

Mazala, Kaonga W. "For Pleasure and Profit: Sex Work in Zambia, c. 1880–1964." MA diss., University of Zambia, 2013.

Money, Duncan. "'No Matter How Much or How Little They've Got, They Can't Settle Down': A Social History of Europeans on the Zambian Copperbelt, 1926–1974." PhD diss., University of Oxford, 2016.

Papstein, Robert J. "The Upper Zambezi: A History of the Luvale People, 1000–1900." PhD diss., University of California, Los Angeles, 1978.

Phillips, John G. "Roan Antelope: Big Business in Central Africa." PhD thesis, University of Cambridge, 2000.

Quick, Grifiths. "Doctor of Iron Stone (*Ng'anga ya Lubwe*)." MSc diss., University of Manchester, 1947.

Rau, William. "Mpezeni's Ngoni of Eastern Zambia, 1870–1920." PhD diss., University of California, Los Angeles, 1974.

Sandifort, Mary-Ann. "World War Two: The Deportation of Polish Refugees to Abercorn Camp in Northern Rhodesia." MA diss., University of Leiden, 2015.

Shackleton, Deborah A. "Imperial Military Policy and the Bechuanaland Pioneers and Gunners during the Second World War." PhD diss., Indiana University, 1997.

Siamwiza, Bennett S. "A History of Famine in Zambia c.1825–1949." PhD thesis, University of Cambridge, 1998.

Simunchembu, Chipo Munzabwa. "Commercial Farming and Social Change in Mkushi District, 1945–1975." MA diss., University of Zambia, 1989.

Tembo, Alfred. "The Colonial State and African Agriculture in Chipata District of Northern Rhodesia, 1895–1964." MA diss., University of Zambia, 2010.

———. "The Impact of the Second World War on Northern Rhodesia (Zambia), 1939–1953." PhD thesis, University of the Free State, 2016.

Index

Abercorn, 64, 65, 66, 67, 75, 99, 101, 105, 113
African Labour Advisory Board (ALAB), 139
African Labour Corps, 139, 140
African Weekly, 27
Afrikaans Newsletter, 28
Afrikaner migrants, 110
Afrikaners, 54, 98
agricultural industry, 59, 61, 62, 70, 72, 76, 155
agriculture, 138, 173. *See also* Department of Agriculture
Alberti, Stefan Fiedler, 100
American Pacific Fleet, 33
Anglo American Corporation, 59
anti-German propaganda, 31
Arakan, 170
army base paymaster, 153
askari, 40, 41–42, 47; definition of, 188n79; demobilization of, 146–48, 150, 153, 154, 164. *See also* servicemen
automobile industry, 128
Axis, the, 4, 5, 24, 29, 43, 53, 55, 81, 142, 171, 173
Axis powers, 24, 43, 57, 119, 171, 173

Bancroft mine, 129
Bantu Mirror, 27
base metal(s), 7, 23, 115–20, 134, 140, 173
Basutoland, 5
Bechuanaland (Botswana), 5, 7, 8, 9, 13, 34, 87, 163
Bedford, Reverend Frank, 124
beeswax, 9, 15, 20, 57, 68–73, 77, 171; trade in, 71–73; uses of, 69
Belgian Congo, 92, 117, 135
Board of Trade, 82
Bombay, 145, 147

Bon Accord Boarding House, 106
Borneo, 56, 58
bowstring hemp, 74
Boycott Control Committee, 94
Bradley, Kenneth, 28
brekweet, 103
British Colonial Supply Mission, 125
British crown, 24, 25, 26, 149
British Empire, 2–4, 5, 14, 18, 24, 25, 28, 41, 54, 81, 112; racial and ethnic stereotyping in, 98, 114, 173; war effort, 118, 136, 174; postwar reconstruction, 141, 145
British foreign secretary, 113
British Metals Corporation, 115
British Ministry of Food, 135
British Ministry of Supply, 15, 21, 59, 126, 171, 173
British War Cabinet, 5
Broken Hill, 53, 54, 75, 86, 91, 96, 107, 108, 111, 118, 121, 148, 149, 151, 153, 155, 157
Brown, Captain J., 139
Burma, 5, 33, 44, 142, 147, 160, 166, 167, 170
Burma complex, 160
Bwana Mkubwa, 99, 101, 104, 109, 110, 113

Calcutta, 75, 145
Canada, 4, 117
Carrier Corps, 48
cenotaph, 169
Central African Federation, 8, 130, 141
Central European evacuees, 98
Ceylon, 147, 166
Chamber of Mines, 94, 120, 146
Chandwe, Francis, 29
chibaro, 136

Index

Chibuluma mine, 129
Child Welfare Association, 106
Chile, 117
Chindwin, 170
Chitimukulu, Chief, 34
Chombola, Rabson, 6, 44, 142–43
cinema van, 28, 32
Civil Recruitment Depot, 46
cobalt, 116, 119, 129
Cold War, 129
Colonial Development and Welfare Act (1940), 65
Colonial Film Unit, 28
Colonial Office, 28, 31, 62, 82, 120, 130, 137, 140, 172
color bar, 120, 124, 160
Commission of Inquiry into the Cost of Living, 92–93
Committee of Action, 121
Committee on the Application for Permanent Residence, 113
comptroller of customs, 119
Conference of East African Governors, 111
consumer goods, 8, 21, 79, 80, 82, 85, 92, 96, 101, 108, 151, 166, 172, 173; causes of shortage of, 80–83; hoarding of, 90–92, 96; rationing of, 87–90
contraband of war, 119
Controlled Materials Plan, 130
controller of prices, 90
copper, 6, 8, 10, 12–18, 21, 115–22, 125–34, 140–41, 159, 173, 175; blister copper, 119, 127, 128; copper mining industry, 115, 130, 141; electrolytic copper, 119, 127
Copperbelt, 17, 18, 27, 39, 41, 53, 67, 87, 92, 93, 104, 110, 121–23, 128–30, 133, 135, 139, 151
cost of living, 85, 92–94, 120, 121, 123, 151, 157; African response to, 93–96; Cost of Living Allowance (COLA), 93, 95, 123; cost of living index, 94–95
Cotton Board, 82
cotton piece goods, 83–84
Cripps, Sir Stafford, 127
Cyprus, 100, 102, 226

Dar-es-Salaam, 12, 123
Defense Production Act (1950), 130
Department of Agriculture, 61, 70, 71, 72, 133
Department of Health, 161
Department of Labour, 159
Department of Public Works, 135

Dickson, Capt. A. G., 36
diplomatic corps, 169
director of medical services, 158, 162
director of war evacuees and camps, 105–6, 111
District After-Care Committee, 157
Dutch East Indies, 56

East African Military Labour Corps, 146
economic challenges, 21, 78, 83, 96
Egypt, 4, 32, 119
Emergency Powers (African Labour Corps) Regulation (1942), 86, 139
Emergency Powers (Conscription of Natives for Farm Labour) Regulation (1942), 139
Emergency Powers (Control of Prices and Hoarding Regulations) (1942), 90
Emergency Powers (Recruitment of Farm Labour) Regulation (1942), 138
Emergency Powers (War Defence) Acts (1939), 138
Empire Air Training Scheme, 13, 136
Enloe, Cynthia, 48, 170
European Mine Workers' Union, 119
Export Licensing Department, 82
export profit tax, 131
Export Prohibition Order (1939), 119

farming implements, 133, 172, 173
Federation of Welfare Societies, 164
fibers, 74
First World War, 1, 25, 48, 59, 126, 155, 171
Food Production Committee, 138
Forster Commission of Inquiry, 93, 122, 123, 124
Fort Jameson, 35, 38, 40, 45, 47, 50, 51, 52, 99, 101, 104, 105, 149
France, 3, 4, 5, 14, 32, 81, 100, 119, 145, 166
Franciszek, Kirkuc, 103
Franklin, Harry, 28, 148
French West Africa, 11–12, 48, 50–51, 136; veterans, 145, 159

George VI, King, 23, 24, 29, 32, 36, 44
German Jews, 98, 99
Germany: British declaration of war on, 24; copper consumption of, 115, 119; defeat of France, 4; entry into Mediterranean and North Africa, 32; invasion of Poland, 3
Girl Guides Association, 106
Gold Coast, 10, 12, 123, 159, 162, 163, 165
Gondar, 170
Gore-Browne, Sir Stewart, 94, 102, 109

Index

Guèye, Lamine, 12
Gurkha syndrome, 48, 170

hemp, 74–76
Hezekiah, Private Alfred, 154
High Commission Territories, 5, 9, 34
Hiroshima, 142
Hitler, Adolf, 29, 39
HMT *Cameronia*, 146
home front, 2, 7, 13, 15, 21, 79, 80, 163, 165, 173
honey, 69–70
honeybee(s), 69
honeycombs, 69
Houphouët-Boigny, Felix, 11
House of Commons, 131
hyperinflation, 15, 79. *See also* inflation

immigration policy, 16, 98–99
Income Tax War Provisions Ordinance, 85
India, 4, 5, 33, 44, 96, 136, 146, 166, 167, 170
Indian-owned shops, 94–96; boycott of, 96
Indian traders, 86–87, 94
Infantry Training Centre, 45–46
inflation, 6–8, 21, 80, 83–85, 96, 120, 123, 151; hyperinflation, 15, 79
Ingutsheni Mental Hospital, 103
inspector of weights and measures, 90
International Labour Organisation (ILO), 136, 174
International Refugee Organisation, 114
Iran, 101
iron, 15, 116, 125, 171; shortage of, 63–65
iron smelting, 63, 64–69, 171
iron tools, 20, 57, 65–66, 68
Italy, 4, 32–33, 119, 167, 177n12

Japan, 3, 9, 14, 32, 33, 56, 58, 117, 126, 142, 146
Java, 56, 58
Jewish refugees, 98, 99
Johnstone, Captain, 162

Kadansa, Chama Mutemi, 3, 5, 44, 147
Kalewa, 170
Kalonga Gawa Undi, 34
Kangwa, Rightson, 39
Karachi, 145
Katanga, 123
Katondwe Mission, 29
Kenya, 5, 8, 10, 13, 17, 40, 58, 113, 135, 135, 146, 147, 150, 155, 157, 163, 170
Kitchin, Major J. E., 160

Kohima, 170
Korean War, 116, 128–29

labor conscription, 13, 17, 50, 67, 116, 135, 139–40, 174; forced labor, 136–41
Labour Party, 107
lead, 118, 119, 121
League of Nations, 136
Legislative Council, 19, 91, 94, 96, 99, 102, 112, 134, 149, 151
Lend-Lease, 72, 93, 125, 126
Lesotho, 9, 34, 150
Lewin, C. J., 59, 61
Litunga, the, 34
Livingstone, 18, 28, 31, 71, 91, 100, 106, 108, 109, 149, 151, 152, 155, 161
Livingstone Mail, 28, 112
Livingstonia Mission, 164
Locke-King, Ethel, 106
London Chamber of Commerce, 82
London Metal Exchange, 8, 118, 173
Lusaka, 5, 19, 27, 40, 45, 46, 48, 52, 53, 54, 69, 74, 84, 99, 100, 101, 103–6, 108, 113, 126, 130, 134, 139, 142, 146, 147, 149, 151, 152, 153, 169
Lusaka Hotel, 108
Lusaka Women's Institute, 106
Lyttleton, Oliver, 82

Macdonald, Malcolm, 58
Macmillan, Harold, 58, 178
Madagascar, 5, 33, 41, 58, 82, 148, 166
maize, 38, 89–92, 96, 133–35, 137–39, 151, 172
maize meal, 90–92, 133, 172
Maize Meal (Wholesale Prices) Order (1942), 91
Makasa, Kapasa, 164
Malaya, 56, 58
Maliselo, Joseph, 146
Manchester Chamber of Commerce, 82
Mankoya, 71, 72, 153
Marrapodi, Mrs. E., 101
martial races, 46–48, 170
martial race theory, 46–48, 170
Masiuk, Bernard, 110
Mawlaik, 170
Maybin, John, Governor, 25, 52, 118
Mazabuka, 139, 140, 149, 154, 158
Mazabuka Farmers' Association, 137
Mazabuka Hotel, 110
Mazoe Valley Agricultural Show, 99
Mbikusita-Lewanika, Godwin, 164
Mckee, Major, 101–2

Index

mechanized farms, 138
medical orderly, 162
Messrs Cavadia and Nephews, 147
Messrs Tarry and Company, 76
Messrs Wilson and Mansfield, 70
Methodist Church, 107
Middle East campaign, 5
Midlands Farmers' Association, 137
military masculinity, 47
miners' strike, 120–21; causes of, 122–24
Ministry of Information, 27
Ministry of Labour and National Service, 144
Ministry of Supply, 9, 15, 21, 59, 60–63, 69, 70, 118, 120, 125–28, 133, 171, 173
Mkushi, 65, 66, 77, 150, 152, 153, 156
Mobile Propaganda Unit, 36, 38
Mombasa, 12, 33, 123, 147
Moore, Sir Leopold, 99
Moyne, Lord, 81
Mpashi, Stephen, 41
Mpezeni, Chief, 25, 34, 38
Mufulira mine, 129
Mulenga, Joseph Chinama, 44, 147
Muliango, Samson, 43, 44
Mussolini, Benito, 4, 32
Mutende, 19, 23–25, 27–29, 32, 36, 88, 152
Mwanachingwala, Chief, 26
Mwase Kasungu, Chief, 27
Mwenzo Welfare Society, 164

Nagasaki, 142
Nairobi, 146, 147, 152, 161
Namwala, 41, 147
Nasson, Bill, 2
National Production Authority, 130
Native Development Board, 65–67, 72, 76
Nazi Party, 29
Nazism, 29, 135
Nchanga mine, 120, 125, 129, 130, 133
Ngangula, Private Levi, 157
Nkana, 27, 59, 110, 120, 122, 123, 124, 127, 129, 131, 149
Nkana mine, 120, 121, 127, 129
North African campaign, 4
Northern Rhodesia: renamed as Zambia, xiii, 5, 178n25
Northern Rhodesia African Congress (NRAC), 164
Northern Rhodesia General Defence Regulations no. 301 (1942), 90
Northern Rhodesia Newsletter, 28, 227
Northern Rhodesia Police, 90

Northern Rhodesia Regiment (NRR), 4–6, 16, 18, 24, 32–36, 39–40, 42, 44, 46–49, 51, 142, 143, 146, 150–54, 159, 162, 166–67, 169–70, 174
Nyasaland, 27, 46, 52, 58, 129, 146, 150, 160

Ossewabrandwag, 54

Palestine, 5, 33, 99, 101, 166
Pay Corps Headquarters, 152
Pearl Harbor, 33
Pemba, 75, 140, 147
Peszkowski, Reverend Z., 113
Philippines, 56, 58, 73, 74
Phiri, Justin Master, 39
plows, 63, 64
Poland, 3, 29, 30, 49, 97, 98, 100, 111, 112, 113, 173
Poles, 16, 21, 29, 97–99, 100–108, 112, 114, 173
Polish refugees, 100–101, 103, 105–9, 111, 114, 173; Cyprus Group, 100; MERRA Group, 101; prostitution among, 99, 106; repatriation of, 111–14
Popiel, Leon, 108
Portugal, 70, 117, 119
postal clerks, 161
postmaster general, 161
Post Office Savings Bank (POSB), 85, 150, 152
potatoes, 135
Prain, Ronald, 131
price control, 90–92
Price Control Office, 90
propaganda: German, 54; Mobile Propaganda Unit, 36, 38; in the recruitment of servicemen, 17, 24–32, 36, 39, 170; war, 6, 17, 21, 136, 171. See also *Mutende*
Public Works Department, 159

Rangoon, 146, 147
rearmament programs, 128
recruitment. *See under* servicemen
Restrictions of Aliens Regulations, 108
Rhodesia Advertiser, 28
Rhodesian Anglo American (RAA), 118, 121, 129, 130, 131, 132
Rhodesian Selection Trust (RST), 118, 129, 130, 131, 132
Rhodes-Livingstone Institute, 31, 38
Rhokana Corporation, 59, 120, 124, 131
Ridgeway, 169
Roan Antelope mine, 121, 122, 131, 132
rope(s), 1, 3, 5, 10–15, 15, 20, 57, 73–76

246

Index

rope-making industries, 171
Royal Commission on Taxation of Profits and Income, 132
rubber, 9, 13, 15, 20, 56–63, 72–73, 77, 83, 136; rubber trade, 61; shortage of, 61–62; uses of, 58; tapped rubber, 60; bark rubber, 60
Russia, 32, 46, 117, 120
Rydarowski, Tadeusz, 108

Saffrey, Lynn A., 93
Second World War, 2, 3, 5–8, 10–18, 20, 22, 24, 39, 41–42, 44, 46–48, 54, 56–58, 79, 96–98, 100, 115–16, 120, 126, 143–44, 148, 164, 168–69, 171, 173, 175
servicemen, 3, 5, 10–11, 12, 14, 19, 22, 43, 48, 146, 149, 150, 152, 153, 157, 159, 166, 167, 168, 169, 174, 175; African agency in recruitment of, 9, 17, 39–44, 117; demobilization of, 12, 19, 22, 44, 142–50, 159–63, 166, 168, 174, 175; political role of, 162–68; propaganda in the recruitment of, 17, 24–32, 36, 39, 170; resistance to the recruitment of, 48–54
Siamaimbo, Timothy, 140
Sichintu, Thomas, 140
signalers, 159, 161
Simwinga, Simon J., 151
Slavery Convention (1926), 136
Smith and Kitchin Company, 161
smuggling, 89, 92
Smyth, Rosaleen, 6, 16
Somaliland: British, 5, 33, 153, 177n12; French, 33; Italian, 4, 153
sorghum, 135
South Africa, 9, 18, 46, 50, 53, 54, 58, 59, 60, 63, 65, 68, 69, 70, 80, 82, 89, 93, 98, 117, 135
Southeast Asia, 9, 13, 14, 31, 20, 33, 56, 57, 58, 69, 81, 129, 153, 171
Southern Rhodesia, 13, 17, 18, 27, 28, 35, 51, 69, 80, 82, 83, 84, 88, 98, 99, 100, 102, 103, 110
Southern Rhodesia Newsletter, 28
Soviet NKVD, 97
Stanley, Oliver, 145
Stephenson, Colonel "Chirupula," 136

sterling: area, 70; convertibility crisis, 80; devaluation of, 89–90, 96, 116, 126–27
string, 20, 57, 73–77
sunhemp, 74
Swaziland, 5, 9, 34, 150
Swazi veterans, 161, 181, 220, 239

Tanganyika, 13, 58, 64, 70, 106, 110, 113, 114, 135, 136
Taung Up, 170
Teheran, 101
Trapnell, C. G., 61
tribal elders, 123
true hemp, 75–76
Tucker, Keith, 82
Tug Argan, 170
Tulasiewicz family, 113
Turkey, 119

Uganda, 16, 26, 46, 52, 58, 106, 110, 150, 163
United States, 2, 63, 68, 93, 116, 117, 119, 125, 126, 127, 128, 156

vanadium, 118, 119
veterans. *See* servicemen

Waddington, John, 134, 140
War Office, 5, 144
War Production Board, 125
War Savings Certificates, 85–86
Welensky, Roy, 111
Whitehall, 13, 21, 62, 135
World War I. *See* First World War
World War II. *See* Second World War
Workers' Compensation Ordinance, 158

Yeta III, Chief, 49

Zaleski, M., 108
Zambia, Northern Rhodesia renamed as, xiii, 5, 178n25
Zambezi Sawmills, 109
Zeesen, 54
zinc, 118, 121
Zulu, Gilbert Malama, 40